Happy Hour
GUIDEBOOK

Portland Happy Hour Guidebook
Eighth Edition
Copyright ©2014 Half-Full Enterprises

ISBN: 978-0-9791201-3-8

Self-published with all content including research, reviews,
illustrations, cover, maps, and design by Cindy Anderson

Editorial assistance by Alethea Smartt LaRowe – Thank you!
You made the book much better! Editing by Mary Beth Saddoris
(writebrainediting@gmail.com) Partial copy once again –
it's always a scramble at the end! Locally printed in the U.S. by
Ink over Ink (www.inkoverink.com) Bill Yancey (503) 680-3128.

Due to the fluid nature of the ever-changing Portland Happy
Hour scene, Half-Full Enterprises cannot accept responsibility
for any complications that may arise from using the information
in this book. Every effort has been made to maintain accuracy,
but things change, and Half-Full Enterprises cannot guarantee
that the information in this book is or will be accurate. The
opinions expressed in this book are just that, opinions of
the author. The author did not receive any endorsement
earnings (or bribes!) from any bar/restaurant/tavern in the
writing of this book. Finally, you are responsible for your
own actions, before, during and after using the information
provided in this book. Drink responsibly! Half-Full Enterprises
is not liable for any irresponsible actions on your part,
including but not limited to drunk dialing, hooking up with
an ex-boyfriend or girlfriend, hurting yourself or hurting
someone else.

*Coupons are provided as a courtesy. Menus may change or
restaurants may close, and neither the author nor the publisher
makes any warranty or representation about the validity or
enforceability of the coupons. Originals only. May not be good
on holidays. Please use coupons wisely — and nicely.*

Half-Full Enterprises / Cindy Anderson
10350 N. Vancouver Way, Suite 173; Portland, OR 97217
Website www.happyhourguidebook.com
Facebook www.facebook.com/HappyHourGuidebook
Twitter twitter.com/PDXHappyHour
Email pdxinfo@happyhourguidebook.com

Contents

Keep smilin'!

- [ ] Step out of your comfort zone and discover a new place you've never tried before. Explore!

- [ ] Revisit a long-time, classic favorite.

- [ ] Hit at least three Happy Hours a month :-)

- [ ] Visit a friend in a different side of town. Try a couple places in a new neighborhood.

- [ ] Play tourist right here in Portland – and go to Happy Hour near your chosen site.

- [ ] Invite a new friend to meet out at Happy Hour.

- [ ] Invite an old friend, or maybe two or three!

- [ ] Ask a networking contact to meet for a drink. Happy Hour can be much more fun than coffee.

- [ ] Make a monthly date night with your special someone. Or maybe make that weekly...

- [ ] Pick up "drinkercising" as a hobby – plan some exercise or walking along with that Happy Hour!

- [ ] Follow **"Portland Happy Hour Guidebook"** facebook page for all kinds of fun ideas!

Map Information

Plus some scattered places "Out & About"
—and—
Beaverton, Lake Oswego, Tigard, Vancouver

- ● Black dots mark restaurant location
- ★ Stars indicate places that go until 7:00pm
- O White dots indicate limited Happy Hour info

★ Rating System ★

As fun as this so-called *job* is, I take it very seriously. I am in a unique positon of having personally analyzed literally hundreds of Happy Hours, and have devised a formula to rate Happy Hours in comparison to others:

Food

Exclusively focused on food served at Happy Hour only. Considers taste, discounts, healthy alternatives, and uniqueness (i.e. not the usual bar menu).

3 – Delicious food, lots of options and discounted well.

2 – Pretty good food food and/or discount.

1 – Negligible discounts, few selections, or possibly bad taste. It will be explained in that section.

Drinks

Not all about being the cheapest, but need discounts!

3 – Good deals, variety, and quality drinks.
2 – Pretty good, but need more variety or discounts.
1 – Eh. Not that impressed. Not trying or expensive.

Atmosphere

Looks matter! As a rule, this book covers the nicer places in town. Good vibes? Stunning decor? What?

3 – Upscale and unique decor and/or gorgeous views.
2 – Nice enough, but not quite stunning.
1 – More of a bar than a restaurant. Low on style and decor. Women may be uncomfortable when alone.

"Magic Points"

An arbitrary point is often added to the overall score to make up for not using half-points. Sometimes a place is better than the sum of three parts! Overall score is shown in large type.

Perfect Tens – You'll see a big star to call it out.

Personal favorites – Three stars and "Favorite!"

Bonus Stars – Sometimes an overall score doesn't quite do the place justice. This especially happens in places that do not offer drink specials. Here and there, I just *had* to assign a star!

Remember to check our website
every once in a while for changes and closures.

www.happyhourguidebook.com

And please let us know if you see
information that needs changing.

• • • • • • • • • • • • • • • • • • •

Mark up your books!

Fold down page corners!

Plan ahead! Make notes!

Notes & Disclaimers

Accuracy of information: Things change! Graciously accept this fluidity and adjust your attitude accordingly. As of this writing, the information herein is current. Every effort has been made to present information accurately. Check the website for updates.

Crowd scene: An element that can greatly vary. I elected not to try to qualify the type of person typically visiting a certain place, but rather encourage you to reserve judgement as well and be accepting and tolerant—and even friendly—to your fellow bar patrons. Also, please be aware that the more popular places get crowded. Be flexible, prompt, and patient. I hope this book will encourage you to get out there and explore! Every place in this book is worth checking out.

Service: I didn't comment on this aspect as "one bad apple doesn't spoil the whole bunch." Be aware that sometimes it's service via bartender only, and you'll have to order at the bar. If things are taking a while, be proactive, yet polite.

Tipping: Servers may have to make just as many trips for you as a regular diner. Please consider the effort—not the totally low bill—and be extra-generous for good service!

Rating and Judging: All judging is based on Happy Hour only. You may find you have different opinions of places. I called 'em as I saw 'em and in comparison to others. Take your own notes for future reference throughout the book. Record your adventures within and it can be a fun walk down Memory Lane!

Do not drink and drive (but of course).

Happy Hours are often relegated to bar area only. Mostly, I've commented on the restaurant atmosphere overall, including outdoor seating (which may not always be available to the Happy Hour crowd). Ask before you are seated to confirm available service.

Factoids & Tipsys

- Be sure to become a **facebook fan!** Get clued in to Happy Hour action and chime in with your opinions and experiences too. Win contests and get deals!

 Portland Happy Hour Guidebook

- Lots of places go all night ('til close) on Sunday or on another weeknight. Look for the ★s in this book to most easily find **extended hours.**

- Check out the website's **MAPS** tab. View these maps on your iPhone! Refer to the restaurant's rating page in book for full information, ratings & exact hours.

- Be aware of the Happy Hour **end-time** and pad your order by at least 10 minutes. Confirm with your waiter if you made it on time.

- Incorporate another **activity** such as a movie, concert, the Chinese Gardens, or a long walk into your night out.

- Not all places can accommodate larger **groups.** Call first. It's fun to organize a get-together!

- Sign up for the **email** list at your favorite restaurants. You'll be in the know about special events and offers. And maybe get a coupon here and there too.

- Live in gratitude—most cities do not have Happy Hours. I know—shocking! And we have the best.

- Things change! Please **report changes** you find to: pdxinfo@happyhourguidebook.com. Also, sign up for the monthly newsletter to be in-the-know.

- Check in with the **website** to keep up with changes!

www.happyhourguidebook.com

Why Trader Vic's?

I love Trader Vic's!

I remember when I was just five years old, being very fascinated with those colorful, little paper umbrellas, plastic swizzle sticks, and the skewer/ swords used with garnishes. And I still love them.

Another early and magical memory is going to Disneyworld's Enchanted Tiki Room. Being a huge "Gilligan's Island" fan, I was enthralled!

Years later, as a young professional in the windy city, I loved going to the legendary Trader Vic's in downtown Chicago, but after nearly 50 years of happy days, they literally paved paradise and put up a parking lot. Popular internationally and founded in 1934, there are actually only *five* Trader Vic's in the United States! Lucky for us, a group of local investors brought Trader Vic's back to Portland in 2011. Mahalo!

It really is the kind of place in which memories are made. Their epic Happy Hour speaks for itself (p.215). Delicious cuisine from around the globe? Yes, please! The home of the Original Mai Tai® and more than 80 tropical cocktails? I'm movin' in...

TRADER VIC'S
TASTE THE WORLD®

Trends, Notes, Faves

Trends and observations from the front line:

• I saw a big increase in the number of places adding mac & cheese to the menu this year. Anti-carb fad be damned, I guess!

• Calamari was added to a lot of menus, but just as often dropped if they already had it. Huh.

• I've never typed "pickle" so many times as this year!

• Arancini is making a comeback. And crostini.

• 2013 was the worst year so far for places closing.

• The more established places are making their Happy Hours better, while the new ones are often starting out as quite the tightwads.

• The big increase in Urban Wineries and Satellite Winery Tasting Rooms is off the charts. Woo hoo!!!

• Our city keeps getting better! :-)

Inevitably, I get asked, **"Got any new favorites?"**

It's such a hard question! A few immediate stand-outs would be **B Squared Wine Bar, Bistro Marquee, Block + Tackle, Cerulean Skies, Oregon Public House, Paley's Place** (started HH this year), **Piattino, Punch Bowl Social, Ración**(!), **Raven & Rose, Saké, Sand Bar,** and **Teote.** Overall, note the places with my handwriting, and exclamation marks.

Look online to see my Official Top 20!

www.happyhourguidebook.com

★ FREE Pizza! ★

Enjoy at: **Amalfi's** (Fremont map)

Buy one delicious Happy Hour item, receive a complimentary HH Pizza!

★ FREE Appetizer ★

Enjoy at: **B Squared** (Pearl map)

Buy one delicious Happy Hour item, get a second one free!

★ FREE Appetizer ★

Enjoy at: **Bazi BierBrasserie** (SE)

Buy one delicious Happy Hour item, get a second one free!

13

Amalfi's Italian Restaurant

4703 NE Fremont
Portland, OR 97213
(503) 284-6747
www.amalfisrestaurant.com

*Buy any Happy Hour food menu item and get receive a
complimentary Happy Hour pizza! Valid only during Happy
Hour. Not good with any other offer or take-out. Limit one
free happy hour menu item per coupon. Limit two coupons
per table. Beverage purchase required. Expires 12/30/14.*

....

B Squared

1966 NW Pettygrove
Portland, OR 97209
(971) 202-7569

*Buy any Happy Hour food menu item and get one of equal
or lesser value free! Valid only during Happy Hour. Not good
with any other offer or take-out. Limit one free happy hour
menu item per coupon. Limit two coupons per table.
Beverage purchase required. Expires 12/30/14.*

....

Bazi Bierbrasserie

1522 SE 32nd Ave.
Portland, OR 97214
(503) 234-8888
www.bazipdx.com

*Buy any Happy Hour food menu item and get one of equal
or lesser value free! Valid only during Happy Hour. Not good
with any other offer or take-out. Limit one free happy hour
menu item per coupon. Limit two coupons per table.
Beverage purchase required. Expires 12/30/14.*

Bistro Marquee

200 SW Market
Portland, OR 97201
(503) 208-2889
www.bistromarquee.com

Buy a Happy Hour food menu item ($8.00 or less) and get one of equal or lesser value free! Valid only during Happy Hour. Not good with any other offer or take-out. Limit one free Happy Hour menu item per coupon. Limit one coupon per table. Beverage purchase required. Expires 12/30/14.

Cerulean Tasting Room

1439 NW Marshall
Portland, OR 97209
(503) 333-9725
www.ceruleanwine.com

Buy any Happy Hour food menu item and get one of equal or lesser value free! Valid only during Happy Hour. Not good with any other offer or take-out. Limit two free happy hour menu items per table. Beverage purchase required. Expires 12/30/14.

Uptown Billiards Club

120 NW 23rd Avenue
Portland OR 97210
(503) 226-6909
www.uptownbilliards.com

Coupon good for one hour of free pool on one table. Minimum $10.00 food purchase required. Not redeemable for cash. Expires 12/30/14.

★ FREE Appetizer ★

Enjoy at: **Equinox** (North/Ne Map)

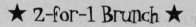

**Buy one delicious Happy Hour item,
get a second one free!**

★ 2-for-1 Brunch ★

Enjoy at: **Equinox** (North/Ne Map)

equinox
RESTAURANT AND BAR

**Buy one delicious brunch item,
get a second one free!**

★ FREE Taco ★

Enjoy at: **Isabel** (Pearl Map)

Buy any food item, get a free taco!

Equinox Restaurant

830 N Shaver St
Portland, OR 97227
(503) 460-3333
www.equinoxrestaurantpdx.com

*Buy any Happy Hour food menu item and get one of equal
or lesser value free! Valid only during Happy Hour. Not good
with any other offer or take-out. Limit one free Happy Hour
menu item per coupon. Limit two coupons per table.
Beverage purchase required. Expires 12/30/14.*

....

Equinox Restaurant

830 N Shaver St
Portland, OR 97227
(503) 460-3333
www.equinoxrestaurantpdx.com

*Buy one select brunch entree and get one of equal or lesser
value free! Maximum value $10.00. Wed-Sun 9:00am-2:00pm
(schedule subject to change). Not good with any other offer
or take-out. One free brunch menu item per coupon. Limit
one coupon per table. Expires 12/30/14.*

....

Isabel

330 NW 10th Ave
Portland, OR 97209
(503) 222-4333
www.isabelscantina.com

*Redeemable at any time with any food purchase of equal or
greater value. Limit one taco per person/coupon. Not good
with any other offer or take-out. Expires Dec. 30, 2014.*

★ FREE Appetizer ★

Enjoy at: **Las Primas** (North/NE map)

**Buy one delicious Happy Hour item,
get a second one free!**

★ FREE Appetizer ★

Enjoy at: **Mama Mia Trattoria**
(Downtown map)

**Buy one delicious Happy Hour item,
get a second one free!**

★ 2-for-1 Brunch ★

Enjoy at: **Mama Mia Trattoria**
(Downtown map)

**Buy one delicious brunch item,
get a second one free!**

Las Primas

3971 N Williams Ave.
Portland, OR 97227
(503) 206-5790
www.lasprimaskitchen.com

Buy any Happy Hour food menu item and get one of equal or lesser value free! Valid only during Happy Hour. Not good with any other offer or take-out. Limit two free happy hour menu items per table. Beverage purchase required. Expires 12/30/14.

....

Mama Mia Trattoria

439 SW 2nd Avenue
Portland, OR 97204
(503) 295-6464
www.mamamiatrattoria.com

Buy any Happy Hour menu food item and get one of equal or lesser value free! Valid only during Happy Hour. Not good with any other offer or take-out. Maximum two free happy hour menu items per coupon. Minimum beverage purchase of $3.00 required per person. Expires 12/30/14.

....

Mama Mia Trattoria

439 SW 2nd Avenue
Portland, OR 97204
(503) 295-6464
www.mamamiatrattoria.com

Buy one select brunch entree and get one of equal or lesser value free! Maximum value $8.95. Weekends 9:00am-1:00pm. Not good with any other offer or take-out. One free brunch menu item per coupon. One coupon per table. Expires 12/30/14.

★ FREE Appetizer ★

Enjoy at: **Mother's** (Downtown map)

Buy one delicious Happy Hour item, get a second one free!

- -

★ FREE Appetizer ★

Enjoy at: **On Deck Sports Bar**
(Pearl Map)

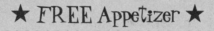

Buy one delicious Happy Hour item, get a second one free!

- -

★ FREE Appetizer ★

Enjoy at: The **Pink Rose** (Pearl Map)

Buy one delicious Happy Hour item, get a second one free!

Mother's Bistro & Bar

212 SW Stark
Portland, OR 97204
(503) 464-1122
www.mothersbistro.com

*Buy any Happy Hour food menu item and get one of equal
or lesser value free! Valid only during Happy Hour. Not good
with any other offer or take-out. Limit one free happy hour
menu item per coupon. Limit two coupons per table.
Beverage purchase required. Expires 12/30/14.*

On Deck Sports Bar & Grill

910 NW 14th Ave
Portland, OR 97209
(503) 227-7020
www.ondecksportsbar.com

*Buy any Happy Hour menu item and get one of equal or
lesser value free! Valid only during Happy Hour. Not good
with any other offer or take-out. Limit one free happy hour
menu item per coupon. Limit one coupon per table.
Beverage purchase required. Expires 12/30/14.*

The Pink Rose

1300 NW Lovejoy
Portland, OR, 97209 USA
(503) 482-2165
www.pinkrosepdx.com

*Buy any Happy Hour food menu item and get one of equal
or lesser value free! Valid only during Happy Hour. Not good
with any other offer or take-out. Limit one free happy hour
menu item per coupon. Limit one coupon per table.
Beverage purchase required. Expires 12/30/14.*

★ FREE Spring Roll ★

Enjoy at: **Saké** (Downtown East Map)

Saké
Japanese & Thai Cuisine

**Enjoy a delicious vegetable spring roll
with any food purchase, at any time!**

- -

★ FREE Appetizer ★

Enjoy at: **Seres** (Pearl map)

申雅 **seres**
restaurant and bar

**Buy one delicious Happy Hour item,
get a second one free!**

- -

★ FREE Coconut Ice Cream ★

Enjoy at: **Thai Bloom!** (Beaverton)

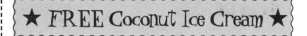

Thai Bloom!

**Enjoy a delicious scoop of Handmade Coconut
Ice Cream with purchase of an entree.**

Saké Japanese & Thai Cuisine

615 SW Park Ave
Portland, OR 97205
(503) 222-1391
www.sakethaior.com

*Buy any food menu item and get a free vegetable spring roll.
Not good with any other offer or take-out. Limit one spring
roll per coupon. Limit two coupons per table. Expires 12/30/14.*

....

Seres Restaurant

1105 NW Lovejoy
Portland, OR 97209
(971) 222-0100
www.seresrestaurant.com

*Buy any Happy Hour food menu item and get one of equal
or lesser value free! Valid only during Happy Hour. Not good
with any other offer or take-out. Limit two free happy hour
menu items per table. Beverage purchase required. Expires
12/30/14.*

....

Thai Bloom!

3800 SW Cedar Hills Blvd
Beaverton, OR 97005
(503) 644-8010
www.thaibloomrestaurant.com

*Buy any dinner entree, and enjoy a free Handmade Coco-
nut Ice Cream scoop absolutley free! Not valid with Happy
Hour. Not good with any other offer or take-out. One free
ice cream per coupon. Limit two free ice cream scoops per
table. Expires 12/30/14.*

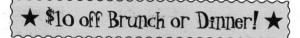

★ $10 off Brunch or Dinner! ★

Enjoy at: **The Central Hotel** (St. John's)

Night or day... save $10.00!

★ FREE Appetizer ★

Enjoy at: **The Slide Inn** (Lloyd Center-ish Map)

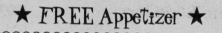

**Buy one delicious Happy Hour item,
get a second one free!**

★ FREE Appetizer ★

Enjoy at: **Touché** (Pearl map)

**Buy one delicious Happy Hour item,
get a second one free!**

The Central Hotel

8608 N Lombard St.
Portland, OR 97203
(503) 477-5489
www.centralhotelstjohns.com

*Spend a minimum of $30.00 on food, and have $10.00
deducted from your pre-discounted total. Not valid at Happy
Hour or with any other offer or take-out. Limit one coupon
per table. Expires 12/30/14.*

....

The Slide Inn

2348 SE Ankeny
Portland, OR 97214
(503) 236-4997
www.slideinnpdx.com

*Buy any Happy Hour food menu item and get one of equal
or lesser value free! Valid only during Happy Hour. Not good
with any other offer or take-out. Limit one free happy hour
menu item per coupon. Limit one coupon per table.
Beverage purchase required. Expires 12/30/14.*

....

Touché Restaurant

1425 NW Glisan St
Portland, OR 97209
(503) 221-1150
www.touchepdx.com

*Buy any Happy Hour food menu item and get one of equal
or lesser value free! Valid only during Happy Hour. Not good
with any other offer or take-out. Limit one free happy hour
menu item per coupon. Limit two coupons per table.
Beverage purchase required. Expires 12/30/14.*

★ 2-for-1 Rate ★

Enjoy at: **Voicebox Karaoke**
(Nob Hill map/Southeast map)

Buy one individual rate hour – get one free.

- -

★ FREE Appetizer ★

Enjoy at: **Wild Abandon** (Southeast Map)

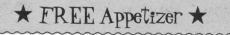

Buy one delicious Happy Hour item, get a second one free!

- -

★ FREE Appetizer ★

Enjoy at: **XV** (Downtown East Map)

Buy one delicious Happy Hour item, get a second one free!

Voicebox Karaoke

2112 NW Hoyt; (503) 303-8220
734 SE 6th Ave; (503) 303-8220
(Coupon valid at either location)
www.voiceboxpdx.com

Good for one guest at the $4 or $7 per hour or $10 Tuesday rate. Maximum value $10. No cash value. Subject to suite availability. Reservations recommended. Party size minimums may apply. Expires 12/30/14.

....

Wild Abandon

2411 SE Belmont
Portland, OR 97214
(503) 232-4458
www.wildabandonrestaurant.com

Buy any Happy Hour food menu item and get one of equal or lesser value free! Valid only during Happy Hour. Not good with any other offer or take-out. Limit one free happy hour menu item per coupon. Limit two coupons per table. Beverage purchase required. Expires 12/30/14.

....

XV (Fifteen)

15 SW 2nd Ave
Portland, OR 97204
(503) 790-9090
www.barfifteen.com

Buy any Happy Hour food menu item and get one of equal or lesser value free! Valid only during Happy Hour. Not good with any other offer or take-out. Limit one free happy hour menu item per coupon. Limit two coupons per table. Beverage purchase required. Expires 12/30/14.

Recommendations

You want cool stuff... and I know good people!

About Face Magazine
Portland's Interview Magazine, highlighting amazing
people and places in and around Oregon.
www.aboutfacemag.com

Alethea Smartt LaRowe
World traveler, connoisseur of Portland food & drink,
and caretaker of Irvington House. Follow her adventures!
www.facebook.com/asmartt1

Azunga Marketing
Online marketing for small business! Responsive & Mobile
Web Sites, Search Engine Optimization, Online Marketing.
www.azunga.com

Christi Fig, Principal Broker
For personal attention to all of your Real Estate needs.
www.christifighomes.com

City Dining Cards & Drink Deck
52 Ways to Save on Portland's best food & drink!
Download the app in iTunes or Google Play and
get the card deck at *www.citydiningcards.com*

Everyday Cooking
Bring the family back to the table! Listen to radio host,
Kristie Greenwood, Saturdays on AM1360 KUIK.
www.facebook.com/pages/Everyday-Cooking

Happy Homes
Large enough to serve you. Small enough to care.
www.happyhomes.com

I Take The Lead Networking Groups
Creating community, one member at a time!
www.itakethelead.com

Wine!

Growing bolder every year,
Portland is now home to more than
a dozen urban wineries.

Explore the best wine bars too!

OREGON **Save 50%!**

Wine Country Guidebook

**Fast-find information on 200+
Oregon wineries. Enjoy exploring!**

www.winecountryguidebook.com

Urban Wineries

For a unique, tasty, and fun experience, tour and taste at working wineries in the city!

Alchemy Wine Productions

3315 SE 19th Ave; (503) 893-4659
www.alchemywineproductions.com
Cute tasting room open Sat-Sun 12:00-5:00pm and by appointment. Focus on Rhone styles with a bit of pinot noir, under their Edwin Dyer label.

Boedecker

2621 NW 30th Ave; (503) 224-5778
www.boedeckerwines.com
Sat-Sun 1:00-5:00pm and by appointment
Sample "dueling wines" from husband and wife, Stewart and Athena Boedecker. Also, conveniently across street from the Portland Brewing Taproom with a great **Happy Hour** (formerly MacTarnahan's).

Burnt Bridge Cellars

1500 Broadway; Vancouver, WA; (360) 695-3363
www.burntbridgecellars.com
Sat-Sun 12:00-5:00pm (and First Fridays 4-8pm)
An urban winery in nearby Vancouver. Cooking classes and event space.

Clay Pigeon Winery

815 SE Oak; (503) 206-8117 **Cyril's** (503) 206-7862
www.claypigeonwinery.com / www.cyrilspdx.com
Food and wines by the glass at their super-cute Cyril's Wine Bar. Very cool place with a delightful patio and epic cheese/meat boards! **Happy Hour** 4:00-6:00pm Tues-Fri $5.00 wine $3.00 cheeses

ENSO Winery
1416 SE Stark; (503) 683-3676
ensowinery.com
Urban Winery & Tasting Lounge 4:00-10:00pm
Daily (2:00pm Sat-Sun) hosts guests, with Enso
and Resonate wines made onsite. **Happy Hour**
4:00-6:00pm Mon-Fri $1.00 off beer, sangria or
wine; $1.00 off salami, cheese and bread plates

Fausse Piste
537 SE Ash, #103; 971-258-5829
www.sauvagepdx.com
Tastes wines by the glass – *and* enjoy a great
Happy Hour! Wines are made on-site, next door to
<u>Sauvage</u> a cozy and intimate wine bar/restaurant
in a renovated, industrial building. See page 321.

Hip Chicks Do Wine
4510 SE 23rd Ave; (503) 234-3790
www.hipchicksdowine.com
Portland's first city winery. Huge tasting/party room
11:00am-6:00pm Daily (Bonus Friday **Happy Hour**
4:00pm-7:00pm with discounts on all wine, plus
sangria and $5.00 off cheese plates).

Jan-Marc Wine Cellars
2110 North Ainsworth; (503)341-4531
www.janmarcwinecellars.com
Small winery in the Overlook neighborhood. Tour
and taste at the winery – call for an appointment.

SE Wine Collective

2425 SE 35th Pl; (503) 208-2061
www.sewinecollective.com
An urban winery extravaganza! Contemporary
yet rustic space with a dedicated tasting bar
serving wine and small plates. **Happy Thursdays**
5:00-7:00pm $2.00 off wines and small bites

www.bowandarrowwines.com
www.divisionwinemakingcompany.com
www.fullertonwines.com
www.helioterrawines.com
www.vincentwinecompany.com

Seven Bridges sevenbridgeswinery.com

2303, N. Harding Ave; (503) 203-2583
Simple urban winery founded in 2008. Focus on
full-bodied reds. Tastings Sat-Sun 1:00-5:00pm.

Saint Johns Cellars

6635 N Baltimore; (503) 789-2009
www.saintjohnscellars.com
Praise be! A very cool winery with tasting room
right in St. John's! Thu-Sun Noon-8:00pm

- -

Cellar 55 Tasting Room

1812 Washington, Vancouver, WA; (360) 693-2700
www.cellar55tastingroom.com
Fri 2:00-8:00pm, Sat 12-7:00pm, Sun 12-6:00pm
No wine-making onsite, but a very unique and
brilliant concept! A co-op featuring four boutique
wineries from Walla Walla and Eastern WA.
Happy Hour 5:00-close Friday; 4:30-6:00 Sun
$1.00-$2.00 off wine and meat & cheese plates

Five Star Cellars (www.fivestarcellars.com)
Gordon Estate (www.gordonwines.com)
Market Vineyards (www.marketvineyards.com)
Purple Star Winery (www.purplestarwines.com)

Winery-Specific Tasting Rooms

Bishop Creek *(at Urban Wine Works)*
1315 NE Fremont; (503) 493-1366
www.urbanwineworks.com
1:00pm-8:00pm Daily (until 6:00pm Sundays)

Cerulean Skies Winery
1439 NW Marshall; (503) 333-9725
www.ceruleanwine.com
2:00-10:00pm Tues-Sat (until midnight Fri-Sat)
Exceptionally cool space! An immediate favorite!
Happy Hour See info on p. 172.

East Fork Winery *(at the Slocum House)*
605 Esther St; Vancouver, WA; (360) 727-3055
www.eastforkcellars.com
Sat 12:00-6:00pm, Sun 12:00-5:00pm
Sweet, renovated Victorian house is a second
home for Ridgefield's East Fork Cellars winery.

Island Mana Wines
526 SW Yamhill; (971) 229-1040
www.islandmanawines.com
Thur-Sun 2:00-7:00pm (later in the summer)
Tropical dry, fruit wines of Hawaii and traditional
Oregon wines. Theme nights and **Happy Hour**!

TeSoAria www.tesoaria.com
4003 N. Williams; (541) 464-0032
1:00pm-9:00 Daily (Fri-Sat until 10:00pm)
A variety of exceptional wines from the Umpqua
Valley paired with small plates in brand-new space.

Viola Wine Cellars *(at Cork Wine Shop)*
2901 NE Alberta; (503) 281-2675
www.corkwineshop.com
Current releases served at Cork Wine Shop.

Wine Bars

Cool places with wines by the glass and/or bottle, and serve food (as opposed to a wine/bottle shop).

1856
1465 NE Prescott; (503) 954-1104
www.1856pdx.com
It's a bottle shop, but with a bar – and beer!
Six wines by the glass and six beers on tap.

Ambonnay Champagne Bar
107 S E Washington; (503) 575-4861
www.ambonnaybar.com
Cool and cozy, quite comfortable, and romantic at night. Champagne and sparklings. Light bites. No Happy Hour, and a bit pricey, but I love it!

Arrivederci
17025 SE McLoughlin Blvd; (503) 659-1143
www.arrivederciwine.com

Happy Hour Wed-Fri 5:00-6:00pm

Food Deals $3.00-$6.00 Amazing menu with 14 delicious items like fondue, calamari, mussels, ravioli, chicken salad, fries, and several pizzas.

Drink Specials $3.50 drafts; $4.00-$5.00 wine; $3.50 wells; $5.00 lemondrops or cosmos

Atmosphere Tuscan tones in gold and terra cotta, fun wine art, and live music nightly. Cozy lounging area, several tables, and welcoming bar.

B Squared
1984 NW Pettygrove; (971) 202-7569

Happy Hour 3:00–6:00pm Daily

Food Deals $3.00-$4.00 Excellent menu for
any restaurant, but especially for a wine bar.
B Squared merits an A+ rating with delicious,
healthy and plentiful food that includes sliders
(pork, bison, lamb), three salad choices (big ones!),
soup of the day, and a special $7.00 flatbread.

Drink Specials $3.00 drafts; $4.00 wine
$5.00-$7.00 cocktails

Atmosphere Open space with friendly, full bar.
Giant walls of windows reach high to the ceiling,
and deep red walls add character and warmth.
They have a coffee shop in same building. Makes
me want to move into the apartments above!

Barrel Fine Wine + Tasting Bar
14740 NW Cornell, Hillsboro; (971) 245-6000
www.barrelfinewine.com
Mostly a wine retail shop, but some small plates
available, and wines by the glass. Contemporary
tasting room with several tables to sit and sip.

Bin 21
5011 NE 21st; (503) 284-4445; www.bin21pdx.com
Happy Hour Drinks only $3.00 drafts; $5.00 wine
Behind Salt & Straw on Alberta (make note)!
Contemporary space with reclaimed woods,
dark gray back wall, and roll-up doors for a nice
breeze. Bistro nibbles and three wines/beers on tap.

Blackbird Wine & Atomic Cheese

4323 NE Fremont; (503) 282-1887
www.blackbirdwine.com

Happy Hours 2:00–5:00pm Tues–Thur; All Sunday

Food Deals $5.00 Salumi plates, cheesemonger's choice (also home to the At omic Cheese Bar), brie crostini, goat cheese samplers, and salad. Small menu, but bonus point for well-chosen wine go-withs.

Drink Specials $3.00 beer; $1.00 off all wine

Atmosphere Go once and it will be a favorite forever. Long wood community table, nice wooden shelving, chalkboard signs, cheese and deli case in back. Outdoor sidewalk seating.

Brewed 360

603 Main Street, Vancouver; (360) 597-3386
www.brewed360.com
Breakfast, lunch and dinner; coffee, beer and wine! Good prices on food, microbrews and growlers, boutique wines out of the Columbia and Willamette Valleys, and Vancouver's Transcendence coffees.

Corkscrew

1665 SE Bybee Blvd; (503) 239-9463
www.corkscrewpdx.com
No Happy Hour, but such a cute place! So cozy and candlelit with reclaimed wood and old world charm. Check website for specials and live music.

Hop & Vine

1914 N Killingsworth; (503) 954-3322
www.thehopandvine.com

Happy Hour 3:00–6:00pm Mon–Sat; All Sunday★
More information in "Beervana" section, page 69.

Korkage Wine Bar & Shop
6320 SW Capitol Hwy; (503) 293-3146
www.korkagewine.com

Happy Hour 3:30-6:00pm Tues-Fri

Food Deals $2.00-$4.25 Cajun fries, white bean hummus, pate, Moroccan lamb sliders. Plus $2.50 off meat and cheese platters for two or more.

Drink Specials $4.00 drafts; $5.00-$6.00 wines

Atmosphere Seafoam-colored stucco walls, a giant wall of bottles presented on black shelves, and a long tasting bar with tables, all tucked neatly within a small strip mall.

La Bottega
1905 Main St., Vancouver; (360) 571-5010
www.labottegafoods.com

Happy Hours 3:00-6:00pm Daily

Food Deals $4.00–$6.00 Small menu with nice little nibbles: veggie plate, antipasti, olives, crostini and bruschetta, baked polenta.

Drink Specials $1.00 off beer; $5.00 house wine

Atmosphere I vaguely remember a bodega being a grocery store in Spanish. Add in lots of bottles for sale and you have bottega! Cute little cafe/store/wine bar that's very European in style.

Lakeside Bistro

8294 SW Nyberg, Tualatin; (503) 486-5464
www.lakeside-bistro.com

Happy Hours 3:00–6:00pm Tues-Sat

Food Deals $5.00-$7.00 Wine go-withs and real meals too: Antipasti plate, bruschetta, Caesar, crab dip, pasta, tacos, hummus, mac & cheese.

Drink Specials $4.00 drafts; $5.00 wines

Atmosphere Cute lakeside bistro! Located in the Tualatin Commons, formerly Parallel 45 Wine Bar. Homey and open, paned windows, and a big bar.

Latte Da Coffeehouse & Wine Bar

205 E 39th St, Vancouver; (360) 448-7651

Cute name, cute space! Tucked inside a neighborhood home with Pottery Barn style. Entry counter, fireplace, and several comfy seating areas. Great outdoor patio!

M Bar

417 NW 21st Ave; (503) 228-6614
Happy Hour 6-8-pm Daily $4 drafts; $3 off wines
Tiny candlelit lounge with a number of wines by the glass, and great "secret" space! Patio too.

Magnolia's Corner

4075 NE Sandy Blvd; (503) 459-4081
www.magnoliascorner.net
Happy Hour 4:30-6:30pm Daily
Drink Specials $3 draft; $4 wine; $5 cocktails.
Sweet place across from the Hollywood theater with good café food (no Happy Hour discount).

Navarre
10 NE 28th Ave; (503) 232-3555
www.navarreportland.blogspot.com
An outstanding place to enjoy wine at the back
bar. Excellent dinner here! But no Happy Hour.

Nebbiolo Wine Bar And Market
800 Main St.; Oregon City; (503) 344-6090

Happy Hour 2:00-5:30pm Tue-Fri ('til 5:00pm Fri)

Food Deals $5.00-$9.00 Nice eats! Calamari,
grilled veggies, salmon tacos, brie & garlic,
greens, flauta, or sandwich of the day. Plus meat
and cheese plates.

Drink Specials $1.00 off beer (two taps) and all
wines by the glass; $2.00 off cocktails

Atmosphere Cool space, especially welcomed
in downtown Oregon City! European flair with
exposed brick walls and ceiling, wooden floors,
and a big tasting bar with lots of tables too.

Niche Wine Bar
1013 Main, Vancouver; (360) 980-8352
www.nichewinebar.com

Happy Hour Mon-Fri 3:00-6:00pm

Food Deals $2.00 off niche plate (salami, cheese,
olives, antipasti); Small menu too, but no discounts.

Drink Specials $1.00 off glass pours
$10.00 select red or white wine paired with cheese

Atmosphere Cozy wine bar that's so cute it looks
staged! Friendly seating at the bar, piano, comfy
couch lounging area, plus a couple tables.

Oregon Wines On Broadway
515 SW Broadway; (503) 228-4655
www.oregonwinesonbroadway.com
More than just a bottle shop with cheese and
salami plates and 40 wines available to try! Cool!

Oso Market + Bar
726 SE Grand; (503) 232-6400
www.osomarket.com
Happy Hours 4:00–6:00pm Mon–Thur
$1.00 off drafts; $2.00 off wine pours; 10% off
six-packs and bottles of wine
New bottleshop, specialty market, and neighborhood
bar all in one. Spartan, diner-esque, rustic, cool.

The Portland Bottle Shop
7960 SE 13th Ave; (503) 232-5202
www.pdxbottleshop.com
Wine and beer on tap. Simple, with nice patio.

Pour Wine Bar
2755 NE Broadway; (503) 288-7687
www.pourwinebar.com

Happy Hours 4:30–6:30pm Mon–Sat

Food Deals $2.00 Very good and insanely inex-
pensive, but limited: cheese panini, marinated
olives, and roasted hazelnuts. Regular menu has
some delicious and affordable options too.

Drink Specials
$3.00 pours of select red and white wines
$5.00 off bottles; $2.00 select beer

Atmosphere Striking and sleek 1960s-style
Space Odyssey lounge; mod design with cool,
white retro chairs and walls; string art mural;
silver, candlelight, and real flowers.

Primrose & Tumbleweeds

248 E Main, Hillsboro; (503) 703-8525
www.primroseandtumbleweeds.com

Happy Hour 3:00-6:00pm Mon-Fri

Food Deals $4.00-$5.00 Top-notch choices!
Brie & apple plate, proscuitto-wrapped pears,
dates with goat cheese, chicken quesadilla, pork
sliders, spinach artichoke dip, or Caesar salad.

Drink Specials $4.00 drafts; $4.00 house wines
$4.00 select cocktails

Atmosphere 4,000 wines and 250 beers! A mixed
space that's hard-edged and more masculine in
appearance, flecked with shopping and flowers.

Red Slate Wine Company

107 SE Washington; (503) 232-3867
www.redslatewine.com
A unique concept and great space! Sign up for
their newsletter for tastes, classes and deals on
very special wines. From the owner of Ambonnay.

Remedy

733 NW Everett; (503) 226-1400
www.remedywinebar.com
No Happy Hour, but many small plates and wines
in a gorgeous space opening up to the park blocks.
Serenely fancy. Same owners as Corkscru.

Renaissance Premium Wines & Cigars

1320 NE Orenco Station Pkwy, Hillsboro
(503) 615-8676
www.renaissancewines.com
Great wine selection and small plates/nibbles.
No Happy Hour. No corkage fee + nice patio = :-)

Shaker & Vine
2929 SE Powell; (503) 231-8466
www.shakerandvine.com

Happy Hour 4:00-7:00 Tues-Sat

Food Deals $3.00-$7.00 A few nice bites like bacon-wrapped dates, steak salad, Caesar, grilled cheese with tomato soup. Plus $10 Cheese plate.

Drink Specials $4.00 drafts or wine; $5.00 wells

Atmosphere Formerly Vino Vixens. Such a cool space! Front retail shop with 500 wines of the world. Three lounges in a giant space. Deep red walls, lots of couches, games, artwork, party space.

Sip D'Vine
7829 SW Capitol Hwy; (503) 977-9463
www.sipdvine.com
Cute little wine shop in Multnomah Village. Check for occasional live music. No food. Spotty service.

Taste on 23rd
2285 NW Johnson; (503) 477-7238
www.tasteon23rd.com

Happy Hours 4:00-7:00pm Daily (closed Tues)

Food Deals $2.00-$6.00 Light bites to taste and nibble while you sip: grilled bread, spiced nuts, warm olives, deviled egg trio, truffle popcorn, wrapped dates or a salami or cheese plate.

Drink Specials $4.00 beer; $5.00 select wines

Atmosphere Wine bar, small plates and bottle shop housed in a sweet green home on 23rd Ave. Head up a half-flight of stairs in a long room with refined, traditional style. Dark woods, cream walls, windows to the street, and pleasant outside patio dining. It's a favorite!

Urban Decanter

2030 Main; Forest Grove; (503) 359-7678
www.urbandecanter.com
Nice wine bar/shop that improves the whole town
of Forest Grove! Nice interior – and patio! Cheese,
meat, & bread plates, soups and salads, and a
few paninis too. **Happy Hour** Mon-Fri 4-6pm
$2.00 off all small plates; $4.00 wine

Vie de Boheme

1530 SE 7th Ave; (503) 360-1233
www.viedebohemepdx.com
Happy Hour (See p.329).

Wine:30

10835 SE Main; Milwaukie; (503) 654-4595
www.wine30bar.com
Happy Hour Tues-Sun 4-6pm $5 Wines; $3 Beer
Greatly needed *good* wine bar in Milwaukee!
Light eats, outside seating, and the best name ever.

WineUp On Williams

3037 N Williams; (503) 236-3377
www.wineuponwilliams.com

Happy Hour 2:00-6:00 Tues-Fri; ★All day Tues

Food Deals $2.00–$6.00 Wide variety of nibbles
like crostini, truffle herb popcorn, caramel corn,
salad, meatballs in marinara, olives, almonds.

Drink Specials $5.00 select house wines
$2.00 off premium wines ($10.00+)

Atmosphere New from the WineWizard! And
he's conjured up a truly wonderful space! Cozy,
but cool, with brick walls, a beautiful bar, dark
shelves of wine lining the entrance, and lots of
parties!

Restaurants

There can be a fine line between what makes a place a "wine bar" vs. what makes it a restaurant. Many are both! Described elsewhere in this book for their **Happy Hours**, these are restaurants that offer a number of wines by the glass, and simply *seem* like a perfect place to drink wine (just probably not where you head to buy your bottles, and they have large menus with great food).

23 Hoyt
Accanto
Aquariva
Bar Avignon
Bar Mingo
Bistro Marquee
Café Nell
Cocotte
Coppia
Farm Café
Five-0-Three (Oregon City)
Five Spice (Lake Oswego)
Gilt Club
Jo Bar
Meriwether's
Noble Rot
Paley's Place
Paragon
Petisco
Press Club
Ringside (all three locations)
Sapphire Hotel
Serratto
Southpark
Tabla
Thirst
Uptown Billiards
Vinotopia (Beaverton/Vancouver)
Wildwood

Wine Shops

Check websites for tasting nights and parties –
Get on their newsletter lists (sometimes tastings
are *free,* and/or great deals on wine to be had)!
Meet your local wine steward and get the best
recommendations about what you'll love:

Cork - A Bottle Shop www.corkwineshop.com
2901 NE Alberta; (503) 281-2675

CorksCru Wine Merchants www.corkscru.biz
339 NW Broadway; (503) 226-9463

Division Wines www.divisionwines.com
3564 SE Division; (503) 234-7281

E & R Wine Shop www.erwineshop.com
6141 SW Macadam; (503) 246-6101

Every Day Wine www.everydaywine.com
1520 NE Alberta; (503) 331-7119

Foster & Dobbs www.fosteranddobbs.com
2518 NE 15th Ave; (503) 284-1157

Frank Wine & Flower Shop frankwineflower.com
3712 SW Bond Ave; (503) 862-9367

Great Wine Buys www.greatwinebuys.com
1515 NE Broadway; (503) 287-2897

Hollywood Beverage and Liquor
3028 NE Sandy (new location); (503) 284-0987
www.hollywoodliquor.net

Liner & Elsen Wine Merchants
2222 NW Quimby; (503) 241-9463
www.linerandelsen.com

Pairings Portland www.pairingsportland.com
455 NE 24th Ave; (541) 531-7653

Portland Wine Merchants
1430 SE 35th Ave; (503) 234-4399
www.portlandwinemerchants.com

Pearl Specialty Market & Spirits
900 NW Lovejoy; (503) 477-8604
www.pearlspecialty.com

Urban Wine Works www.urbanwineworks.com
1315 NE Fremont; (503) 493-1366

Vino
137 SE 28th Ave; (503) 235-8545; vinobuys.com

Vinopolis www.vinopoliswineshop.com
1025 SW Washington; (503) 223-6002

The Wine Cellar www.portlandwinecellar.com
525 NW Saltzman; (503) 643-5655

Woodstock Wine & Deli
4030 SE Woodstock Blvd; (503) 777-2208
www.woodstockwineanddeli.com

World Class Wines
269 A Ave, Lake Oswego; (503) 974-9841
www.worldclasswinesoregon.com

And don't forget about...

Go local with **New Seasons or Zupan's! Fred
Meyer,** especially the one on Hawthorne, offers
knowledgeable help and a wide selection. **Trader
Joe's** has a big selection of value-priced wine.
And of course our best selves love **Whole Foods**.
And if you appreciate cuteness, hit an **Elephants
Deli! And HEY! Get out to Wine Country!**

Beervana!

Beervana Map

(Near Downtown)

Brewpubs (On-site Breweries)

4th Street Brewing

Gresham 77 NE 4th Street; (503) 669-0569
www.4thstreetbrewing.com

Hoppy Hours 4:00–6:00pm and 9:00–11:00pm Daily
★ All day Sunday and starts at 2:00pm on Saturday

Food Deals $2.95–$4.95 Big bar menu with soup
or salad, fries or chips or dips, cheese plate, giant
pretzels, nachos, sliders, skewers

Drink Specials $3.00 drafts; $4.00 wines; $3.00 wells

Atmosphere Nice brewery with bar and brewing in
back, and dining in front. Nine big-screen TVs and pool.

Alameda Brewhouse

Fremont Map 4765 NE Fremont; (503) 460-9025
www.alamedabrewhouse.com

Hoppy Hours 3:00–6:00pm Mon-Fri; 9:00pm–close Daily

Food Deals $5.00 Pretty much half-off a dozen or
so well-portioned appetizers: ravioli, cajun calamari,
hummus, quesadillas, pizza, nachos, spinach dip, wings.

Drink Specials $3.00 house ales; $3.95 wines

Atmosphere Interior leans more towards a nicer
restaurant than a casual microbrewery with clean,
contemporary lines, colors, and stylings. Outdoor
seating on active sidewalk at Happy Hour.

Amnesia Brewing

1834 Main, Washougal; (360) 335-1008
www.amnesiabrews.com

Moved up north for bigger digs and will even be selling
six-packs! Food served here (salads and sandwiches),
but no Happy Hour. New brewery coming to their old
Mississippi Ave. location in the Spring – **Stormbreaker,**
with Amnesia's former brewer Rob.

B.J.'s Brewhouse www.bjsrestaurants.com

Waterfront Map 12105 N. Center; (503) 289-5566
7390 NE Cornell, Hillsboro; (503) 615-2300

Hoppy Hours 3:00–7:00pm Mon–Fri and
10:00–close Sun–Thur

Food Deals $4.00-$6.00 Bar menu of 10 items

Drink Specials $4.00 drafts; $6.00 wines; $4.00 wells
$5.00 mojitos and martinis

Atmosphere Warm and friendly pub with golden
beer-colored walls, red brick, big ol' beer vats and
a long bar. Big – 143 National locations.

Breakside Brewery www.breaksidebeers.com

Northeast (off map) 820 NE Dekum; (503) 719-6475

* Plus added in early 2013 – a new taproom and
brewery in Milwaukee at 5821 SE International Way

Hoppy Hours 3:00–6:00pm and 9:00–close Mon–Thur

Food Deals $2.00–$6.00 About 10 or so beer bites:
wings, hummus, salads, pretzel, nachos, grilled
cheese & soup, chips & salsa, burgers, slider trio.

Drink Specials $3.75 drafts; $5.50 house wines

Atmosphere A fresh and clean take on the standard
brewery trends of cement floors, giant wood beams,
and garage-style roll-up doors. Outdoor picnic tables.

Bridgeport Brewpub

Pearl Map 1313 NW Marshall; (503) 241-3612
www.bridgeportbrewandalehouse.com

Hoppy Hours 4:00–6:00pm Mon-Fri: ★All day Mon

Food Deals $3.00–$6.50 Giant menu with about 20
top choices: Cheeseburgers, brats, mac & cheese,
pizza, wings, salads, nachos, and more!

Drink Specials $3.50 Imperial pints

Atmosphere Slick, big-city-style brewery, bakery and
coffee shop in renovated loft building; cavernous open
area with the brick, iron and wood; outdoor seating.

Burnside Brewing

Central Eastside Map 701 E Burnside; (503) 946-8151
www.burnsidebrewco.com

Hoppy Hours 3:00-6:00pm Mon-Thurs; ★All day Sun

Food Deals $3.00-$10.00 Frequently changing
menu with some very obscure items that somehow
match the place: pickled veggies, olives, roasted beet
salad, burger, cheese curds, duck confit cohiba/crepe.

Drink Specials $4.00 drafts (20 oz. Imperial pints
$3.00 all day on Wed); $5.00 house wines

Atmosphere Big, open room with cement floors
(much like most breweries), with added character
from massive wood beams overhead, black walnut
tables and designerly L-shaped bar. Very cool, and
huuuge, chalkboard framed sign. Patio.

Cascade Brewing Barrel House

Southeast Map 939 SE Belmont; (503) 265-8603
www.cascadebrewingbarrelhouse.com

Hoppy Hours 4:00–6:00pm Daily $1.00 off drafts

Lots of barrels, 16 taps, and cheap grub at all times
– and lots of it! Bright green walls and visible barrels,
picnic table seating, and outdoor patio.

Coalition Brewing

Lloyd Center-ish 2724 SE Ankeny; (503) 894-8080
www.coalitionbrewing.com

Hoppy Hours 3:00–6:00pm Tues-Sun

Food Deals $2.00–$4.00 Ultra-cheap beer go-withs!

Drink Specials $3.50 pints; $10.00 pitchers;
$5.00 house wines

Atmosphere Cozy little neighborhood place with
good beer (with local, hand-picked guest home brews)
located in the old Noble Rot space. It's both a pub and
10-barrel brewery. Come thirsty!

Columbia River Brewing

Northeast (off map) 1728 NE 40th; (503) 943-6157
www.columbiariverbrewpub.com

Hoppy Hours 3:00–6:00pm and 9:00pm–close Daily
★All day Monday

Food Deals $3.50–5.50 Big menu of little eats:
ravioli, nachos, artichoke dip, pizza, wings, hummus
plate, fries, tots, poppers.

Drink Specials $1.00 off drafts; $5.00 wines
$4.00-$5.00 wells

Atmosphere Nice, open brewpub with refinished
wood floors and tables, separated bar area, views of
the "Brew House" beer vats, but all a bit too brightly lit.

Deschute's Brewery

Pearl Map 210 NW 11th Ave.; (503) 296-4906
www.deschutesbrewery.com

Hoppy Hours 4:00–6:00pm Mon–Fri

Food Deals $3.00–$4.50 Mini-meals like ribs, pizza,
sloppy joes, mac & cheese, salads, pretzels, soup.

Drink Specials $3.50 beer-of-the-day (half-liter)

Atmosphere A "don't miss" for both visitors and locals.
Very popular! Cavernous interior captures the spirit of
the Pacific NW. Totem poles, brick, and lots of wood.

Ecliptic Brewing

North/NE Map 825 N Cook; (503) 265-8002
www.eclipticbrewing.com

Hoppy Hours 3:00–6:00pm Daily

Food Deals $2.00–$10.00 Menu will rotate every six
weeks reflecting seasonal changes: burgers, Caesar
salad, drumsticks, daily soup, fried russet potatoes.

Drink Specials $1.00 off drafts and house cocktails

Atmosphere It's an epic approach to Ecliptic's giant
blue building that houses both its brewing facilities
and their cool and comfortable restaurant. Named for
the yearly path around the sun. Big place. Big menu.

Golden Valley www.goldenvalleybrewery.com

Beaverton 1520 NW Bethany Blvd.; (503) 972-1599

Hoppy Hours 3:00–6:00pm Daily

Food Deals $2.95–$4.95 A bit of everything: sliders, ribs, shooters, tacos, hummus, veggie quesadilla, fries.

Drink Specials $2.00 Beaverton Blonde
$3.00 drafts; $4.00 house wines

Atmosphere A beacon in Beaverton that calls out for an immediate detour! Warm and woody in floors, tables, trim, bar, bar stools, and ceiling rafters.

Hair of the Dog Brewery

Southeast/CES Map 61 SE Yamhill; (503) 232-6585
www.hairofthedog.com

Hoppy Hours No Happy Hour (Eight beers on tap)
Big tasting room for one of our founding microbrewies (1993), with full kitchen and big, garage-style pub.

Harvester Brewing
2030 SE 7th Ave; (503) 928-4195; harvesterbrewing.com

Dedicated gluten-free brewery! No Happy Hour, but taproom open 3:00-9:00pm Thurs-Sun. Gluten-free gastropub offers a big menu with full entrees, sandwiches, pizzas, and salads. Simple golden-walled tasting room, tables inside and out.

Fire on the Mountain

3443 NE 57th Ave; (503) 894-8973; portlandwings.com
4225 N Interstate / 1708 E Burnside (503)280-9464

Hoppy Hours 3:00-6:00pm

Drink Specials Daily $1.00 off pints and $3.00 off pitchers; All day Monday $ 2.50 pints and $9 pitchers

Food Deals Wide variety of pub grub (wings, pizzas, burgers, salads), but no food discounts at Happy Hour.

Fun, fiery, and funky, family-friendly restaurants. The 57th/Fremont location is the largest with a full bar and excellent outdoor patio with fireplace.

H.U.B. (Hopworks Urban Brew)

www.hopworksbeer.com

Bike Bar 3947 N. Williams; (503) 287-6258

Urban Brewery 2944 SE Powell Blvd; (503) 232-4677

Hoppy Hours 3:00–6:00pm and 9:00pm–close Daily

Food Deals $2.50-$5.75 A dozen or so tasty bar treats to complement award-winning beers, plus a couple of desserts: pizza, giant pretzels, outstanding chicken wings, big salads, hummus, and soups.

Drink Specials $.75 cents off drafts

Atmosphere Organic beer, sustainable food. Bike-, banquet-, baby- and beer-garden-friendly. Lots of natural woods and light inside. Nice beer gardens. Bike frames overhang the bars. And there's 99 bottles of beer on the walls!

Kells, McMenamins Breweries, Old Town Brewing (Old Town Pizza)

Beer brewed on-site. See index for Happy Hour info.

Laurelwood Brewpubs

www.laurelwoodbrewpub.com

5115 NE Sandy; (503) 282-0622
6716 SE Milwaukie Ave; (503) 894-8267
PDX Airport Concourse A (503) 493-9427 (No HH)
PDX Airport Concourse E (503) 281-6753 (No HH)
1401 SE Rasmussen; Battleground, WA (360) 723-0937

Hoppy Hours 3:00–6:00pm and 9:00–close Daily

Food Deals $4.00–5.00 Nine bar bites: burgers (meat or veggie), Caesar, garlic fries, pork sliders, nachos, artichoke dip, and hummus.

Drink Specials $3.00 drafts

Atmosphere Since 2001, neighborhood-, family- and friend-focused. Casual, neighborhood hangouts. "Portland's Original Certified Organic Brewery."

Lompoc Brewpubs

www.newoldlompoc.com

Hedgehouse
3412 SE Division; (503) 235-2215

Hoppy Hours 4:00–6:00pm and 10:00pm–close Daily
Beer special: $3.50 pints; $2.50 pints on Tuesdays
Food deals: $2.00–$5.00 Seven snacks like Welsh
rarebit, nachos, beer cheese dip, and hummus.

Family- and dog-friendly. Fun, super-big patio area
outside; cute & cozy converted craftsman interior.

Lompoc Fifth Quadrant & Sidebar Tasting Room
3901 N. Williams; (503) 288-3996
Hoppy Hours 4:00–6:00pm and 10:00pm–close Daily
Beer special: $3.50 pints ($2.50 pints all day Tuesday)
$1.00 off cocktails; Plus $3.00 Bloody Mary Sunday
Food deals: $5.00 select appetizers (burger, wings,
nachos, salad, hummus, beer cheese dip, fries).

Fresh and colorful, loft-style brewpub; long wooden
booths for socializing; outdoor covered patio open to
restaurant. Sidebar bonus room!

Lompoc Tavern
1620 NW 23rd Ave; (503) 894-9374
Hoppy Hours 4:00–6:00pm and 10:00pm–close Daily
Beer special: $3.50 drafts; $1.00 off cocktails
Food deals: None as of press time

Reminiscent of the former New Old Lompoc, but
spiffed up a bit, with much of the same adornments.

Oaks Bottom Pub
1621 SE Bybee; (503) 459-4988

Hoppy Hours 3:00–6:00pm and 9:00pm–close Daily
Beer special: $3.50 Lompoc pints ($2.50 Mondays);
$1.00 off wine and wells; $3.00 Bloody Mary Sunday
and mimosas too!
Food deals: $4.00–$5.00 Best totchos ever! Plus
pita-za hummus platter, shrooms, sliders, wings, fries.

Small but popular neighborhood haunt with a café
appeal and outside seating on back patio.

Lucky Labs www.luckylab.com

Lucky Labrador Brew Pub
915 SE Hawthorne; (503) 236-3555

Lucky Labrador Beer Hall
1945 NW Quimby; (503) 517-4352

Lucky Labrador Public House
7675 SW Capitol Hwy.; (503) 244-2537

Lucky Labrador Tap Room
1700 North Killingsworth; (503) 505-9511

Miser Mondays for $1.00 off beers (Hawthorne and Killingsworth) and Tuesdays at Capitol Hwy or Quimby. No food HH deals. Casual favorites in big, woody spaces. Big rooms, dog- and family-friendly.

Mashtun Brewpub

North/NE Map 2204 NE Alberta; (503) 548-4491
www.themashtunbrewpub.com

Hoppy Hours 3:00–6:00pm Daily

Food Deals $2.50–$5.00 Tasty basics that go well with beer and pool. Generous servings of tots!

Drink Specials $3.50 drafts and wells

Atmosphere Very casual and warehouse-y pub with big patio. Large and open garage-like space.

Max's Fanno Creek

Tigard 12562 SW Main St; (503) 624-9400
www.maxsfannocreek.com

Hoppy Hours 3:00–6:00pm and 9:00pm–close Daily

Food Deals $2.00–$5.00 A good 15 bar eats like hummus, quesadillas, mushrooms, mac & cheese, nachos, Caesar, fish & chips, sliders, artichoke hearts.

Drink Specials $1.00 off drafts (8 taps)

Atmosphere Very casual brewpub with central hand-painted pillar and few other quirky art pieces. Exterior looks almost like a convenience store.

Migration Brewing

Lloyd Center-ish 2828 NE Glisan Street; (503) 206-5221
www.migrationbrewing.com

Hoppy Hours 3:00–6:00pm Mon-Fri (and all Blazer and Timbers games)

Beer special: $3.50 pints; $1.00 off wine

Food Deals: $3.00-$5.00 Good eats grub

Atmosphere Casual and low-key PDX-style micro-brewery with large TV (movie nights) and outdoor picnic tables. Seven brews with a few guest taps.

Old Ivy Brewery & Taproom

Vancouver Map 108 W Evergreen; (360) 993-1827
www.salmoncreekbrewpub.com

Hoppy Hours 3:00–6:00pm Tues–Fri

Food Deals $3.00–$5.00 Pub munchies made for beer: chips & salsa, quesadilla, pork sliders, chili.

Drink Specials $3.50 pints on Tuesdays only

Atmosphere Formerly Salmon Creek Brewery with new owners. A cozy little pub interior with hunter green walls, café curtains, tin ceilings, memorabilia and art, and twinking white lights everywhere. Charming, private patio with brick walls covered in ivy.

Old Market Pub & Brewery

Garden Home 6959 SW Multnomah; (503) 244-2337
www.drinkbeerhere.com

Hoppy Hours 2:00-6:00pm and 9:00-close Daily

Food Deals $2.00-$4.75 Extensive pub food menu

Drink Specials Rotating daily drink deal
Note: Their beer is also served at The Broadway Grill 1700 NE Broadway; (503)284-4460
Atmosphere Big red barn exterior, and decorated like a pub, and an old market. Go figure! Casual and nice, wood booths and tables, outdoor patio.

Pints www.pintsbrewing.com

Old Town Map 412 NW 5th Ave.; (503) 564-2739

Hoppy Hour 3:00-6:00pm Daily; ★Noon-9:00pm Sun

Beer special: $3.50 pints

Food Deals: $3.00-$4.00 Small menu of basics: Chicken tenders, fries, flatbread, sliders, hummus.

Atmosphere Coffeehouse by day, urban taproom by night (find the cozy second back room with brick walls and working brewery). Locally roasted coffee *and* NW craft beers. What a perfect Portland concept!

Portland Brewing Taproom

NW/Nob Hill 2730 NW 31st Ave.; (503) 228-5269
www.macsbeer.com

Hoppy Hours 3:00–6:00pm and 9:00pm–close Daily

Food Deals $3.00–$5.00 A dozen big bar bites like burgers (meat or SW bean/veggie), pork sliders, tacos, corndogs, Caesar, fries, hummus, Scottish pie – and desserts too!

Drink Specials $3.50 drafts; $10.50 pitchers
$4.00 house wine or mimosas

Atmosphere Formerly MacTarnahan's. Also Pyramid Ale House. A little bit of everything strewn throughout 3-4 rooms, with the patio being a highlight. Cozy and pubby back room, TVs and views of beer vats in front.

Raccoon Lodge

7424 SW Beaverton-Hillsdale Hwy.; (503) 296-0110
www.raclodge.com

Hoppy Hours 4:00–6:00pm / 9:00pm–close Daily
All day 10:00am–2:00pm Sat–Sun (in the Den only)

Food Deals: $3.00–$7.95 Big bar menu has it all

Drink Specials $3.50 three select microbrews (20 oz.)

Atmosphere Home of Cascade Brewing Company (since 1998). Simple, clean, basic pub with pool and TV. Popular and enjoyable outdoor beer garden!

Ram Brewery www.theram.com

29800 SW Boones Ferry; Wilsonville (503) 570-0200
9073 SE Sunnyside; Happy Valley (503) 659-1282
(30 locations throught the U.S.)

Hoppy Hours 3:00–6:00pm and 9:00pm–mid Daily
(10:00-mid Fri-Sat)

Food Deals $2.99–$5.99 Three styles of sliders, three
kinds of fries, calamari, potato skins, nachos, spinach
dip, hummus, and armadillo eggs!

Drink Specials $3.25 drafts, wines, or wells

Atmosphere Big, bold, and woody befitting the
Big Horn Brewing Company name and corporate style.
Sports, family-friendly and outdoor eating area.

Rock Bottom www.rockbottom.com

Downtown East Map 206 SW Morrison; (503) 796-2739
(34 locations throughout the U.S.)

Hoppy Hours 2:00–6:00pm Mon–Fri
9:00pm–close Sun–Thurs; 11:00pm–close Fri & Sat

Food Deals $1.95–$4.95 17 appetizer goodies!

Drink Specials $1.00 off pints, wine, cocktails (early)

Atmosphere Corporate-style open brewery; warm
coppers mixed with wood under soaring lofted ceilings;
bustling big bar area; sidewalk dining.

✳   ✳

✳ Remember to check our website
every once in a while for changes and closures.

www.happyhourguidebook.com

And please let us know if you see
information that needs changing.

Rogue Ales www.rogue.com

"Meeting Halls" are each different, and visiting each at least once should be on every beer lover's bucket list.

Portland Locations

Rogue Hall 1717 SW Park Ave; (503) 219-8000

Hoppy Hours 3:00–5:00pm Mon–Fri (food only)
Food Deals: $3.00–$5.00 bar food basics
Located in the heart of the PSU campus in the Vue Tower (formerly Paccini's). College bar casual with coffee too. Occasional Tiki Tuesdays (aloha shirts).

Rogue Ales Public House

1339 NW Flanders; (503) 222-5910

Hoppy Hours 3:00–5:00pm Mon–Fri (food only)
Food Deals: $3.00–$5.00 bar food basics
38 taps! A fun and rouge-ish interior with several bawdy bar rooms befitting the name and attitude.
Often a much-welcomed retreat from all the Pearliness nearby. Fun outside seating in the summertime. Occasional Tiki Tuesdays (aloha shirts).

Green Dragon 928 SE 9th Ave.; (503) 517-0606

Also home to Buckman Botanical Brewing
(503) 241-3800; www.buckmanbrewery.com

Hoppy Hours 4:00–6:00pm Daily
Food Deals $3.00–$5.00 Fresh, tasty bar bites
Drink Specials No drink discounts, but 62 taps!!
Atmosphere Open, garage-style brewery with a most heavenly beer selection of perfectly selected, rotating taps. Nice big beer garden! Next to the Q-hut.

Visit them at PDX! Concourse D (503) 282-2630

Visit them on the Coast!

Brewer's on the Bay
2320 OSU Drive; Newport, OR; (541) 867-3664

Rogue Ales Public House
748 SW Bay Blvd; Newport, OR; (541) 265-3188

Sasquatch Brewery

Out and About Map 6440 S.W. Capitol Highway
(503) 402-1999; www.sasquatchbrewery.com

Hoppy Hours 3:00–5:00pm and 9:00pm–close Daily

Food Deals $2.00–$6.00 Good beer go-withs like giant
pretzel, herbed popcorn, cheese or meat plates, soup,
greens, beet fritter, olives, fries or burger.

Drink Specials $3.50 beer of the Day; $4.00 wines

Atmosphere Casual brewery in converted craftsman
house. Traditional dining room with wood floors and
green walls. Summer fun on the new outdoor deck!

Stickmen Brewery & Skewery

Lake Oswego Map 40 N State: Lake Oswego
(503) 344-4449; www.stickmenbeer.com

Hoppy Hours 3:00–6:00pm / 9:00pm-close Mon–Fri

Food Deals $3.00–$7.00 Nice menu of soup, salads,
fries, poppers, spinach dip, burger, and chicken wings.
Check skewers on regular menu!

Drink Specials $3.50 pints; $1.00 off wines;
$6.00-$7.00 cocktails

Atmosphere It's right on the lake! This is the former
Oswego Lake House. They've really brightened up the
place. Traditional, somewhat nautical decor.

Tugboat Brewing Co.

Downtown East Map 711 SW Ankeny; (503) 226-2508
www.d2m.com/Tugwebsite

Hoppy Hours 4:00–6:00pm Mon–Fri
Beer Special: $4.00 drafts; $4.00 wines

Downtown Portland's oldest microbrewery and the perfect rainy-day hideout. Completely cozy with lots
of dark woods, loads of old books, and well-loved board
games. A secret treasure for dark days and nights. Per
their website: "nightly live jazz music, cool munchies,
and nice beer for nice people."

Widmer Gasthaus www.widmer.com

North/NE Map 929 N Russell; (503) 281-3333

Hoppy Hours 2:00–5:00pm Mon–Fri ('til 10pm Mon)
11:00am–close Sun

Food Deals $3.00–$8.00 ($2.00 off burgers Sun–Mon)
Bar menu with lots of food to go with beer, but without
the higher prices: BBQ pork sandwiches, pretzels,
salads, hummus, fondue, soup, wings, burgers.

Drink Specials $1.00 off pints

Atmosphere One of Oregon's biggest and best.
Nice looking space with bricks, wood pillars and trim,
and beer-colored walls. Fun – and free – tours Fri-Sun
(reservations are required).

• •

Volcanic Brewery!?

**Guest beers on tap?
Find it in a Tiki Hut?**
My very favorite Portland
brewery! Lively brews by
savage hop heads, Edward
Querfeld and Steve Woods.

www.facebook.com/
VolcanicBrewing

Small Microbreweries

No food served, but growler fills encouraged!
Can usually bring your own food from the outside.

13 Virtues Brewing Co.
6410 SE Milwaukie Ave; (503) 239-8544
www.13virtuesbrewing.com
Hoppy Hour 5:00-10:00pm Tues & Thur $2.95 pints
New brewery behind Philadelphia's Steaks & Hoagies

Ambacht Brewing
Hillsboro 1060 NE 25th Ave ; (503) 679-0710
www.ambacht.us
Tasting room open Tu-Fri 4:00-8:00pm

Base Camp Brewing
Southeast Map 930 SE Oak St; (503) 477-7479
www.basecampbrewingco.com
Hoppy Hour All day Mon, 3:00-6:00pm Tues-Fri,
Open-3:00pm Sat-Sun $1.00 off pints; $2.00 off
pitchers; Mon & Thurs $2.00 off growler fills
Very cool base camp decor for the adventurous.
Food carts outside: Pizza Box and Gonzo

Captured by Porches
Several locations (off map); (971) 207-3742
www.capturedbyporches.com
Following in the food cart distribution plan, but with
beer – and buses! Check website to find them. Genius!

The Commons Brewery
Southeast (off map) 1810 SE 10th Ave; (503) 343-5501
www.commonsbrewery.com
Eight house taps with occasional guests. Limited hours.

Gigantic Brewing
Southeast (off map) 5224 SE 26th Ave; (503) 208-3416
www.giganticbrewing.com
Cool tap room with funny flair here and there. Garage
style with outdoor picnic tables.

The Hoppy Brewer

Gresham 328 N Main Ave; (503) 328-8474
www.oregonshoppyplace.com
Homebrew supply shop plus bar with 12 taps.
Currently brewing three beers. Courtyard seating

Loowit Brewing

Vancouver 507 Columbia; (360) 566-2323
www.loowitbrewing.com
Tap room open Thurs-Sat (6 taps)

Mt. Tabor Brewing

Vancouver 113 W 9th St; (360) 696-5521
www.mttaborbrewing.com
Tasting room open Thurs & Fri only (9 taps)

Occidental Brewing Co.

North (off map) 6635 N. Baltimore; (503) 719-7102
www.occidentalbrewing.com
Simple tasting room in St. John's with a small bar area
open the the brewing warehouse. Tiny beer museum!

Three Mugs Brewing

Hillsboro 2020 NW Aloclek Dr.; (971) 322-0232
www.threemugsbrewing.com
Open every day. Same owners as Brew Brothers
Homebrew Products.

Upright Brewing

North/NE 240 N Broadway; (503) 735-5337
www.uprightbrewing.com
Bare-bones tasting room to enjoy samples, full beers,
and occasional live music.

Vertigo Brewing

Hillsboro 21420 NW Nicholas Ct; (503) 645-6644
www.vertigobrew.com
Big warehouse tasting room with barrel, picnic, and
metal tables. Stand steady or sit and sip a spell.

Happy Beer Pubs

All about beer and food – and Happy Hour too!

Bazi Bierbrasserie   Top cover fave 2013!

Southeast Map 1522 SE 32nd Ave; (503) 234-8888
www.bazipdx.com

Hoppy Hours 3:00-7:00 pm Daily (plus 10:00pm–close)
★All day Sunday

Food Deals $3.00-$8.00 Wide-ranging menu of 10
items: kale chips, veggie or carnivorous burgers,
pork belly skewers, charcuterie board, and merguez
sausage with creamy polenta.

Drink Specials $1.00 off most beers; $1.00 off wine
$3.50 wells; $5.00 cocktails (full bar including award-
winning signature BEER cocktails!)

Atmosphere *The* place for Belgian beers on tap!
They rotate 17 taps in all, and have over 50 bottles
and growlers. Nice back bar area; lounge area with
couches and tables up front. Roll-up garage door and
lots of light. "A wine bar of beer."

Birra Deli

Tualatin (Off map) 18749 SW Martinazzi; (503) 486-5172
www.birradeli.com

Hoppy Hours 2:00-5:00pm amd 8:00-11:00pm Daily

Food Deals $1.50-$3.50 Get a buck off chicken or
cheese quesadillas or chips & salsa

Drink Specials $1.00 off drafts

Atmosphere Named for the Italian word for beer.
Lotsa sandwiches, loads of beers. TVs and beer swag
cover the walls. Monthly beer tasting parties.

Caps & Corks

1000 NW 17th Ave; (503) 222-6435
www.capsandcorks.com

Hoppy Hours 3:00–6:11pm Daily (they cut ya slack :-)
Plus late-night the last hour before closing

Food Deals $3.00–$5.00 Wide array with the usual
bar line-up, plus some fancy stuff like steak bites and
baked brie. About 15 menu items.

Drink Specials $3.50 select beer; $4.00 house wines
$4.00 wells

Atmosphere Formerly the Emanon, now a popular
stop on the super-fun BrewCycle tour. They have several
coolers packed with hundreds of beers, plus a great
wine shop. Extremely casual, especially for the Pearl.
They have 7 taps and 350 bottles of beer and wine!

Concordia Ale House

North/NE (off map) 3276 NE Killingsworth
(503) 287-3929; www.concordia-ale.com

Hoppy Hours 3:00–6:00pm Mon–Fri; $2.00 Tuesdays
(noon–mid Your choice of 20 bottles)

Food Deals $3.75 About 10 bar apps cover all the
bases: nachos; plain, veggie or cheeseburgers; BBQ
pork sandwich; chili cheese fries, wings, tots, mac &
cheese; quesadillas, or healthy salads.

Drink Specials Sadly, no drink deals.

Atmosphere A visit to Concordia's Great Wall of
Taps is a feast for the eyes and a touch of paradise
for the discriminating beer palate. Bar in back with
22 taps and over 150 bottles. Pool tables, keno et al.,
and TVs. Up front, family-friendly, neighborhood place.

Henry's Tavern

Pearl Map 10 NW 12th Ave.; (503) 227-5320
www.henrystavern.com

Hoppy Hours 3:00–6:00pm Daily; 9:00pm–close
Mon–Thur; 10:00pm–mid Fri–Sat; ★All day Sunday

Food Deals $3.95–$6.95 About 12 items: a couple salads, soup, mac & cheese, sushi roll, burger, killer Gorgonzola fries(!), prawns, hummus, dip, and more.

Drink Specials $1.00 off drafts; $4.00 wines, wells

Atmosphere A popular, long-time Portland favorite. Warm, but very spacious ex-brewery; open two-story seating; huge center bar; loft-style bricks & iron; patio (now allows HH seating). More than 100 beers on tap with refrigerated bar top to keep them chilled!

Highland Stillhouse

Oregon City Map 201 S. 2nd Street; (503) 723-6789 www.highlandstillhouse.com

Hoppy Hours 3:00–6:00pm Tues–Fri

Food Deals $4.00–$5.00 If you love haggis balls, you'll love the Highland Stillhouse! Or on the possibly less-interesting side, there's also wings, rings, shrimp cocktail, fried mushrooms, coconut prawns, mac & cheese, and sliders.

Drink Specials $1.00 off beer and wine (rotating beer specials with 18 choice taps)

Atmosphere Step inside and sample a whisky (there's more than 400 to try)! Stay and relax – the wall-to-wall Scottish decor transports you to a whole other time and country, and the upstairs is especially loaded with true tavern character. Outside patio.

Hop & Vine   www.thehopandvine.com

North/NE Map 1914 N Killingsworth; (503) 954-3322

Hoppy Hours 3:00–6:00pm Mon–Sat;
★3:00pm–close Sunday

Food Deals $2.00–$8.00 Limited Happy Hour menu: Olives, popcorn of the day, butter lettuce salad, cheeseburger, tomato soup with grilled cheese.

Drink Specials $1.00 off beer and wine

Atmosphere Everything to make a hoppy beer lover happy. And a large wall of wine makes it a bottle shop heaven too! Simple and mellow backyard picnic table seating, with hops and vines. Coffeehouse-like interior.

Hophouse(s) www.oregonhophouse.com

Hawthorne Map 4111 SE Hawthorne; (503) 477-9619
North/NE (off map) 1517 NE Brazee; (971) 266-8392

Hoppy Hours 3:00–6:00pm and 9:00pm–close Daily
★3:00pm–close Sunday

Food Deals $3.00-$7.00 Good for beer drinkin' food, plus a little more: cheese curds, poutine, fries, crostini, chicken satay, deviled eggs, sliders.

Drink Specials $1.00 off select beer

Atmosphere The 15th Ave. location hosts 33 local taps and has outside seating. Hawthorne Hophouse, has "only" 24 taps. Not an overdose of personality to these places, but they are fun!

Oregon Public House

North/NE (off map) 700 NE Dekum; (503) 828-0884
www.oregonpublichouse.com

Hoppy Hours 2:00-6:00pm & 9:00pm-close Daily

Food Deals $3.50-$6.00 Good food that covers the basics: cheeseburger, garden burger, hummus plate, chicken or vegetarian nachos, fries, cheesy bread.

Drink Specials $1.00 off drafts

Atmosphere Such a cool space and an immediate new fave! Brick walls, cement floors, reclaimed wood tables, outside seating, 12 taps, family-friendly. "Have a Pint – Change the World"! 100% of net profits go to various non-profits; run/staffed by volunteers.

Saraveza www.saraveza.com

North/NE Map 1004 N Killingsworth; (503) 206-4252

Happy Hours: 4:00-6:00pm Mon-Fri $1.00 off drafts

Food Deals $3.50-$5.50 Six or seven items on a rotating menu. Overall, their menu focuses on pasties, pickling, house meats, and Midwest treats.

Drink Specials $1.00 off beer and wine

Atmosphere 200+ bottles and 10 rotating taps! Very cool neighborhood pub! Fun, bottle-cap tables. A bit of a Packer bar, with raving fans of its own!

More Pubs with a Big Beer Focus

Dublin Pub
6821 SW Beaverton-Hillside Hwy.; (503) 297-2889
www.dublinpubpdx.com
Happy Hours: 3:00–7:00pm and 10:00pm-close Daily
$.75-$1.50 off pints; $1.00 off wells $3-$5 HH food

59 beers on tap; over 30 more in bottles. Since 1983,
a very popular Irish pub in Southwest PDX. Pool and
frequent live music. Ultra-casual bar. Cheap grub.

Horse Brass Pub www.horsebrass.com
4534 SE Belmont; (503) 232-2202
No Happy Hour Legendary English Pub style and has
59 taps! "It's #7 of the 125 places to have a drink in
the world before you die" ~ All About Beer Magazine

Moon & Six-Pence
2014 NE 42nd Ave; (503) 288-7802
No Happy Hour Super-casual and somewhat old, but
that makes it seem more British, in a good way.

Prost! www.prostportland.com
4237 N. Mississippi; (503) 954-2684
No Happy Hour Highly popular place and worth going.
Nice German pub w/over-sized beer mugs—and boots!

Roscoe's www.roscoespdx.com
8105 SE Stark; (503) 255-0049
Happy Hours: 2:00–6:00pm Daily; $3.00 wells;
$3.00-$5.00 food menu. Big and well-chosen tap line-up.

Rose & Thistle Pub
2314 NE Broadway; (503) 287-8582
Happy Hours: 3:00-7:00pm Mon-Fri
$2.75 well, $4.00 20 oz micros
Haggis, scotch eggs, character, and a great patio!

Bottle Shops & Taprooms

1856
1465 NE Prescott; (503) 915-0135; www.1856pdx.com
Beer, wine, cider, vermouth, bitters, books. Tiny place with 350 beers, wine, and six rotating taps.

Apex
1216 SE Division; (503) 273-9227; www.apexbar.com
Enjoy 50 taps with a wide variety of beer styles.
No food served, but next to a Mexican take-out. Giant patio, small bar. Bike friendly, but no dogs or kids.

Bailey's Tap Room
213 SW Broadway; (503) 295-1004 baileystaproom.com
20 Rotating Taps of Craft Ales and Lagers. Prime location downtown and really cool place!

Beer Bunker
7918 SE Stark St; (503) 254-8200
Old tin signs, office chairs, and hanging beer-can lights.

BeerMongers
1125 SE Division; (503) 234-6012 thebeermongers.com
500+ beers and 8 rotating, mostly local taps.

Belmont Station
4500 SE Stark; (503) 232-8538 belmont-station.com
1,000 beers in the store; Italian Market next door. Patio.

Beer
1410 SE Stark; (503) 233-2337
www.facebook.com/BeerPortland
Small bar and bottle shop next to Meat Cheese Bread.

Bottles
5015 NE Fremont; (503) 287-7022 www.bottlesnw.com
<u>Happy Hour:</u> 3:00–6:00pm Mon-Fri
$4.00 drafts
Cool and very casual neighborhood bottle shop with ribs, wings, sliders, eight rotating taps, and hundreds of bottles. Great outdoor beer garden!

Bridgetown Beerhouse
915 N Shaver; (503) 477-8763
www.bridgetownbeerhouse.com
Tiny, northeast bottleshop. Five taps, growler fills.

By the Bottle
104 W. Evergreen, Vancouver, WA (360) 696-0012
www.www.bottledbrews.com
A store, taproom, a sight to see. Over 600 types of beer!

Hop Haven
2130 NE Broadway; (503) 287-0244
150 bottles of beer & cider to stay or go
HH Daily until 8:00pm and all Sunday; $0.50 off drinks
Late night "Color" Happy Hour - They pick a color and
then if it's on bottle label, tap handle, beer style, etc. you
get the $0.50 discount
"Double" Happy Hour until 6:00pm on weekdays
$1.00 off (drafts, wells, ciders)
*Small bar with four taps, sidewalk seating, no food but
you can bring from outside.*

Imperial Bottle Shop and Taproom
3090 SE Division 971-302-6899
www.imperialbottleshop.com
Happy Hour Monday only $3 imperial pints

*Hundreds of bottles of the best American craft beer,
16 local beers on tap. Grower fills, sidewalk seating.*

John's Marketplace
3535 SW Multnomah Blvd; (503) 244-2617
www.johnsmarketplace.com
*More than 800 different bottled beers and lots of kegs
too. Plus – they carry over 400 different wines!*

Northwest Liquid Gold
11202 NE Fourth Plain Blvd; (360) 326-4281
www.northwestliquidgold.com
Happy Hour 2:00-4:00pm Mon-Fri; $1.00 off drafts
Enjoy 20 taps of NW beers and growlers. TVs. Patio.

NW Growlers
6141 SW Macadam Ave #101; (503) 245-4509
www.nwgrowlers.com
30 rotating taps!

N.W.I.P.A.
6350 SE Foster; www.nwipapdx.com
*Bottle shop specializing in IPA's; six taps, growler fills,
also serves wine, coffee, soda*

Plew's Brews
8409 N. Lombard; (503) 283-2243
www.plewsbrews.com
<u>Happy Hour</u> 4:00–7:00pm Mon–Fri $1.00 off drafts
*Funky and fun tasting room and possibly the best place
in town to fill your growlers (only eight bucks)!*

Portland Bottle Shop
7960 SE 13th Ave; (503) 232-5202
www.pdxbottleshop.com
*Outside patio, weekly wine & beer tastings, four taps.
Sells fine wines & specialty beers plus snacks (olives,
meats, cheeses, etc.)*

Portland U-Brew & Pub
6237 SE Milwaukie; (503) 943-2727
www.portlandubrewandpub.com
<u>Happy Hour</u> 3-6pm $.50-$1.00 off beer; $4.00 wines
$1.50-$3.00 Pretzels, nachos, sliders, pizza.
*Make your own beer! Learn new important skills from
friendly and knowledgeable staff. Brew on premises with
everything you'll need. Stocked-up for home brewing.*

Tin Bucket
3520 N Williams; (503) 477-7689; www.tin-bucket.com
36 craft beers + 4 ciders on tap

Uptown Market
6620 SW Scholls Ferry Rd; (503) 336-4783
www.uptownmarketpdx.com
<u>Happy Hour</u> $3.00 drafts Mondays; $10 growler fills
*Specialty brew store with 700 bottles and six taps too.
Homebrew and kegerator experts, consultants, and
suppliers.*

McMenamins Hotels

Crystal Hotel
303 SW 12th Ave.; Downtown Portland; (503) 972-2670
Right across the street from the Crystal Ballroom.
Houses Al's Den for live music and the Zeus Café too.

Edgefield
2126 SW Halsey; Troutdale; (503) 669-8610
38-acre renovated "Poor Farm;" golf course, movie
theater, beer garden, casual and fine-dining, wine bar,
Jerry Garcia bar, Little Red Shed Pub, and Spa.

Gearhart Hotel
1157 N. Marion Ave; Gearhart (coast); (503) 717-8150
Eighteen guestrooms on a golf course with pub.

Grand Lodge
3505 Pacific Ave.; Forest Grove; (503) 992-9533
Stately ex-Masonic lodge and nursing home near
Wine Country; restaurants, bars, movies, soak tub.

Hotel Oregon
310 NE Evans Street; McMinnville; (503) 472-8427
Weekend get-away in wine country; rooftop bar (great
for viewing UFOs), pub, back bar, Cellar Bar, billiards.

Kennedy School
5736 NE 33rd Ave.; Portland; (503) 249-3983
Detention Bar, Honors Bar, Boiler Room Bar, movies,
soaking pool, beer garden, party rooms, restaurant.

Old St. Francis School
700 NW Bond; Bend; (541) 382-5174
Old 1936 Catholic schoolhouse transformed into
a heavenly entertainment complex.

White Eagle
836 N. Russell; Portland (503) 335-8900
A small "rock 'n' roll hotel" with resident "spirits"
(it's reportedly haunted), nightly bands, saloon,
and outdoor, seasonal beer garden.

McMenamin's Pubs

Select favorites – see their website for all pubs.

Bagdad Theater/Greater Trumps
3702 SE Hawthorne; (503) 236-9234
Arabian-Nights-inspired movie theater and secret pub.

Blue Moon Tavern
432 NW 21st Ave.; (503) 223-3184
Meandering bar with table-top fireplace in the round
and pool tables; outdoor sidewalk seating.

Chapel Pub
430 N Killingsworth; (503) 286-0372
A sanctuary with lots of cozy rooms. Outdoor patio.

Crystal Ballroom
1332 W Burnside; (503) 225-0047
Awesome place to see concerts! The ballroom floor
is spring-loaded so it bounces slightly, and there's
'80s nights downstairs at Lola's (check calendar).

McMenamins on the Columbia
1801 SE Columbia River Dr.
Vancouver, WA; (360) 699-1521
Brews with views! See full review on page 86.

McMenamins Tavern & Pool
1716 NW 23rd Ave.; (503) 227-0929
Heated outdoor tables; big pool room.

Mission Theater
1624 NW Glisan; (503) 223-4527
$3.00 movies in old Swedish evangelical mission.

Ram's Head
2282 NW Hoyt; (503) 221-0098
Sophisticated manly-man haven.

Ringler's Pub
1332 W. Burnside; (503) 225-0627
Funky ex-auto garage.

Zeus Café
303 SWt 12th Ave.; (503) 384-2500
The latest and greatest in the brand-new Crystal Hotel.

Distilleries

All listed below have tasting rooms.

Big Bottom Whiskey www.bigbottomwhiskey.com
21420 NW Nicholas Ct, Suite D-9 Hillsboro
(503) 608-7816

Bull Run Distilling Co. www.bullrundistillery.com
2259 NW Quimby; (503) 707-1619

Clear Creek Distillery www.clearcreekdistillery.com
2389 NW Wilson; (503) 248-9470

Eastside Distilling www.eastsidedistilling.com
1311 SE 9th Ave; (503) 234-2513

House Spirits www.housespirits.com
2025 SE 7th Ave; (503) 235-3174

Indio Spirits www.indiospirits.com
7272 SW Durham Rd #100; (503) 620-0313

McMenamins Edgefield Distillery
2126 SW Halsey,Troutdale; (503) 492-5444
www.mcmenamins.com/edgefield

McMenamins Cornelius Pass Roadhouse
www.mcmenamins.com/cpr
4045 NW Cornelius Pass; Hillsboro; (503) 640-6174

New Deal Distillery www.newdealdistillery.com
900 SE Salmon St; 503-234-2513

Rogue Distillery www.rogue.com
1339 NW Flanders; (503) 222-5910

Rolling River Spirits www.rollingriverspirits.com
1215 SE 8th Street: (503) 236-3912

Stone Barn Brandyworks
www.stonebarnbrandyworks.com
3315 SE 19th, Suite B; (503) 775-6747

Vinn Distillery www.vinndistillery.com
833 SE Main St. Suite 125; (503)807-3826

Cideries

These places have tasting rooms unless otherwise noted.

Reverend Nat's Hard Cider
1813 NE 2nd Ave; (503) 567-2221
www.reverendnatshardcider.com

Bushwhacker
6710 N Catlin Ave; (503) 283-4335
www.bushwhackercider.com

Finnegan
P.O. Box 2185 Lake Oswego; (503) 703-6786
www.finnegancider.com
No tasting room

Portland Cider Co.
275 Beavercreek Rd Oregon City; (503) 908-7654
www.portlandcider.com
No tasting room

Square Mile Cider Co.
929 N. Russell Street; (503) 281-2437
www.squaremilecider.com
*Launched by Craft Brewers Alliance/Widmer Bros.
and shares their address.*

Outcider
1313 NE Lombard Pl, Unit B; (503) 719-3402
www.glutenfreeoutcider.com
No tasting room

Cider Riot
Location: Abram Goldman-Armstrong's garage
www.ciderriot.com
Launch date January 2014. No tasting room.

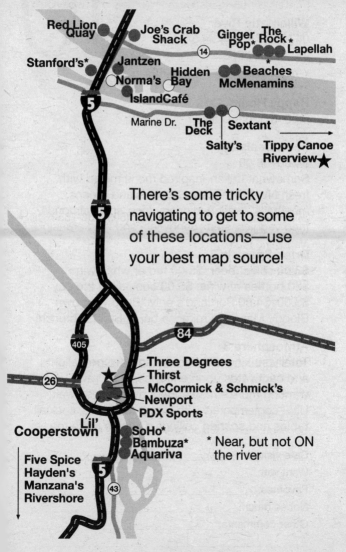

Red Lion Quay

Joe's Crab Shack

Ginger Pop*

The Rock *

Lapellah

(14)

Stanford's*

Jantzen

Hidden Bay

Beaches

McMenamins

Norma's

IslandCafé

Marine Dr.

The Deck

Sextant

Salty's

Tippy Canoe

Riverview ★

There's some tricky
navigating to get to some
of these locations—use
your best map source!

84

405

(26)

Three Degrees

Thirst

McCormick & Schmick's

Newport

PDX Sports

Lil'
Cooperstown

SoHo*

Bambuza*

Aquariva

* Near, but not ON
the river

Five Spice
Hayden's
Manzana's
Rivershore

(43)

Aquariva

Willamette River
0470 SW Hamilton Ct
(503) 802-5850
www.aquarivaportland.com

Happy Hours
3:00–6:30pm Daily

Food Deals 3
$4.00–$8.00
Somewhat Italian-inspired menu mixed with
fresh NW influences: Sauvie Island greens,
meatballs, seasoned crispy fries, spicy almonds,
fried veggies, steak sandwich, and fried arancini.

Drink Specials 3
$3.00 select beer; $5.00 red or white wine
$20 bottles of wine; $6.00 cocktail of the day
$3.00–$4.00 Portland's only "Build your own"
Bloody Mary and mimosa bar at Sunday brunch!

Atmosphere 3
Totally striking architecture and design delights
and captivates upon entrance, and draws you in
wanting more – resplendent river views await!
Ultra-contemporary with comfy couch pits, cocktail
tables and soaring ceilings. Outside patio too.

Date visited: _____ **My Rating:** _____
Went with: _____
Favorites: _____
Not so much: _____
Other comments: _____
_____

Bambuza

Just off Willamette River
3682 SW Bond Ave.
(503) 206-6330
www.bambuza.com

Happy Hours
4:00–6:00pm Mon–Sat

Food Deals 3
$3.00–$5.00
About 20 delicious Vietnamese small plates!
Several salad rolls and spring rolls, skewers,
soups, wontons, coconut shrimp and fresh
salads.

Drink Specials 3
$3.00 NW bottled beers; $4.00 house wines
$5.00 select cocktails

Atmosphere 2
Colorful and bright, simple, quiet Asian bistro.
Open room with hanging orange lanterns, green
walls with bamboo stalks, lots of light from two
walls of windows. Not on the water, but close
enough to walk. Needs a full-page shout-out!

Date visited: _____ **My Rating:** _____
Went with: _____
Favorites: _____
Not so much: _____
Other comments: _____
_____

Beaches

Columbia River (Vancouver)
1919 SE Columbia River Dr.
(360) 699-1592
www.beachesrestaurantandbar.com

<u>PDX</u> Main Terminal Pre-Security; (503) 335-8385
3:00–6:00pm and 9:00-10:00pm Daily

Happy Hours
3:00–6:00pm Daily; ★3:00–10:00pm Mondays
9:00–11:00pm Daily ('til 10pm Sun-Mon)

Food Deals 3
$2.99-$4.99
Huge menu with 23 items! First off, there's a
brownie; also chipotle hummus, wings, taquitos,
BBQ chicken pizza, mac & cheese, burgers, tots,
fish & chips, rice bowls, and salads.

Drink Specials 3
$3.99 beer; $4.75 wines; $3.99 daily cocktail

Atmosphere 3
SO nice along the river here, but Happy Hour
is in the inside bar area only. Overall, has a fun,
but refined beach bar motif, wall-to-wall giant
windows for river peeks and big stone fireplace.

Date visited: _____ **My Rating:** _____
Went with: _____
Favorites: _____
Not so much: _____
Other comments: _____

_____

Five Spice

Lake Oswego Map
315 First St., Ste 201
(503) 697-8889
www.fivespicerestaurant.com

Happy Hours
3:00–6:00pm Daily ('til 5pm on outside deck)

Food Deals 3
$2.00–$9.00
About a dozen delicious delights with items like oysters on the half-shell, soup, satay, coconut shrimp, spring rolls, crab cakes, field greens, burgers. Plus $12 meat or cheese plates.

Drink Specials 3
$5.00 selection of wines, cocktails and drafts; plus 1/2 off bottles of wine on Sundays

Atmosphere 3
Head upstairs to their lounge area for Happy Hour and sit outside if possible for views of the lake! Inside, it's pleasant as well, with Northwest-natural stylings, lots of light and huge windows. Relaxing fireplace with lounge area and couches.

Date visited: _____ **My Rating:** _____

Went with: _____

Favorites: _____

Not so much: _____

Other comments: _____

_____

Jantzen Beach Bar&Grill

Columbia River
909 N Hayden Island Drive
(503) 283-4466
www.redlionontheriver.com

Happy Hours
3:00–6:00pm and 9:00–11:00pm Daily

Food Deals 2
$2.00–$10.00
About $2.00 off select appetizers: items like
goat cheese crostini, burgers, calamari, hummus,
dungeness crab cakes, clams, beef skewers.

Drink Specials 3
$3.00 daily draft; $5.00 wines
$4.00 cocktail of the day

Atmosphere 3
Wall-to-wall windows frame excellent river views!
Large black & white photos reveal scenes of bygone
glory days of Jantzen Beach Amusement Park.
Enjoy Happy Hour seating anywhere in the
understated, fine-dining restaurant or out on the
long, outdoor patio. Fully remodeled and nicely
appointed. Shenanigan's used to be next door.

Date visited: _____ **My Rating:** _____
Went with: _____
Favorites: _____
Not so much: _____
Other comments: _____
_____

Joe's Crab Shack 9

Columbia River (Vancouver)
101 SE Columbia Way
(360) 693-9211
www.joescrabshack.com

Happy Hours
4:00-7:00pm and 9:00-close Mon-Fri

Food Deals 3
$4.00-$7.00
Half off the entire appetizer (Get Started) menu!
Featuring over a dozen yummy seafood-centric
items like crab nachos, crispy calamari, garlicky
mussels, soup, dips, and clam strips.

Drink Specials 2
$3.00 all drafts; $3.00 hurricanes and well
Margaritas; $5.00 Patrón margaritas

Atmosphere 3
Extremely colorful and lively place, all decked
out in full-on crabby, shabby chic! Great views
of the river, where you can Happy Hour outside
in the summer (and in the bar). Family-friendly
restaurant side has dancing servers on the hour
and are a big hit with the kids.

Date visited: _____ **My Rating:** _____
Went with: _____
Favorites: _____
Not so much: _____
Other comments: _____
_____

Lil Cooperstown

9

Waterfront Map
1831 SW River Dr; (503) 719-5394
www.lilcooperstown.com

<u>Hillsboro</u>: 2947 SE 73rd Ave; (503) 718-7513
<u>Oregon City</u>: 19352 Molalla Ave; (503) 305-6954
<u>West Linn</u>: 1817 Willamette Falls; (503) 655-1995

Happy Hours
3:00–6:00pm and 9:00pm–close Daily

Food Deals 2
$1.99–$4.99
About a 20 item list covering all the bases: wings, rings, nachos, burger, fish & chips, pasta, tacos, quesadilla, pork sliders, salad soup, fries and more!

Drink Specials 3
$2.99–$5.49 domestics, micros and mondos!
$1.00 off all wines; $3.79 wells; $3.99 cocktails

Atmosphere 3
One of five locations, the Waterfront location is in the former Stanford's spot (near, but not on, the water). Patio! Overall, the restaurant sides are decked out with full throttle sports memorabilia, but bar side decor (with Happy Hour) may be more for the B team.

Date visited: _____ **My Rating:** _____

Went with: _____

Favorites: _____

Not so much: _____

Other comments: _____

Manzana's

Lake Oswego Map
305 1st St.
(503) 675-3322
www.manzanagrill.com

Happy Hours
4:00–6:00pm and 9:00pm–close Daily

Food Deals 3
$3.95–$6.95
Pork quesadilla, citrus honey chicken wings, BBQ sandwich, hummus, Caesar, sliders, seafood cakes, pork quesadilla, chimichangas.

Drink Specials 3
$1.00 off drafts; $4.00 red & white wine
$5.00 wells; $5.00 featured cocktails

Atmosphere 3
Mmmm... the rotisserie smell! Deep, dark, rich wooden booths and walls (new and modern). Big space attracts a crowd. Located right on the lake, but Happy Hour seating inside only. Part of the beloved Restaurants Unlimited Group.

Date visited: _____ **My Rating:** _____
Went with: _____
Favorites: _____
Not so much: _____
Other comments: _____
_____

McCormick&Schmick's
Harborside Pilsner Room

Willamette River
0309 SW Montgomery
(503) 220-1865
www.mccormickandschmicks.com

Happy Hours
3:00–6:00pm and 9:00pm–close Daily
10:00pm–close Fri–Sat (in the summer)

Food Deals 3
$2.99–$5.99

#1 Happy Hour in America!
–USA Today

A dozen or so items with a menu that changes
a bit every month, with items like sliders, tacos,
artichoke dip, wings, calamari, or hummus plate,
but then you almost always have to get the
famous cheeseburger and fries for only $3.95!

Drink Specials 3
$4.00 drafts; $5.00 wine; $6.00–$7.00 cocktails

Atmosphere 3
Gorgeous and stately restaurant overlooking the
Willamette River! Impressive, traditional-style.
Happy Hour inside, on bar side. Classy, but fun.

Date visited: _____ **My Rating:** _____

Went with: _____

Favorites: _____

Not so much: _____

Other comments: _____

_____

McMenamins
on the Columbia

• • • • • • • • • • • • • • • • • • **10**

Columbia River (Vancouver)
1801 S.E. Columbia River Dr.
(360) 699-1521
www.mcmenamins.com

Happy Hours
3:00–6:00pm / 10:00pm–close Daily

Food Deals 3
$2.00–$5.00
NOT just the usual line-up! On board with some unique, trending NW goodies like a kale Caesar, grilled asparagus, pickled veggies, pork sliders, steamer clams.

Drink Specials 3
$3.75 drafts ($10 pitcher); $6.00 wines
$3.75 wells; $5.00 cocktails
Deals on taster flights for both beer and wine

Atmosphere 3
An especially nice McMenamins with an onsite brewery for brews with views. Traditional spin to the interior, but it's all about being *outside* at Happy Hour!

Date visited: _____ **My Rating:** _____
Went with: _____
Favorites: _____
Not so much: _____
Other comments: _____
_____

Newport Seafood Grill

Willamette River
0425 SW Montgomery
(503) 227-3474
www.newportseafoodgrill.com

Happy Hours
3:00–6:00pm Daily (closed in the winter months)

Food Deals 3
$2.99–$5.99
Cheap and delicious menu with fish & chips, burger, chowder, tacos, pear and pecan salad, oyster shooters, teriyaki salmon.

Drink Specials 3
$3.99 draft beer, wines and wells, cocktails

Atmosphere 3
Located right out over the river amidst the yachts, docks and ducks in the marina. This is one of the best places in Portland to kiss! Get there early and hope for one of the few spots available outside on the patio (Happy Hour is upstairs in bar area).

Date visited: _____ **My Rating:** _____
Went with: _____
Favorites: _____
Not so much: _____
Other comments: _____
_____

The Quay

10

Columbia River (Vancouver)
100 Columbia
(360) 750-4940
www.redlion.com

Happy Hours
4:00–7:00pm Mon-Fri; ★2:00-7:00pm Sat
★All day Sunday

Food Deals 3
$2.50–$5.50
Half-off a dozen items! Plentiful and cheap with some key specialties like gorgonzola bacon cheese fries, butternut squash ravioli, fish tacos, crab cakes, calamari, flatbreads, salads, quesadilla.

Drink Specials 3
$3.00-$4.00 drafts, $4.50 house wines
$4.00 wells

Atmosphere 3
Rehab planned soon, but for now, it's a house-boat-like interior with dark woods everywhere, huge sailboat pulleys and thick ropes. River views, but more industrial looking as the I-5 bridge blocks things a bit.

Date visited: _____ **My Rating:** _____

Went with: _____

Favorites: _____

Not so much: _____

Other comments: _____

_____

Riverview

Sandy River / Troutdale
29311 SE Stark
(503) 661-FOOD (3663)
www.yoshidariverview.com

Happy Hours
4:00–7:00pm Daily; All night Tuesday★

Food Deals 3
$3.00–$5.00
Nice mix of bar menu faves done gourmet-style and switched out seasonally: BBQ ribs, Caesar, chowder, sliders, calamari, wontons, steak bites.

Drink Specials 3
$4.00 beer; $5.00 wine; $5.00 martinis / cocktails

Atmosphere 3
An absolutely gorgeous place! Fine dining with views of the Sandy River and surrounding forest. The Happy Hour area is in the lounge side, and patio tables no longer host Happy Hour seating. Keep it in mind after a Sunday Gorge hike (unless your shoes are muddy 'cause it's fancy here)! Frequent live music.

Date visited: _____ **My Rating:** _____
Went with: _____
Favorites: _____
Not so much: _____
Other comments: _____
_____

Salty's

Columbia River
3839 NE Marine Drive
(503) 288-4444
www.saltys.com/portland

Happy Hours
4:00–6:00pm Mon–Sat; 4:30pm-6:00 Sun
Weekend hours may vary depending on season

Food Deals 3 *2012 Happy Hour of the Year!*
$2.00–$9.00
More than a dozen superb menu items including a
cup of award-winning seafood chowder (yum!),
blackened salmon Caesar, fish & chips, oysters,
chilled or coconut prawns, calamari, fish tacos,
and the *best* bacon cheeseburgers around!

Drink Specials 3
$3.00 select beer; $6.00 wine selections
$5.50 Select boat drinks

Atmosphere 3+
Fine-dining waterside restaurant; wall-to-wall
giant windows and stellar outdoor deck; yacht
club motif. Gorgeous scenery along the river,
and a great place to watch the sunset!

Date visited: _____ **My Rating:** _____
Went with: _____
Favorites: _____
Not so much: _____
Other comments: _____
_____

Thirst

Willamette River
0315 SW Montgomery (RiverPlace)
(503) 295-2747
www.thirstwinebar.com

Happy Hours
3:00–6:00pm Tues–Sun (All day Sun)

Food Deals 3

Top cover fave 2013!

$2.00–$6.00
Delicious nibbles perfect with wine (plan and pair your choices): hot crab dip, baked brie, stuffed and wrapped dates, chili, salads and soups. Plus sharable charcuterie and cheese plates and flat iron steak with mashed potatoes ($9.00).

Drink Specials 3
$3.00 beer; $5.00 select wine (try the $9.00 flight)
$5.50 cocktail of the day

Atmosphere 3
Right on RiverPlace Esplanade with huge windows and sidewalk seating for people and river-gazing; lovely lounge area with comfy couch and fireplace. A truly enjoyable wine bar, now with a separate NW wine tasting room!

Date visited: _____ **My Rating:** _____

Went with: _____

Favorites: _____

Not so much: _____

Other comments: _____

_____

Three Degrees

10

Willamette River
1510 SW Harbor Way (RiverPlace)
(503) 295-6166
www.threedegreesrestaurant.com

Happy Hours
4:00–7:00pm Daily

A Happy Hour favorite!

Food Deals 3
$3.00–$5.00
Menu covers basic demands in bar food with
grilled cheese or a cheeseburger, plus some
more healthy snacks like edamame, chicken
satay, hummus plate or a mixed green salad.

Drink Specials 3
$4.00 drafts; $4.00 red or white wine
$4.00 wells; $6.00 cocktail of the day

Atmosphere 3
Romantic upscale perfection; river view with lots
of windows, cushy seats, and a cozy fireplace.
Summer weather treats us to their outstanding
outdoor deck. Free valet parking!

Date visited: _____ **My Rating:** _____
Went with: _____
Favorites: _____
Not so much: _____
Other comments: _____
_____

Tippy Canoe

9

Sandy River / Troutdale
28242 E Historic Columbia Hwy.
(503) 492-2220
www.shirleysfood.com

Happy Hours
3:00–6:00pm Mon-Fri

Food Deals 3
$3.00–$4.00
Half-off appetizers: BBQ beef, jalapeno poppers,
wings, spinach artichoke dip, fried mushrooms,
or a quesadilla. Or just split a GIANT sandwich
(no HH discounts).

Drink Specials 3
$2.00 domestics; $3.00 micros; $3.75 wells

Atmosphere 3
Also known as Shirley's Tippy Canoe Bar & Grill
on the Sandy River. Remodeled and re-opened
in early 2009, it still retains the look and feel of a
1940's woodsy, riverside lodge. Enjoy the patio
out back in the summer! Perfect location and
vibe when coming back from a hike in the Gorge.

Date visited: _____ **My Rating:** _____
Went with: _____
Favorites: _____
Not so much: _____
Other comments: _____
_____

The Deck www.thedeck.bz

Columbia River 33rd & Marine Dr.; (503) 283-6444
Happy Hours 12:00-6:00pm Daily★
Seasonal/Outdoor (mid-April – end of September)

Food Deals 2 $4.00-$7.75 Bar eats with emphasis
on seafarer's grub; shrimp, fish tacos, chili, nachos.

Drink Specials 2 $2.95-$3.95 beers; $5.00 wine
$4.25 wells; $4.50 margaritas

Atmosphere 3 Floating deck on the river (you'll feel
it move)! Down the ramp from McCuddy's parking lot,
past the harbor boats, to a slice of PDX paradise.

Island Café www.islandcafepdx.com

Hayden Island 250 NE Tomahawk.; (503) 283-0362

Happy Hours 3:00-6:00pm Mon-Fri
Seasonal/Outdoor (mid-April – mid-October)

Food Deals 2 $2.00-$5.00 Basic and limited pub grub

Drink Specials 1 Daily beer specials

Atmosphere 3 Totally tropical! Well, as much as you
can get in Portland anyway. A favorite treasure that's
worth fighting horrific traffic heading north on I-5.
They re-did the place, so may be open weekends.

Portland Sports Bar

Willamette River 1811 SW River Dr.; (503) 222-2027
www.portlandsportsbarandgrill.com

Happy Hours 3:00–6:00pm Daily

Food Deals 3 $3.00-$5.00 About a dozen menu
items, many with some real substance: philly cheese
steak, cheeseburger and fries, gyros, chicken coco
bowl, polish dogs, salad, hummus, fries and wings.

Drink Specials 3 $3.75 beers; $5.00 wines; $4.50
wells; $4.50 martinis (a very wide and fun variety)

Atmosphere 2 It's a small place for a sports bar, but
as such, it's a very nice one. Colorful jerseys hang from
the ceiling everywhere, there's a view (peek) of the river
outside in the summer, and good TV set-up inside.

Rivershore Bar and Grill

Willamette River / Oregon City
1900 Clackamette Dr.; (503) 655-5155
www.rivershorerestaurant.com

Happy Hours 3:00–6:00pm and 8:00–9:00pm Daily

Food Deals 2 $2.95–$4.95 More than a dozen bar
& grill items for a wide range of eats

Drink Specials 3 $2.00 domestics; $4.00 house
wines; $3.50 wells; $4.50 cocktail

Atmosphere 3 Wonderful outside deck here with a
beautiful view of the Willamette, but most of the year
Happy Hour is inside in the very casual bar area.

Soho Asian Fusion www.sohopdx.com

Just off Willamette River
3500 SW River Parkway; (503) 467-7533

Happy Hours 4:00pm–close Daily (Bar area)

Food Deals 3 $1.99–$6.99 Bar menu currently offers
22 tasty nibbles, plus 10 kinds of sushi (rolls and
nigiri). Enjoy fried tofu, wings or calamari, miso soup,
salads, mixed tempura, gyoza, sweet potato fries.

Drink Specials 3 $1.00 off drafts or wells; $6.00 wines
$4.00 sake; $6.00-$7.00 cocktails

Atmosphere 3 Large, open space with big, blocky
sandstone bricks, giant TV screen, and silky, wavy,
white back wall. Not on the water, but close enough to
walk. Soho can be translated into the saying "when you
smile, good things will happen."

On the Columbia

Hidden Bay
Waterside Map (Portland)
515 NE Tomahawk Island Dr; (503) 240-1871
Casual, with elevated views of river and marina.

Mark's on the Channel
Scappoose, OR
34326 Johnsons Landing Rd; (503) 543-8765
www.marksonthechannel.com
Cute place out on the docks in a floating home.

Norma's Kitchen
Waterside Map (Portland)
12010 N Jantzen Dr; (503) 240-3447
www.normaskitchen.org
N'awlins down-home cooking with views of the moorage below, but from inside (no deck).

Puffin Cafe
Washougal, WA
24 S "A" St; (360) 335-1522
www.puffincafe.com
Fun place out on the docks in a floating home.

Sextant
Waterside Map (Portland)
4035 NE Marine Dr.; (503) 281-5944
Casual, affordable watering hole on the river.

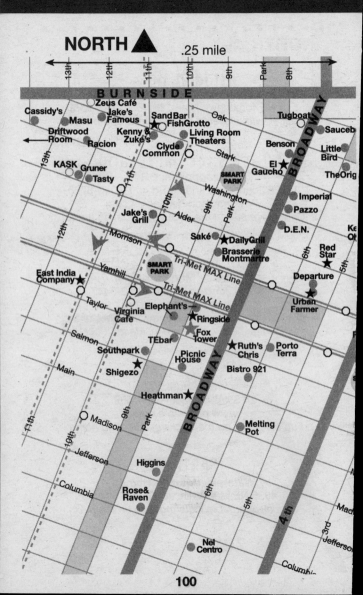

Downtown-East

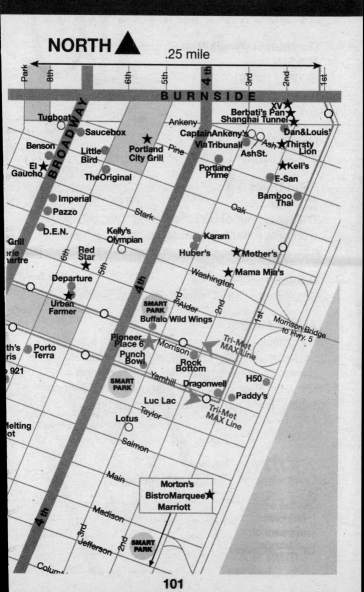

Bamboo Thai

10

Downtown (West) Map
108 SW Pine
(503) 241-2691
www.bamboo-thai.com

Happy Hours
3:00–6:00pm Mon-Sat

Food Deals 3
$2.00-$5.00
The full gamut of goodness: egg rolls, prawns,
wontons, meatballs, sausage, pad thai, fried
rice, pad see ew, satays, and papaya salad.

Drink Specials 3
$3.00 drafts; $5.00 wines; $5.00 cocktails

Atmosphere 3
A gorgeous and huge space with artful sensitivity
to design. Bamboo divider walls, big planters,
paintings, pillows, exposed brick, and soft
curtains. Several serene seating areas, plenty of
tables, giant bar, and room for a party!

Date visited: _____ **My Rating:** _____
Went with: _____
Favorites: _____
Not so much: _____
Other comments: _____
_____

Benson Hotel 10

Downtown (East) Map
309 SW Broadway
(503) 228-2000
www.bensonhotel.com

Happy Hours
4:00–6:00pm and 9:00pm–close Daily

A Happy Hour favorite!

Food Deals 3
$4.00-$6.00
Yay! A giant upgrade in their menu with some
great basics and other goodies: Caesar, clam
chowder, fries, fried veggies, wedge salad,
grilled cheese, crabcake sliders, grilled shrimp
with sweet chili, calamari, baked brie and pears.

Drink Specials 3
$2.00 off all beer and wine
$5.00-$6.00 cocktails

Atmosphere 3+
Historic and Fancy with a capital "F," their Palm
Court Bar in the hotel lobby offers the opportunity
to dine in high-style at a great value. Perfect place
to pretend you're Thurston or Lovey Howell.
It's simply fabulous, dahling! And whatever you do,
never ever miss it at Christmas time!

Date visited: _____ **My Rating:** _____
Went with: _____
Favorites: _____
Not so much: _____
Other comments: _____
_____

Bistro Marquee

Downtown (East) Map
200 SW Market
(503) 208-2889
www.bistromarquee.com

Happy Hours
4:00–7:00pm Mon–Fri *A Happy Hour favorite!*

Food Deals 3 $2.00-$7.00
French/wine bar basics and specialties with an
occasional creole spin. Changes a bit seasonally:
Soup, fries, hush puppies, salad, steak bites,
po' boys, lamb meatballs, fried chicken, sauteed
shrimp, mac & cheese, glazed carrots, beans.
Array of charcuterie, cheese, nibbles $2.50 each.
Half-price burgers 4:00-5:00pm (bar only).

Drink Specials 3
$3.00 drafts; $5.00 wines/sangrias; $5.00 wells

Atmosphere 3
Applause! This Happy Hour is a big hit with stellar
reviews all over the place! Located near the
Keller Auditorium in the former Carafe space.
Charming and relaxing outdoor courtyard patio,
and contemporary-yet-cozy bistro with comfy
cushioned booths. Same owners as Thirst.

Date visited: _____ **My Rating:** _____
Went with: _____
Favorites: _____
Not so much: _____
Other comments: _____
_____

Brasserie Montmarte

Downtown (West) Map
626 SW Park Avenue
(503) 236-3036
www.brasserieportland.com

Happy Hours
★2:30-6:30pm and 9:00pm-close Daily

A Happy Hour favorite!

Food Deals 3
$2.00-$7.00
Big and delicious Happy Hour menu! About half-off a dozen or so menu items with five kinds of flavored "frites" (duck fat with rosemary, pork belly w/tarragon, truffle fries, garlic aioli), salads, mac & cheese, frog legs, calamari, and burgers.

Drink Specials 3
$1.00 off drafts; $4.00 wine; $4.00 wells

Atmosphere 3
The new owners have hit it out of the park! Rather than jazzing things up, they've toned things down on a more country-rustic note. Giant gold mirrors over the bricked back bar, checkerboard floors, white-washed walls, cozy booths, and candlelit.

Date visited: _____ **My Rating:** _____
Went with: _____
Favorites: _____
Not so much: _____
Other comments: _____
_____

Clyde Common

Downtown (West) Map
1014 SW Stark
(503) 228-3333
www.clydecommon.com

Happy Hours
3:00–6:00pm Daily
11:00pm–close Mon–Sat (food only)

Food Deals 3
$3.00–$6.00
Dozen-item bar menu includes both unique and
mainstream treats like popcorn, pickled veggies,
burger, fries, grilled cheese, salad, and cookies.

Drink Specials 3
$3.50 drafts; $5.00 select wines
$5.00 fun and funky cocktails

Atmosphere 3
Big, open warehouse space like an unfinished, art
school gallery. Rough wood floors, banged-up
bar stools, stenciled signage, and butcher paper
walls give it a working-man edge. Popular social
scene with community table seating.

Date visited: _____ **My Rating:** _____
Went with: _____
Favorites: _____
Not so much: _____
Other comments: _____
_____

D.E.N. (Drink.Eat.Network)

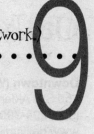

Downtown East
520 SW Broadway
(503) 552-2220
www.marriottportland.com

Happy Hours
4:00–6:00pm Daily

Food Deals 2
$4.00–5.00
The standard options on the typical bar menu, but they have standards, so the quality is there: wings, hummus, quesadilla, onion rings, Caesar, and a cheese plate.

Drink Specials 3
$5.00 drafts, wine, or wells

Atmosphere 3
Formerly the Mez, on the very grand gallery-like mezzanine level of the Marriott. Rich dark woods, decorative moldings, and a rotating artist showcase set the stage for elegance. Or hang out in the beautiful, typically empty lobby area. Makes me want to be all business-y to drink, eat, and network. Or maybe just do the first two.

Date visited: _____ **My Rating:** _____
Went with: _____
Favorites: _____
Not so much: _____
Other comments: _____
_____

Daily Grill

9

Downtown (West) Map
750 SW Alder
(503) 294-7001
www.dailygrill.com

Happy Hours
4:00–7:00pm Daily

Food Deals 2
$6.00–$8.00
Several at each price point: fries, rings, hummus;
quesadilla, wings, calamari, cheeseburger slider,
popcorn or coconut shrimp, pot pies, ahi sashimi.

Drink Specials 3
$4.00 drafts; $6.00 wine $6.00 wells
$7.00 cocktails; $10.00 build your own martini

Atmosphere 3
Newly remodeled bar is now accessible from
both restaurant-side as well as hotel lobby,
creating a more open, swanky feel with great art
and Chihuly-inspired glass fixtures. Sit in front
of the bartop fire and get online at one of the
iPad stations. Or, go for one of the cozy chairs
and put your feet up.

Date visited: _____ **My Rating:** _____

Went with: _____

Favorites: _____

Not so much: _____

Other comments: _____

_____

Departure

Downtown (East) Map
525 SW Morrison; Rooftop
(503) 222-9996
www.departureportland.com

Happy Hours
4:00–6:00pm Mon–Sat

Food Deals 3

A Happy Hour favorite!

$3.00–$9.00
Giant, mostly Asian-inspired menu with things
like maki rolls, edamame, wings, skewers, salads,
udon noodles, fried rice and much more!

Drink Specials 3
$5.00 beer; $6.00 wine; $20 bottle of bubbly
$6.00 cocktails/sake of the day

Atmosphere 3+
It's a departure from Portland norm in every
way! From the funky elevator entrance and
Space-Mountain-style exit, you know you're
someplace different. Warm weather offers three
top-floor patio seating areas with stellar views
of the city below and mountains in the distance.
Website has spectacular photography for a pre-tour.

Date visited: _____ **My Rating:** _____
Went with: _____
Favorites: _____
Not so much: _____
Other comments: _____
_____

Dragonwell

Downtown (East) Map
735 SW First Ave.
(503) 224-0800
www.dragonwellbistro.com

Happy Hours
★2:30–6:30pm Mon–Fri; 4:00pm–close Sun★
9:30–11:30pm Fri–Sat

Food Deals 3+
$1.00–$6.00

A Happy Hour favorite!

Phenomenal food! And 25+ choices! Amazing line-up of *everything:* General Tso's, orange, or sesame chicken; several versions of fried rice, lo mein, or salt & pepper dishes; several kinds of noodle dishes; salad or spring rolls, and more!

Drink Specials 3
$1.50 Sapporo; $5.00 red and white wine
$5.00 Happy Sake or Cocktail of the Day

Atmosphere 3
Serene, upscale restaurant with a wonderful mix of understated elegance, Asian simplicity and exceptional design. Bright by day, dark and intimate by night. Flexible group seating.

Date visited: _____ **My Rating:** _____
Went with: _____
Favorites: _____
Not so much: _____
Other comments: _____
_____

Driftwood Room

Downtown (West) Map
729 SW 15th Ave.
(503) 223-6311
www.hoteldeluxeportland.com

Happy Hours
★2:00–6:30pm and 9:30pm–close Daily

A Happy Hour favorite!

Food Deals 3
$4.00–$7.00
Outstanding menu with more than a dozen
choices: grilled portobello mushroom or Oregon
beef burgers, Caesar and mixed greens salads,
skewers, mac & cheese, flatbreads, fries.

Drink Specials 3
$4.00 daily draft; $6.00 wines
$20.00 bottle of wine (red or white)
$6.00 champagne cocktails

Atmosphere 3+
Off the very impressive grand lobby of the Hotel
deLuxe, the Driftwood has a dark, discreet, and
fancy ratpack appeal in a kidney-shaped, dimly-
lit, wooden room with NW touches. LOVE it!

Date visited: _____ **My Rating:** _____
Went with: _____
Favorites: _____
Not so much: _____
Other comments: _____
_____

East India Company

9

Downtown (West) Map
821 SW 11th Ave.
(503) 227-8815
www.eastindiacopdx.com

Happy Hours
5:00–7:00pm Mon–Sat

Food Deals 3
$3.00–$5.00
Expanded menu with old favorites and several
new ones: eggplant dip, wings, fish fingerlings,
veggie fritters, potato croquettes, spicy peanuts,
channa chaat, bhel puri.

Drink Specials 3
$4.00 drafts; $5.00 house wine
$1.00 off all drinks; $6.95 specialty cocktails

Atmosphere 2
Nice enough overall, but the front bar decor and
ambiance at Happy Hour pales in comparison
to the dark, rich, romantic restaurant in back.
But if you get a group of 6-8 together and call
ahead, you can get a nice table in the restaurant.
Otherwise, tables are made for 2-3 people up
front in the bar.

Date visited: _____ **My Rating:** _____

Went with: _____

Favorites: _____

Not so much: _____

Other comments: _____

_____

El Gaucho

Downtown (East) Map
319 SW Broadway
(503) 227-8794
www.elgaucho.com

Happy Hours
5:00–7:00pm Mon–Fri; 10:00pm–close Mon-Sat
★5:00pm-close Sun

Food Deals 3
$6.00–$18.00
Nine delicious menu items – on the spendy side,
but marked down from regular menu: steak w/
frites, cheddar bacon burger, fish & chips, beef
tenderloin kebabs, pasta, salad, cheese plates.

Drink Specials 3
$4.00 select beer; $6.00 red or white wine
$7.00 cocktails (four)

Atmosphere 3
Notably classy, classic steakhouse. Enjoy a
memorable evening in their dramatic lounge.
See a celebrity or just feel like one yourself.
(Author note: I think they have the best steaks
in the city! Worth the occasional splurge. BYOW
corkage fee $20.00)

Date visited: _____ **My Rating:** _____

Went with: _____

Favorites: _____

Not so much: _____

Other comments: _____

_____

Grüner

Downtown (West) Map
527 SW 12th Avenue
(503) 241-7163
www.grunerpdx.com

Happy Hours
4:30–6:00pm Mon–Fri

Food Deals 3
$2.00-$5.00
Nibbles of Germany, Austria, Hungary, and Romania. Food here is funky, but top marks for being unique! Roasted pumpkin seeds, soup, bratwurst, grilled gruyere sandwich, charcuterie plate, cheeses, beet-pickled hard-boiled eggs.

Drink Specials 2
$5.00 drafts; $6.00 red or white wine
$6.00–$7.00 array of theme cocktails

Atmosphere 3
Simple NW style and not a lot of flourish. Deep blue-gray walls, sleek woods and limited bar/ HH seating inside. Sidewalk Happy Hour allowed.

Date visited: _____ **My Rating:** _____
Went with: _____
Favorites: _____
Not so much: _____
Other comments: _____

H5O Bistro

Downtown (East) Map
50 SW Morrison
(503) 484-1415
www.hotelroseportland.com

Happy Hours
4:00–6:00pm and 9:00pm–close Mon–Sat;
★All day Sunday (noon–close)

Food Deals 3
$1.00–$4.00
New owners bring an all-new Happy Hour. BIG
changes ahead, as they make the full conversion
to the Hotel Rose. Duck liver mousse, chicken
bites, pork belly tacos, hummus, shrimp cocktail.

Drink Specials 3
$1.00 off beer; $6.00 wines; $6.00 wines

Atmosphere 3+
Ultra-mod with knock-out design: contrasts of
geometric shapes in decor and plates; sleek,
clean, and linear, yet inviting and friendly; open
fireplace; stellar ambiance! Great for groups.
Renovations January 2014.

Date visited: _____ **My Rating:** _____
Went with: _____
Favorites: _____
Not so much: _____
Other comments: _____

Heathman Hotel

7

- -

Downtown (West) Map
1001 SW Broadway
(503) 241-4100
http://portland.heathmanhotel.com

Happy Hours
2:00pm–close Daily (bar menu)
4:00–6:00pm / 9:00pm–close Daily (drinks & burger)

Food Deals 2
$3.00–$8.00
All day Bistro menu with more than a dozen
unique, gourmet samplings that change just
a bit seasonally: Oysters, beet salad, terrines,
crepes, cheese or meat plate, rissotto, salad,
bruschetta. Plus HH burger special for $6.95.

Drink Specials 1
$6.00 house wines

Atmosphere 3
Two traditional upscale rooms: the quiet, romantic
Tea Court in back with giant, marble fireplace,
and the well-stocked Marble Bar, very popular
with the after-work crowd. A landmark since 1927.

Date visited: _____ **My Rating:** _____
Went with: _____
Favorites: _____
Not so much: _____
Other comments: _____
_____

Higgins

Downtown (West) Map
1239 SW Broadway
(503) 222-9070
www.higginsportland.com

Happy Hours
4:00–6:30pm Sun–Fri

Food Deals 2
$4.00–7.00
Bonus points for fancy food that changes every
day. Minus points for offering only 2-4 choices
as listed on the blackboard menu. It's Higgins
though – rest assured it will be good. Like spicy
duck wings, duck confit, or duck liver mousette.

Drink Specials 2
20% off drafts and wells; $5.00 house wines

Atmosphere 2
Happy Hour is served in the bar, which is a
separate tap room, which isn't nearly as nice as
the adjacent, elegant, and expensive restaurant.
Old-school, excellent service with black tie wait-
staff. Cool place to go.

Date visited: _____ **My Rating:** _____
Went with: _____
Favorites: _____
Not so much: _____
Other comments: _____
_____

Huber's

Downtown (East) Map
411 SW 3rd Ave.
(503) 228-5686
www.hubers.com

Happy Hours
4:00–6:30pm Daily; 9:30pm–close Daily

Food Deals 3
$1.95–$5.95
Giant menu with wide variety of appetizers
with a good mix of options: turkey (sandwich,
enchilada or quesadilla), wings, calamari, burger,
salads, house-smoked salmon plate, shrimp
cocktail, nachos, skewers, ahi, mussels, soup.

Drink Specials 0
Sadly, no drink specials

Atmosphere 3
Historic architecture and design; giant, domed,
stained-glass ceiling; open tables and cozy
booths make it a pleasant, warm meeting place.
Watch the Spanish coffee "shows!" Portland's
oldest restaurant, so it's very famous. Est.1879!

Date visited: _____ **My Rating:** _____
Went with: _____
Favorites: _____
Not so much: _____
Other comments: _____
_____

Imperial

Downtown (East) Map
410 SW Broadway
(503) 228-7222
www.imperialpdx.com

Happy Hours
2:00–6:00pm Daily

Food Deals 3
$3.00–$10.00
Too-cool-for-old-school menu: burger, fries, nuts, wings, rolls, steamer clams, salad, meat and cheese plates, oysters, grilled sausage.

Drink Specials 2
$5.00 select imperial pints; $8.00 wines
$5.00 cocktails (choice of two)

Atmosphere 3
Quality restaurant in Hotel Lucia brought to us by Vitaly Paley (Paley's Place). Formerly Typhoon, and the talk of the town upon opening, they started a much-heralded Happy Hour! Loft style with cement beams, wood floors, and brick-like tiles in browns and tans. Unique wallpaper.

Date visited: _____ **My Rating:** _____
Went with: _____
Favorites: _____
Not so much: _____
Other comments: _____
_____

Jake's Famous Crawfish

Downtown (West) Map
401 SW 12th Ave.
(503) 226-1419
www.jakesfamouscrawfish.com

Happy Hours
3:00–6:00pm Daily; 9:00pm–close Sun–Thurs
10:00pm–close Fri–Sat

Food Deals 3+   *A Happy Hour favorite!*
$2.95–$5.95
22 items and outstanding, hearty sizes: Enjoy
the ever-famous cheeseburger with fries only
$3.95(!), or chicken sandwiches, fish tacos,
calamari, gumbo, sushi rolls, salmon cake, wings.

Drink Specials 2
$5.75-$6.75 wines; $6.50 cranberry sangria

Atmosphere 3
Old-school fun with traditional class; outdoor
sidewalk dining. Considered one of the top
seafood restaurants in the nation, Jake's has been
a downtown landmark for more than 110 years.
Location not to be confused with Jake's Grill
(see next page).

Date visited: _____ **My Rating:** _____
Went with: _____
Favorites: _____
Not so much: _____
Other comments: _____
_____

Jake's Grill

10

Downtown (West) Map
611 SW 10th Ave.
(503) 220-1850
www.jakesgrill.com

Happy Hours
3:00–6:00pm Mon–Fri; 9:00pm–close Daily
★1:00–4:00pm Saturday; ★3:00pm–close Sun

Food Deals 3+
$2.95–$5.95

A Happy Hour favorite!

Changing menu of 14 items with outstanding, hearty sizes: wings, cheeseburger with fries, ribs, hummus, pizza, pork sliders, fish taco, oyster shooters, chicken Caesar wrap, frito misto.

Drink Specials 3
$4.00 drafts; $6.00 red or white wine; $4.00 wells

Atmosphere 3
Stately and traditional with convivial class; fancy, white jacket and bowtie servers; connected with impressive Governor Hotel. Wildly popular and like Jake's Famous, pretty much always packed.

Date visited: _____ **My Rating:** _____
Went with: _____
Favorites: _____
Not so much: _____
Other comments: _____
_____

Karam Lebanese 9

316 SW Stark
(503) 223-0830
www.karamrestaurant.com

Happy Hours
2:00–6:00pm Mon–Fri

A Happy Hour favorite!

Food Deals 3+
$2.50
Deals on the basics and some mysteries: falafel, hummus, baleela (ultra-yummy, warmed, almost fluffy hummus), the best taboule, feta, fries, veggie kibbee nayee, arnabeet mekle, kafta.

Drink Specials 2
$3.00-$4.00 select beer; $5.00 red or white wine

Atmosphere 3
A low-key and serene respite from the hussle of the downtown streets. Hand-painted mural art depicting ancient ruins, carpeted floors and nice wooden tables. Good for groups. (Author note: Look up their online reviews on your favorite critique source – they are *all* quite full of stars!)

Date visited: _____ **My Rating:** _____
Went with: _____
Favorites: _____
Not so much: _____
Other comments: _____
_____

Kenny & Zuke's

Downtown West
1038 SW Stark; (503) 222-3354
www.kennyandzukes.com

NW/Nob Hill 2376 NW Thurman; (503) 954-1737
www.kennyandzukes.com/bagelworks

North/NE Map 3901 N Williams; (503) 287-0782
www.kennyandzukes.com/delibar

Happy Hours
3:00–6:00pm Mon–Fri

Food Deals 2
$3.00-$7.00
In general, about $2.00 off on bar menu items:
Sliders, sandwiches, burgers, hotdogs, Caesar.
Big enough to share!

Drink Specials 2 $3.00 drafts; $5.00 wine

Atmosphere 3 A real New York deli in Portland
(and now there's three of them), with a twist of
being fresh and clean, bright and upbeat, retro
and modern at the same time.

Date visited: _____ **My Rating:** _____
Went with: _____
Favorites: _____
Not so much: _____
Other comments: _____
_____

Little Bird

8

Downtown (East) Map
219 SW 6th Ave.
(503) 688-5952
www.littlebirdbistro.com

Happy Hours
2:30-5:00pm Mon-Fri and 10:00pm-mid Daily

Food Deals 1
$4.00–$12.00
A total favorite of foodies with HH menu hosting
a smaller version of the dinner menu with same
prices on salads, sides, appetizers and desserts.
(So overall, not all that happy). You'll hear raves
about the famous "Le Pigeon" burger for $12.

Drink Specials 3
$1.00 off draft beer; $5.00-$6.00 wines
$5.00 specialty cocktails

Atmosphere 3
Sweet petite space with both French charm and
Parisian cool thrown in. Robins-egg light blue walls
give it a mellow vibe, with giant antlers adding
some edge. Upstairs, lofted dining area and
outside sidewalk seating too. Le Pigeon owners.

Date visited: _____ **My Rating:** _____
Went with: _____
Favorites: _____
Not so much: _____
Other comments: _____
_____

Living Room Theaters

Downtown (West) Map
341 SW 10th Ave.
(971) 222-2005
www.livingroomtheaters.com

Happy Hours
4:00–6:00pm Mon–Fri

A Happy Hour favorite!

Food Deals 3
$4.00
Delicious, inexpensive and healthy movie food:
Small menu of Spanish-style tortillas, mezza plate,
pizza, chicken skewers. Plus a $5.00 burger.

Drink Specials 3
$3.00 select beer; $4.00 white or red wine
$5.00 ginger mojo, pomegranate martini,
or Spanish coffee

Atmosphere 3
Sleek, urban/retro stylings with low tables,
fuzzy pillows and glowing, backlit "mood" bar;
enjoy top-quality high-def movies in recliners
with drink in hand. Get on their email list –
they show the most interesting movies here!

Date visited: _____ **My Rating:** _____
Went with: _____
Favorites: _____
Not so much: _____
Other comments: _____
_____

Lúc Lác

• •

Downtown (West) Map
835 Sw 2nd Ave.
(503) 222-0047
www.luclackitchen.com

Happy Hours
4:00–7:00pm Daily

Food Deals 3+
$2.00-$3.00
Insanely cheap, and 20-items on HH menu!
Great food, and on the nice and healthy side
with four salads (steak, papaya, chicken, tofu),
spring or crispy rolls (pork, shrimp, tofu, veggie),
skewers (pork, chicken, shrimp), wings, and more!

Drink Specials 3
$4.00 drafts; $4.00 wines; $6.00 daily cocktail

Atmosphere 2
A funky place... Wildly popular, but an awkward
ordering process with front counter service, long
lines and payment upon ordering. You'll be your
own waiter in this hipster-ish lounge reminiscent
of a loud, but authentic, Vietnamese street pub.

Date visited: _____ **My Rating:** _____
Went with: _____
Favorites: _____
Not so much: _____
Other comments: _____
_____

Mama Mia Trattoria

Downtown (East) Map
439 SW 2nd Ave.
(503) 295-6464
www.mamamiatrattoria.com

Happy Hours
4:00–7:00pm Mon–Sat
★All night Sunday (4:00–close)

Food Deals 3

Top cover fave 2013!

$2.00-$4.00
Several options at each price point for an amazing menu featuring 20+ items! Features the full range of pasta dishes, several salads, one of Portland's best cheeseburgers, plus desserts! Outstanding!

Drink Specials 3
$3.50 select beer; $4.50 wines; $5.50 cocktail

Atmosphere 3
Mama mia! Now that's Italian! Dripping in old world ambiance with 20 chandeliers, mirrors and frames, white marble tables, and romantic candlelight. Happy Hour is in the front bar area only, plus seasonal sidewalk al fresco dining. Group availability possible (must call ahead).

Date visited: _____ **My Rating:** _____

Went with: _____

Favorites: _____

Not so much: _____

Other comments: _____

_____

Masu

8

Downtown (West) Map
406 SW 13th Ave;
(503) 221-6278
www.masusushi.com

Happy Hours
3:00–6:00pm Daily; 10:00–11:00pm Mon–Thurs
10:00pm–mid Fri–Sat

Food Deals 3+
$3.00–$9.00
Possibly the best sushi in the city! And about half
of it is half-off at Happy Hour! Nigiri and sushi
maki rolls, plus ramen noodles.

Drink Specials 1
$3.50 Sapporo

Atmosphere 3
Unique retro-Asian lounge; open and boxy with
Jenga-style wood blocks covering the walls
and back bar; stunning, colorful, hand-painted
mural. Ultra cool!

Date visited: _____ **My Rating:** _____
Went with: _____
Favorites: _____
Not so much: _____
Other comments: _____
_____

Melting Pot 10

Downtown (West) Map
1001 5th Ave. (entrance at 6th & Main)
(503) 517-8960
www.meltingpot.com

Happy Hours
4:00-6:30pm Mon–Fri

Food Deals 3
$3.00–$5.00 (plus $12.00 cheese fondues)
Big discounts on great food: several salad
selections ($3.00 each); artichoke and spinach dip;
shrimp cocktail; smoked salmon cheese ball;
mushroom paté; lobster, shrimp and caviar cups.

Drink Specials 3
$3.50 draft beer; $5.50 red or white wine
$5.50 daily cocktail

Atmosphere 3
Subterranean entrance leads to clean and simple
windowless batcave perfect for celebrating
cold winter nights or escaping summer heat.
More stark and sleek than romantic, but dark.

Date visited: _____ **My Rating:** _____
Went with: _____
Favorites: _____
Not so much: _____
Other comments: _____
_____

Morton's

Downtown (East) Map
213 SW Clay St
(503) 248-2100
www.mortons.com

Happy Hours
4:45–6:30pm and 9:00pm–close Sun–Fri

Food Deals 3
$6.00–$7.00
They've really quite outdone themselves – steak lovers, rejoice! You'll get a platter of four steak sandwiches, three 5" high slider burgers or four salad wedge bites; crab cakes, artichoke dip, house-made potato chips, or ahi tuna tacos.

Drink Specials 2
$5.50 drafts; $7.00 red and white wines
$8.00 martinis (on the spendy side, but good!)

Atmosphere 3
Enjoy the dark, rich ambiance in the bar area of this top-notch, manly-man steakhouse near the Keller Auditorium. Small bar area will fill up fast, so grab a table early.

Date visited: _____ **My Rating:** _____
Went with: _____
Favorites: _____
Not so much: _____
Other comments: _____

_____

Mother's

Downtown (East) Map
212 SW Stark
(503) 464-1122
www.mothersbistro.com

Happy Hours
3:00–7:00pm Tues–Fri

A Happy Hour favorite!

Food Deals 3
$3.50
Fried ravioli, chicken quesadilla, mini-burgers,
deviled eggs, hummus, fries, chopped liver,
pulled pork sliders, and little teenie weenies :-)

Drink Specials 3
$4.00 microbrew pints; $6.00 wines
$5.00 array of infused cocktails

Atmosphere 3
Their "Velvet Lounge" bar side steps back in
time and looks much like a wealthy, Southern
grandmother's home. High ceilings, brick walls,
ornate gilded mirrors, chandeliers, and flocked
wallpaper everywhere. Cool space!

Date visited: _____ **My Rating:** _____
Went with: _____
Favorites: _____
Not so much: _____
Other comments: _____
_____

Nel Centro

Downtown (West) Map
1408 SW 6th Avenue
(503) 484-1099
nelcentro.com

Happy Hours
4:00–6:00pm Daily

Food Deals 3
$4.00–$7.00
Seasonal 20-item menus from one of Portland's most respected kitchens: delicious gourmet-style pizza, lamb burger or meatballs, mussels, soup, pork slider, calamari, and salads.

Drink Specials 3
$4.00 drafts; $5.00 house wines and prosecco
$5.00 featured cocktail or well drinks

Atmosphere 3
One of the most enjoyable patios in town where you can enjoy Happy Hour too! Next to the Hotel Modera with mod, contemporary courtyard and long fire pits. Inside, the decor is sleek and stylish, with a giant open bar and globe lights.

Date visited: _____ **My Rating:** _____
Went with: _____
Favorites: _____
Not so much: _____
Other comments: _____
_____

The Original 10

Downtown (East) Map
300 SW 6th Ave.
(503) 546-2666
www.originaldinerant.com

Happy Hours
2:00–6:00pm Mon–Fri

Food Deals 3
$2.00–$6.00
A dozen or so American diner food items with
some Happy Hour oddities: chex mix, poutine,
hotdogs, chicken waffle sliders, donut burger,
french fries, and pie!

Drink Specials 3
$3.00 drafts; $4.00 wines/wells; $5.00 punch

Atmosphere 3
Very mod, retro and contemporary restaurant/
diner (aka "dinerant"). Amazingly giant, floor-
to-ceiling, wall-to-wall windows that are two
stories high, and run the length of the building.
Sleek interior blends downtown, city-cool with
the charm of 1950s greasy spoon lunch counters.

Date visited: _____ **My Rating:** _____
Went with: _____
Favorites: _____
Not so much: _____
Other comments: _____
_____

Pazzo

Downtown (East) Map
627 SW Washington
(503) 228-1515
www.pazzo.com

Happy Hours
2:30–6:00pm Daily

Food Deals 2
$2.00–$8.00
Simple, mostly Italian-style bar eats: artisan-cured meat plates, manicotti, salad, brick oven pizzas, stromboli, spiced nuts, and olives.

Drink Specials 3
$3.00 drafts; $5.00 wines; $5.00 cocktails

Atmosphere 3
The PazzoBAR side of Pazzo's Ristorante is stately and traditional in tone, rather than country-side Italian. It hosts a low-key and popular after-work bar scene.

Date visited: _____ **My Rating:** _____
Went with: _____
Favorites: _____
Not so much: _____
Other comments: _____
_____

Picnic House

9

Downtown (West) Map
723 SW Salmon; (503) 227-0705
www.picnichousepdx.com

Happy Hours
3:00–6:00pm Mon–Sat

Food Deals 2 $3.00–$5.00
Great food here, but too-limited Happy Hour menu.
Seasonal changes to reflect picnicing weather
with things like a soup & sandwich, chips &
dips, unique crostinis, grilled asparagus, and
some kind of treat like a chocolate pudding.

Drink Specials 3
$4.00 drafts; $15.00 bottle of wine; $4.00 wells
$5.00 special cocktail of the day

Atmosphere 3
Very unique! A step back in time in this former
grand hotel from 1926. Gorgeous tile work, thick
dark wood moldings, and two-story ceilings.
The front is kind of a coffee shop/luncheonette
set-up with a lot of empty space. Overall decor
has split personalities, so head to the back bar,
ideally at dusk, for maximum cuteness factor!

Date visited: _____ **My Rating:** _____

Went with: _____

Favorites: _____

Not so much: _____

Other comments: _____

_____

Portland City Grill

10

Downtown (East) Map
111 SW Fifth Ave., 30th Floor
(503) 450-0030
www.portlandcitygrill.com

Happy Hours
4:00–7:00pm and 9:00pm–close Mon–Sat
4:00pm–close Sunday★

Food Deals 3+
$4.25–$9.25

A Happy Hour Favorite!

About 15 high-quality and beautifully-presented
apps like salmon cakes, spring rolls, blue cheese
fries, cheeseburger, spicy basil chicken, fish &
chips, peanut noodle salad, plus their famous
steak & frites ($7.25!) and kung pao calamari.

Drink Specials 3
$5.25 beer and special cocktails; $6.25 wines

Atmosphere 3+
Get there early and try to get a window seat!
Enjoy amazing views of the our city, river, hills,
Mt. Hood, sunsets, and occasional full moons.
Giant central bar, full walls of windows, raw
timber beams, marble cocktail tables, and live
music. Impressive! Not fair to compare. They
blow the curve for everyone else.

Date visited: _____ **My Rating:** _____
Went with: _____
Favorites: _____
Not so much: _____
Other comments: _____
_____

Portland Prime

10

Downtown (East) Map
121 SW 3rd Ave.
(503) 223-6200
www.portlandprime.net

Happy Hours
3:00–6:00pm Daily; 11:30–5:00pm Sunday

Food Deals 3
$5.00-$7.00
Prime bar menu offers a wide array of tasty apps:
wedge salad, crab cakes, beef sliders, calamari,
chicken wings, shrimp cocktail, eggplant stack,
fries, and pizza.

Drink Specials 3
$5.00 drafts; $6.00 house wines
$6.00 wells and signature cocktails

Atmosphere 3
Located in Embassy Suites – enter through the
lobby as it's majestic! Rich mahogany woods
and private booth seating; enjoy elegant restaurant dining on the cheap! Several hi-def TVs.

Date visited: _____ **My Rating:** _____
Went with: _____
Favorites: _____
Not so much: _____
Other comments: _____
_____

Porto Terra

9

Downtown West
830 SW 6th Ave.
(503) 944-1090
www.portoterra.com

Happy Hours
3:30–6:00pm / 9:00–11:00pm Mon–Fri

Food Deals 3
$3.00–$7.00 They've improved even more this
year with more than a dozen apps: Bruschetta,
gnocchi, Caesar, calamari, hot wings, smoked
trout, mac & cheese, paninis, pizzas (deep dish
version too!), hummus, and a burger.

Drink Specials 3
$5.00 drafts; $6.00 house wine; $1.00 off wells

Atmosphere 3
Hilton hotel bar with Tuscan countryside modern
motif; an upscale, contemporary slice of Italy.
Cool black and silver bar hosts a large number
of wines by the glass, and does flights too.

Date visited: _____ **My Rating:** _____
Went with: _____
Favorites: _____
Not so much: _____
Other comments: _____
_____

Punchbowl Social 9

Downtown (East) Map
340 SW Morrison, Third Floor
(503) 334-0360
www.punchbowlsocial.com/pdx

It's like ten bars in one!

Happy Hours
3:00–6:00pm and 10:00pm-close Daily

Food Deals 3
$2.50-$7.00
Bar basics with some twists: oyster nachos, deviled or pickled eggs, wings, fries, tacos.

Drink Specials 2
$3.00 "Old Man Cans"; $6.00 wines; $4.00 wells
$6.00 specialty house cocktails

Atmosphere 3
This place has a WOW! Factor I haven't seen in Portland for quite some time. Retro, playful atmosphere that changes with each turn in this 32,000 sq. ft. funplex at the top of Pioneer Place Mall. Creative design, conversation/couch areas, cocktail tables, three big bars, three private bowling areas, karaoke, darts, and shuffleboard. "Imagine Paul Bunyan meets Don Draper."

Date visited: _____ **My Rating:** _____

Went with: _____

Favorites: _____

Not so much: _____

Other comments: _____

_____

Ración

Downtown (West) Map
1205 SW Washington
(971) 276-8008
www.racionpdx.com

Happy Hours
5:00–6:00pm Tues-Sat

A Happy Hour favorite!

Food Deals 3
$7.00
Ever-changing menu of six or so Spanish tapas taken to new heights of deliciousness, quality, and creativity! Artistic presentations are a sheer joy to behold. Innovative mixing of ingredients will delight your tastebuds. Savor and enjoy!

Drink Specials 3
$3.00 draft cider; $5.00 wines; $6.00 cocktail

Atmosphere 3
Modern and boxy, with slatted wood walls, floor-to-ceiling windows, hanging plants, and miniature window gardens. Sit at the big, central bar/kitchen to see the skilled chefs in action. It's fascinating!

Date visited: _____ **My Rating:** _____

Went with: _____

Favorites: _____

Not so much: _____

Other comments: _____

_____

Raven & Rose

Downtown (East) Map
1331 SW Broadway
(503) 222-7673
www.ravenandrosepdx.com

Happy Hours
3:30–5:00pm Mon–Fri

Food Deals 3

A Happy Hour favorite!

$2.00-$6.00
About 10 gastropub offerings like olives, glazed nuts, fries, pickled veggies, salad, terrine, soup, and a house-specialty plate of the day.

Drink Specials 3
$5.00 drafts or spritzers; $6.00 cocktail; $7.00 wine

Atmosphere 3
A marvelous renovation of this historic carriage house (a.k.a. mansion)! The place is rich but welcoming, and absolutely gorgeous. Elegant, farmhouse style that's traditional in tone with dark woods and slate floors. The first level restaurant hosts a hand-crafted bar, big open kitchen, and chef's table. Cool bar upstairs too!

Date visited: _____ **My Rating:** _____
Went with: _____
Favorites: _____
Not so much: _____
Other comments: _____
_____

Red Star Tavern

Downtown (East) Map
503 SW Alder
(503) 222-0005
www.redstartavern.com

Happy Hours
4:00–8:00pm Daily ★

Food Deals 3
$5.00–$9.00
New menu with about a dozen bar bites: poppers, glazed nuts, olives, fries, focaccia, lamb skewers, greens, french fry nachos (yum!), and burgers. They'll switch things up occasionally, to varying degrees of deliciousness and success.

Drink Specials 3
$4.50 drafts; $5.00 wines; $5.00 wells
$6.00 cocktails (6)

Atmosphere 3
Romantic and upscale with just a touch of rustic charm, interesting street-scape viewing, and big booth options for some serious lounging. Nice!

Date visited: _____ **My Rating:** _____

Went with: _____

Favorites: _____

Not so much: _____

Other comments: _____

_____

Ringside Fish House

● ● ● ● ● ● ● ● ● ● ● ● ● ● ● ● ● ● ● ●

NW/Nob Hill Map
838 SW Park Ave. (Fox Tower)
(503) 227-3900
www.ringsidefishhouse.com

Happy Hours
3:00pm–7:00pm and 9:00pm-close Daily
★3:00–11:00pm Sunday

A Happy Hour favorite!

Food Deals 3+
$2.95–$4.95
Big menu of 12 or so items: steak bites (YUM!),
steamed mussels, shrimp, fried oysters, Caesar
salad, burger, fish tacos, clam chowder, fried
oysters, deviled eggs, calamari, or French dip

Drink Specials 3
$1.00 off drafts; $2.00 off wine or cocktails

Atmosphere 3
The temporary relocation of their steakhouse
brought us a whole new Ringside! Contemporary,
upscale, toned-down interior with Happy Hour
in bar area only. Illuminated, colorful ceramic
fish and giant whale bone decorate the walls.

Date visited: _____ **My Rating:** _____
Went with: _____
Favorites: _____
Not so much: _____
Other comments: _____
_____

Ruth's Chris

10

Downtown (East) Map
850 SW Broadway
(503) 221-4518
www.ruthschris.com

Happy Hours
4:00–7:00pm Sun-Fri

A Happy Hour favorite!

Food Deals 3
$7.00
Seven high-quality apps like seared ahi tuna,
prime burger, tenderloin skewer salad, crab BLT,
steak sandwich, spicy lobster, smoked salmon.

Drink Specials 3
$3.00 domestics; $7.00 red or white wine
$7.00 select cocktails

Atmosphere 3
This new and upgraded location gives us a
wonderful and *bright*, richly-appointed, fine-
dining steakhouse. Enjoy a very affordable,
fancy evening out when you go here for their
Happy Hour. Big cheers to the good life!

Date visited: _____ **My Rating:** _____
Went with: _____
Favorites: _____
Not so much: _____
Other comments: _____
_____

Saké

Downtown (West) Map
615 SW Park Ave
(503) 222-1391
www.sakethaior.com

Happy Hours
3:00–6:00pm and 9:00pm-close Daily
★6:00pm-close Sundays

Food Deals 3
$2.00-$5.00

A Happy Hour favorite!

Several options at each price point. A mix of
Japanese and Thai cuisine includes: spring rolls,
salads, gyoza, crab rangoon, spicy wings, tom
yum, tom kha, pad thai, steamed mussels, bok
choy, grilled salmon, soba, onigiri. Plus buy one,
get one when you mix and match sushi rolls.

Drink Specials 3
$3.00-$4.00 beer; $5.00 wine; $5.00 cocktails

Atmosphere 2
Not incredibly polished on the outside, but a
hidden gem on the inside! Serene with gold
walls and a big front bar. Group space in back.

Date visited: _____ **My Rating:** _____
Went with: _____
Favorites: _____
Not so much: _____
Other comments: _____
_____

Sand Bar (at Fish Grotto)

Downtown (West) Map
1035 SW Stark
(503) 226-4171
www.fishgrotto.com/sandbar

Happy Hours
4:00-7:00pm Daily

A Happy Hour favorite!

Food Deals 3 $5.00
Appropriately fun names and a festive feast:
Captain Cobb or Galley salads, Man Overboard
nachos, Fisherman's fondue, Beach Bowls, plus
a variety of tacos, chowder, crab dip, and fries.

Drink Specials 3
$3.00 beer; $3.00 wine; $3.00 cocktail

Atmosphere 3
New this year, it's a very welcomed, more casual
addition to the Fish Grotto restaurant next door.
Well-designed, with tropical traveler embel-
lishments, it's a smallish, but very fun, beachy,
bamboo-y, and Jimmy Buffett-y bar, without being
over the top. Cool place – I love it! Fish Grotto
shares their same menu for cool, old-school bar
action right next door. Just one more?

Date visited: _____ **My Rating:** _____

Went with: _____

Favorites: _____

Not so much: _____

Other comments: _____

_____

Saucebox

10

• •

Downtown (East) Map
214 SW Broadway
(503) 241-3393
www.saucebox.com

Happy Hours
4:30-6:30pm Mon-Fri; 5:00-6:30pm Sat
10:30pm-mid Tues-Thur; 11:00pm-close Fri-Sat

Food Deals 3
$1.00–$5.00
Huge menu of about 20 mostly Asian-inspired
fusion dishes, that impresses every time: crispy
brussel sprouts, miso soup, taro chips, papaya
salad, pad thai, salad, spring, or hand rolls, pork
noodle, squash curry, and the best burgers!

Drink Specials 3
$3.00 select beer; $5.00 wine; $4.00 saké
$5.00 daily cocktail; $5.00 boxcar or daiquiri

Atmosphere 3
Big and open, boxy, saucy lounge; chocolate-
browns and greys; looming giant art murals with
personality overlook the entire room. Upstairs and
sidewalk dining too. Cool bathroom entrance!

Date visited: _____ **My Rating:** _____
Went with: _____
Favorites: _____
Not so much: _____
Other comments: _____
_____

Shigezo

Downtown (West) Map
910 SW Salmon
(503) 688-5202
www.shigezo-pdx.com

Happy Hours
4:00pm–close Sun-Thur (Sun 2:00–close);
4:00–6:00pm and 9:00pm–close Fri–Sat

Food Deals 3
$1.00–$3.00 About ten rolls and ten tapas: salads,
wings, veggies, squid, miso soup. Plus $5.00
salmon carpaccio, ceviche, or ebi mayo.

Drink Specials 3
$5.00 drafts (22 oz.); $5.00 wines or sake
$2.00 off specialty cocktails

Atmosphere 3
Seemingly authentic like you're really in Japan.
Happy Hour is casual bar side of restaurant.
Big fish mural, hanging paper lanterns, and
character stamps.

Date visited: _____ **My Rating:** _____

Went with: _____

Favorites: _____

Not so much: _____

Other comments: _____

_____

Southpark

10

Downtown (West) Map
901 SW Salmon
(503) 326-1300
www.southparkseafood.com

Happy Hours
3:00–6:00pm Daily

Food Deals 3
$3.00–$8.00
Special Happy Hour menu with nine fine menu
items: olives, spiced nuts, pork cracklings,
salad, calamari, fries, smoked trout, oysters,
meatbals, and cheeseburgers.

Drink Specials 3
$1.00 off drafts; $5.00 red, white or sparklings
$4.00 glass of sangria ($10.00 carafe)

Atmosphere 3
Southpark has been a perennial favorite of
many a Portlander, myself included. It just works
on so many levels. Be aware that it's more of a
bar than a romantic wine-date place and that it
can get crowded. Outstanding wine selection.

Date visited: _____ **My Rating:** _____

Went with: _____

Favorites: _____

Not so much: _____

Other comments: _____

_____

Tasty n Alder

10

North/NE Map
580 SW 12th Ave.
(503) 621-9251
www.tastyntasty.com

Happy Hours 2:00–5:30pm Daily

Food Deals 3
$1.00–$9.00
A bit different menu than their northside original,
Tasty n Sons has going. Same owners of Toro
Bravo (look for their new cookbook). Changing
menu, but well-attended to online. Hush puppies,
paté or cheese boards, fried chicken, chili dog,
egg dishes, fries, phenomenal steak sandwich.
It's all so very tasty!!!

Drink Specials 3
$2.00 mugs (3); $6.00 wines
$7.00 tasty cocktail specials (4)

Atmosphere 3
Trendy Northwest stylings much like the other
Tasty. Reclaimed woods, open ceiling rafters and
visable ducts, silver metal accents and lights,
wood benches and white chairs. Great back bar!

Date visited: _____ **My Rating:** _____
Went with: _____
Favorites: _____
Not so much: _____
Other comments: _____
_____

TE:bar

Downtown (West) Map
909 SW Park
(503) 243-5991
www.tastingeast.com

Happy Hours
3:00–6:00pm and 10:00pm–close Fri-Sat

Food Deals 3
$.95-$6.95
Greatly expanded Happy Hour includes pretty
much everything except sushi. About 18 items
cover all other Asian food bases! Soups, salads,
tempura, pot stickers, asian nachos, poke, ribs.

Drink Specials 3+
4.00 drafts; $3.50 house wines; $4.00 wells
$4.50 cocktail of the day

Atmosphere 3
TE:bar is the bar side of Tasting East, formerly
Dragonfish. Old, dark wood planks cover the
walls, bar, tables, and pillars, giving the place a
kind of Asian street scene essence. Cool,
artistic paper lanterns, low street level views,
and big square bar.

Date visited: _____ **My Rating:** _____
Went with: _____
Favorites: _____
Not so much: _____
Other comments: _____
_____

Urban Farmer

● ●

10

Downtown (East) Map
525 SW Morrison
(503) 222-4900
www.urbanfarmerrestaurant.com

A Happy Hour favorite!

Happy Hours
3:00–6:00pm and 10:00pm–close Daily

Food Deals 3 $2.00–$8.00
Giant menu with over 20 items! Farm-fresh NW
delights and seasonal updates, and changing
options from the earth, ocean and range – plus
several desserts! Chicken pops, bangers & mash,
sliders, burgers, ribs, skewers, oysters, shrimp,
deviled eggs, pork, and soup (but no salads).

Drink Specials 3
$5.00 drafts; $6.00 house wines
$5.00 cocktail of the day

Atmosphere 3
Absolutely stunning! The number one decor
award winner! Truly a Portland stand-out in the
giant, cavernous atrium of the Hotel Nines with
cozy, mini-atrium seating areas. Ultra-modern
style with subtle rustic touches. Coolest at night!

Date visited: _____ **My Rating:** _____
Went with: _____
Favorites: _____
Not so much: _____
Other comments: _____
_____

Via Tribunali

8

Old Town Map
36 SW 3rd Ave.
(503) 548-2917
www.viatribunali.net

Happy Hours
4:00–6:00pm and 10:00pm–close Daily

Food Deals 2
$5.00
Choose from three tasty wood-fired pizzas
(pepperoni, cheese or marinara), antipasto plate,
or chocolate nutella calzone (pastry) dessert.

Drink Specials 3
$3.00 select draft; $8.00 house wine carafe;
$5.00 well drinks

Atmosphere 2
Small and skinny bar room with old-time charm,
super-high ceiling, and upstairs mezzanine.
A second, somewhat cozier area in back and
sidewalk seating in the thick of some of Portland's
weirdest action.

Date visited: _____ **My Rating:** _____
Went with: _____
Favorites: _____
Not so much: _____
Other comments: _____
_____

Berbati's www.berbati.com

Downtown East 19 SW 2nd Ave, ; (503) 248-4579

Happy Hours 4:00–7:00pm Daily; 3:00–8:00pm Sun★

Food Deals 3 $3.00–$7.00 New, big menu! Four kinds of gyros, Greek salad, tzatziki or feta dip, rings, rings, calamari, hummus, soup, chicken souvlaki.

Drink Specials 2 $2.00–$3.00 drafts; $3.00 wells

Atmosphere 2 Greek arches over doors, faux-aged walls, funky Aladdin lamps, cool, copper-studded floor, and original artwork. Outdoor patio seating.

Bistro 921

Downtown West 921 SW 6th Ave; (503) 220-2685 www.bistro-921.com

Happy Hours 3:30-6:00pm Mon–Fri

Food Deals 2 $3.00–$6.00 Bar food basics like wings, salad, fries, quesadilla, calamari, burgers, pizza.

Drink Specials 2 $5.00 drafts; $6 wine; $1.00 off wells

Atmosphere 2 In the Hilton near the Schnitz. Nice restaurant area, but Happy Hour in the Bistro Bar only. Enter through the glamorous lobby and restaurant.

Buffalo Wild Wings See page 240.

Downtown East 327 SW Morrison; (503) 224-1309

Cassidy's www.cassidysrestaurant.com

Downtown West 1331 SW Washington; (503) 223-0054

Happy Hours 4:00–6:00pm & 10:00pm–2:00am Daily

Food Deals 3 $6.50 Big, full-size servings of items like several salads, soups, burgers, pizzas, calamari, chicken fried pork belly, grilled portobello sandwich.

Drink Specials 0 Sadly, no HH drink specials

Atmosphere 2 Inside an old, historic building with lots of character on the inside too (and it's perfectly positioned behind the Crystal Ballroom).

Dan & Louis' Oyster Bar

Downtwn East 208 SW Ankeny; (503) 227-5906
www.danandlouis.com

Happy Hours 4:00–6:00pm Mon–Fri

Food Deals 3 $4.00-$10.00 Optional wine pairings:
Mussels (white wine), fried clams (red beer), pickled
veggies (PBR), oysters (red wine), and small plates
like steak, jumbo prawns or fish or chicken tacos.
Plus $2.00 oyster shooters and deals on the half-shell.

Drink Specials 1 Special pairings menu

Atmosphere 2 Happy Hour is in the bar area of this
historic Old Town restaurant. Unique space with
small-town, East-Coast, casual, crabbing charm.
Cozy, candlelit, ship-like hideaway that's loaded with
portside personality. Best at night (but that's after HH).

Elephants Deli Fox Tower

Downtown (West) Map
877 SW Taylor; (503) 546-3166
www.elephantsdeli.com

Happy Hour Drinks: 4:00–6:00pm Mon–Sat;
3:30pm–close (7:30pm) Sun
$1.00 off beer and wine

Happy Hour Food: 6:00–7:30pm Mon–Sat;
3:30pm–close (7:30pm) Sun
1/2 off sandwiches and hot plates

Cute place to shop or grab lunch, but bizarrely, their
Happy Hour times don't match up to eat & drink!

Elephants in the Park

812 SW Park; (503) 937-1073 www.elephantsdeli.com

Happy Hour 4:00-6:00 Mon-Sat; All day Sun
No Food Deals / Drink Specials $.50 off beer in
bottles; $1.00 off 22 oz. size

Looks like a train station entrance on the outside,
and a fast-food breakfast diner on the inside. Great
people watching through the all-glass building, and
very enjoyable outdoor plaza seating in the summer!

E-San Thai www.e-santhai.com

Downtown East 133 SW 2nd; (503) 223-4090
North location: 8233 North Denver Ave; (503) 517-0683

Happy Hours 2:30–6:00pm and 9:00–10:00pm Daily

Food Deals 3 $2.00–$5.00 A whopping 22 Thai basics:
egg rolls, wontons, an array of satays, pad thai, salads,
tom kha soup, chicken skewers, and more.

Drink Specials 3 $4.00 drafts; $4.00 well drinks

Atmosphere 2 Casual, comfortable, colorful Thai
restaurant without any over-the-top styling, but up-top
dining space for the huge crowds flooding in at lunch.

Kells Irish Pub www.kellsirish.com

Downtown (East) Map 112 SW 2nd; (503) 227-4057

Happy Hours 4:00–6:30pm Mon–Fri;
10:00pm–close Mon–Thurs

Food Deals 3 $3.00–$5.00 Forever menu of faves
like Irish nachos, wings, BLTC, burger, sandwiches,
fries, quesadilla, oyster shooters, sweet potato fries.

Drink Specials 0 Sadly, no drink specials

Atmosphere 3 You know a good time is to be had by
all at this infamous Portland Institution! Fun bar with
an upbeat Irish vibe, traditional decor, and crinkled
dollar bills covering the ceiling.

Marriott Bistro www.marriott.com

Downtown (East) Map
1401 Southwest Naito Parkway; (503) 226-7600

Happy Hours 4:00–6:00pm Daily

Food Deals 2 $2.50–$4.00 Food from Truss. Eight
typical upscale bar items: onion dip, soup, hummus,
fried kale, veggie crudite, pico de galloo, pickles.

Drink Specials 3 $3 daily draft; $5 wines; $7 cocktail

Atmosphere 3 Striking, very contemporary hotel
lounge with community couch seating with big-
screen TV; big, central long bar table; and several
quiet booths (plus the usual two- and four-tops).

Leaky Roof www.theleakyroof.com

Downtown (off map)
1538 SW Jefferson St; (503) 222-3745

Happy Hours 3:00–6:00pm Mon–Fri

Food Deals 2 $2.95–$5.50 Cheap, nice, and tasty pub food (may vary seasonally): A dozen items including Irish stew, burgers, hummus plate, risotto, wings, quesadillas (three kinds), tacos, calamari.

Drink Specials 2 $1.00 off beer, wine, or wells

Atmosphere 2 Very cozy Irish pub, especially on a dark, cold night! Traditional, forest green walls, open fireplace and wooden booths and tables.

Paddy's www.paddys.com

Downtown (East) Map 65 SW Yamhill; (503) 224-5626

Happy Hours 4:00–6:30pm/10:00pm–2:00am Daily

Food Deals 3 $5.00–$6.00 Expanded bar menu, now with *nine* kinds of flavored mac & cheese! Also hummus, pork or corned beef sliders, nachos, poppers, calamari, shepherd's pie, wings, Guinness chili fries, hush puppies.

Drink Specials 1 Occasional, random specials

Atmosphere 3 Warm, upscale Irish pub with a very impressive turn-of-the-century bar stacked sky-high with spirits of all sorts. Seasonal sidewalk seating.

Shanghai Tunnel Lounge

Downtown East 211 SW Ankeny; (503) 220-4001

Happy Hours 5:00–7:00pm Daily

Food Deals 3 $2.00–$6.00 Yummy pot stickers, quesadillas, chips, veggie or chuck burgers, fries.

Drink Specials 3 $1.00 off drafts, $5.00 wine; $2.00 off wells

Atmosphere 2 Built over the underground Shanghai tunnels; painted murals and simple Asian touches. Sidewalk Happy Hour.

Thirsty Lion Pub

Old Town Map 71 SW 2nd Ave.; (503) 222-2155
www.thirstylionpub.com

Happy Hours 3–7pm Mon–Fri; 9:00pm-close Daily

Food Deals 2 $3.95–$5.95 Scotch eggs, fries, Caesar, pork or burger sliders, nachos, calamari, onion rings, mozzarella sticks, and soft pretzel fondue.

Drink Specials 2 $4.00 daily pints/wine; $3.00 wells

Atmosphere 2 Neighborhood English Pub theme, being more new, yuppie and huge. Food, spirits, ales, live music, and sports on several TVs.

West Café

Downtown Map 1201 SW Jefferson; (503) 227-8189
www.westcafepdx.com

Happy Hours 4:00-close Mon-Sat

Food Deals 2 $2.00-$7.00 Extensive menu of 14 fresh, gourmet and unique items: snacks, soups, salads, sliders, veggie dishes, skewers, dip, quesadilas.

Drink Specials 1 $1.00 off beer and wine

Atmosphere 3 They do lunch, dinner and brunch and fit somewhere between being a nice restaurant and cozy café. Elegant touches mix with diner styles. For Happy Hour, sit on the bar side.

XV (15)

Old Town Map 15 SW 2nd Ave; (503) 790-9090

Happy Hours 4:00–7:00pm Daily

Food Deals 2 $2.00–$5.00 Big selection of good cheapies: yam fries, pork or beef sliders, tacos, three kinds of satays, mac & cheese, salads.

Drink Specials 2 $1.50 PBRs; $3.00 drafts $4.00 wells; $6.00 cocktails

Atmosphere 2 Black and more black; regular bar area, but cool restaurant/candlelit lounge in adjacent room. Couches line the wall for kicking back. Crowded and different vibe late-night.

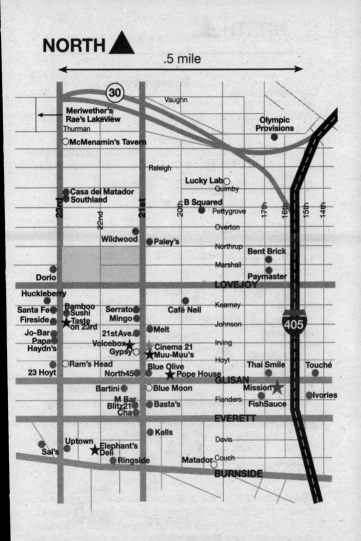

NORTH ▲

.5 mile

30

Vaughn

Meriwether's
Rae's Lakeview
Thurman

Olympic
Provisions

○ McMenamin's Tavern

Raleigh

Lucky Lab ○
Quimby

● Casa del Matador
● Southland

● B Squared
Pettygrove

20th
17th
16th
15th
14th

23rd
22nd
21st

Overton

● Wildwood
● Paley's

Northrup

Bent Brick ●

Marshall

Paymaster ●

● Dorio

LOVEJOY

Huckleberry ●

Santa Fe ●
Bamboo
Sushi
Fireside ●
★ Taste
on 23rd

Serrato ●
Mingo

Café Nell ●

Kearney

Jo-Bar ●
Papa
Haydn's ●

21stAve. ●
Voicebox ★
Gypsy ○

● Melt

Johnson

405

★ Cinema 21
★ Muu-Muu's

Irving

○ Ram's Head

● Blue Olive

Hoyt

Thai Smile ●
Touché ●

23 Hoyt ●
North45 ●
★ Pope House

GLISAN

Bartini ●
○ Blue Moon

Mission ★

● Ivories

M Bar
Blitz21 ●
Cha

● Basta's

Flanders
FishSauce ●

EVERETT

● Kells

Davis

Sal's ●
Uptown ●
★ Elephant's
Deli
● Ringside

Matador ● Couch

BURNSIDE

159

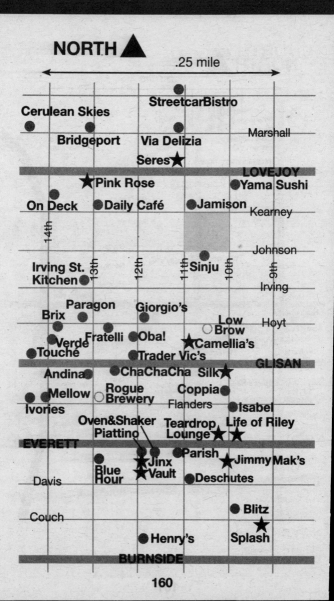

NORTH

.25 mile

StreetcarBistro

Cerulean Skies

Bridgeport   Via Delizia   Marshall

Seres ★

LOVEJOY

★ Pink Rose   Yama Sushi

On Deck   Daily Café   Jamison   Kearney

14th

Johnson

Irving St.   13th   12th   11th   Sinju   10th   9th
Kitchen

Irving

Paragon   Giorgio's

Brix   Low   Hoyt
        Fratelli   Oba!   Brow

Verde   ★ Camellia's
Touché   Trader Vic's

GLISAN

Andina   ChaChaCha   Silk ★

Mellow   Rogue   Coppia
        Brewery
Ivories   Flanders   Isabel

Oven&Shaker   Teardrop   Life of Riley
Piatting   Lounge ★ ★

EVERETT

               Parish   ★ Jimmy Mak's
       ★ Jinx
Blue   ★ Vault
Hour   Deschutes

Davis

Couch   Blitz

         Henry's   ★ Splash

BURNSIDE

Old Town

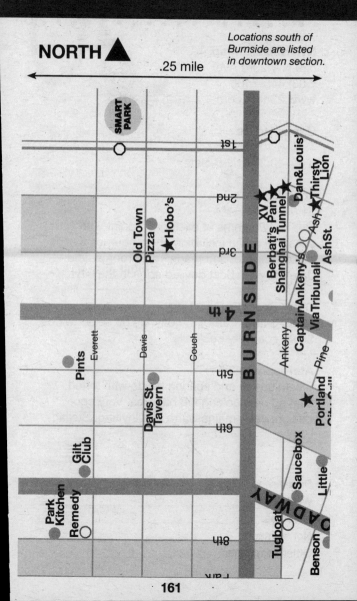

NORTH ▲

.25 mile

Locations south of Burnside are listed in downtown section.

SMART PARK

1st

2nd

3rd

Old Town Pizza

★ Hobo's

XV ★★★

Berbati's Pan

Shanghai Tunnel

Dan&Louis'

★ Thirsty Lion

Ash

AshSt.

CaptainAnkeny's

ViaTribunali

4th

BURNSIDE

Everett

Davis

Couch

Ankeny

Pine

Pints

5th

Davis St. Tavern

★ Portland City Grill

6th

Gilt Club

Saucebox

Little

Park Kitchen

Remedy

Tugboat

Benson

ADWAY

8th

Park

23 Hoyt

10

NW/Nob Hill Map
529 NW 23rd Ave.
(503) 445-7400
www.23hoyt.com

Happy Hours
4:00–6:30pm Daily
9:00–10:30pm Fri–Sat

Food Deals 3
$1.00–$7.00
One or two items at each price point with
seasonal menu including cheeseburger, salad,
mac & cheese, flatbreads, mushrooms, and
dare I say the best deviled eggs in the city!

Drink Specials 3
$3.50-$4.00 draft of the day; $5.00 select wines
$6.00 specialty cocktails

Atmosphere 3
Sleek, stylish and soaring inside with lofted
seating overlooking the bar area. Very cool
design, yet remains warm and inviting. Stellar!

Date visited: _____ **My Rating:** _____
Went with: _____
Favorites: _____
Not so much: _____
Other comments: _____
_____

Andina

8

Pearl Map
1314 NW Glisan
(503) 228-9535
www.andinarestaurant.com

Happy Hours
4:00–6:00pm Daily

Food Deals 2
Skewers Sm $6.50 / Med $13.00 / Lrg $26.00
Choose from kebobs (chicken, beef heart, or
grilled octopus), $7.00 beet salad or $1.50 raw
bar oysters. Low on choices, hence a deceptively
lower score here, but a top PDX place! Just go
full-throttle and go for dinner.

Drink Specials 2
$6.00 house wines; $7.50 specialty cocktails

Atmosphere 3
One of Portland's most renowned restaurants
and a most active Happy Hour bar scene.
High, wooden-beamed ceilings, copper-topped
tables, painted stucco walls, fireplace.

Date visited: _____ **My Rating:** _____
Went with: _____
Favorites: _____
Not so much: _____
Other comments: _____
_____

Bamboo Sushi

10

NW/Nob Hill Map
836 NW 23rd Ave; (971) 229-1925

310 SE 28th Ave; (503) 232-5255
www.bamboosushipdx.com

Happy Hours
4:00–6:00pm Mon–Fri (4:30 SE location)

Food Deals 3
$1.00–$6.00
The food at Bamboo Sushi is soooo goood! To list in plain English: house-pickled veggies, seafood pancake, seaweed salad, mushrooms, salad, veggie tofu crisped noodles, grilled peppers, plus nigiri set, daily hand rolls, and veggie rolls.

Drink Specials 3
$3.00 Sapporo; $4.00 wine; $4.00–$7.00 sake

Atmosphere 3
NEW! Very similar in layout and overall style to original location in SE Portland. Serene and cozy with focus on sustainability and Japanese simplicity. Natural, neutral woods, pillows on bench seating and fascinating artwork. Happy Hour is in the lounge areas only.

Date visited: _____ **My Rating:** _____

Went with: _____

Favorites: _____

Not so much: _____

Other comments: _____

_____

Bar Mingo

9

NW/Nob Hill Map
811 NW 21st Ave
(503) 445-4646
www.barmingonw.com

Happy Hours
4:00–6:00pm Daily

Food Deals 3
$6.00
Expanded menu delivers a nice field green salad, cheese and meat plates, manilla clams, calamari, baked polenta, or lamb meatballs and the ever-elusive and delicious goat cheese in spicy tomato sauce with bruschetta!

Drink Specials 2
$5.00 beer (kind of... two PBRs); $5.00 wines
$5.00 daily martinis or bellinis

Atmosphere 3
Big in size and style with modern, Italian design and some groovy West Elm touches. Warm, harvest tones with cool, giant wooden doors imported from Italy. Several pillowy conversation pits. Outdoor sidewalk seating at HH.

Date visited: _____ **My Rating:** _____
Went with: _____
Favorites: _____
Not so much: _____
Other comments: _____

Bartini

NW/Nob Hill Map
2108 NW Glisan
(503) 224-7919
www.bartinipdx.com

Happy Hours
4:00–6:30pm and 9:30pm–close Daily
4:00pm–close Sunday and Monday ★
9:30pm–close Fri-Sat (food only)

Food Deals 3
$3.00–$7.00
Literally 25 gourmet choices, plus fondue: three
kinds of salads, ahi tuna pork or chicken sliders;
crab cakes; coconut shrimp, shrimp tacos,
several flatbreads and satays, burgers, soup,
hummus, pork tacos, mashed potato martini.

Drink Specials 3
Half-off signature martinis (full menu of 80!)

Atmosphere 3
Black, black and more black; small & intimate
martini lounge; best appreciated after sunset.
Truly a classic and all-time fave of so many fans!
Sidewalk seating at Happy Hour.

Date visited: _____ **My Rating:** _____
Went with: _____
Favorites: _____
Not so much: _____
Other comments: _____
_____

Bent Brick

10

· · · · · · · · · · · · · · · · · · · ·

Pearl Map
1639 NW Marshall
(503) 688-1655
www.thebentbrick.com

Happy Hours
4:00–6:00pm Tues–Sat

Food Deals 3
$2.00-$6.00
Follows (and helps establish) the trending,
funky-fresh, Northwest foodie thing. Duck fat jo-
jos, hush puppies, ham & black-eyed pea soup,
charred veggies, smoked salmon chips.

Drink Specials 3
$3.00 HUB cans; $5.00 house wines
$5.00 select cocktails (old-fashioneds on tap!)

Atmosphere 3
Rustic and warm with brick walls (but of course)
and an upscale angle on a neighborhood tavern.
It's not a big place, and there's a well-designed
waiting/lounge area at the entrance with a cool,
artsy wooden "tree" to sit beneath. Park Kitchen
chef/owner (and James Beard Award nominee).

Date visited: _____ **My Rating:** _____
Went with: _____
Favorites: _____
Not so much: _____
Other comments: _____
_____

Bluehour

10

Pearl Map
250 NW 13th Ave.
(503) 226-3394
www.bluehouronline.com

Happy Hours
4:00–6:30pm Mon–Sat

Food Deals 3
$1.00–$9.00
Keeping us happy after all these years with a super-extensive menu of 14 items. Seasonal focus, with things like pork belly, sliders, pasta of the day, fried blue cheese stuffed olives, burgers, pizzetta, cheese or meat plates.

Drink Specials 3
$5.00 draft beers; $6.00 house wines
$20 select bottle wine; $6.00 specialty cocktails

Atmosphere 3+
Impressive lofted interior; very well-designed — a Portland standout! Trés trendy and active scene (can be a touch loud). Happy Hour sidewalk patio dining allowed — and totally enjoyed! Ultra cool lighting effects at night, LOVE it!

Date visited: _____ **My Rating:** _____
Went with: _____
Favorites: _____
Not so much: _____
Other comments: _____
_____

Brix

Downtown (East) Map
1338 NW Hoyt
(503) 943-5995
www.brixtavern.com

Happy Hours
3:00–6:30pm and 9:30pm-mid Daily
★All night Monday

Food Deals 3
$2.95-7.95
18 items with seasonal variations of gastropub food: sliders, ribs, soups, salads, wings, yummy Brix chips, cheddar fries, burger, tacos, pizza.

Drink Specials 3
$1.00 off drafts (or try one of 30 cans of beer)
$1.00 off wine; $4.00 cocktails (nice, wide array)

Atmosphere 3
A welcomed new sportsbar/restaurant/lounge in the Pearl's old Olea space. The front half is very social with brick walls, extra-long bar, and chalkboard menu. Back half hosts the dining crowd and has a couple of pool tables too. Plus, an elevated private loft space for small groups.

Date visited: _____ **My Rating:** _____
Went with: _____
Favorites: _____
Not so much: _____
Other comments: _____
_____

Café Nell

NW/Nob Hill Map
1987 NW Kearney
(503) 295-6487
www.cafenell.com

Happy Hours
3:00–6:00pm Mon–Sat; ★All night Wed

Food Deals 3
$2.00–$7.00
Diverse menu with seasonal spins and items like soups, salad, oysters, mac & cheese, tacos, or clams, flatbreads, walnuts, or risotto.

Drink Specials 3
$1.00 off drafts; $5.00 wine; $5.00 bubbles or champagne cocktails; $5.50 martinis/cocktails

Atmosphere 3
Cute, little hidden gem tucked away on a quiet tree-lined street. A welcoming brasserie both day and night. Tiny Parisian-style bar with big cushy couch and cafe windows opening to the outside. The kind of place you could stay all day into the night!

Date visited: _____ **My Rating:** _____

Went with: _____

Favorites: _____

Not so much: _____

Other comments: _____

_____

Casa Del Matador 7

NW/Nob Hill Map
1438 NW 23rd Ave.; (503) 228-2855
Lloyd Center Map
2424 East Burnside; (503) 719-5757
www.matadorseattle.com (small local chain)

Happy Hours
4:00–6:00pm & 10:00pm–1:00am Daily

Food Deals 3
$5.00
Four kinds of quesadillas, choice of six tacos, and
even more: nachos, habanero or garlic prawns,
soups, chili, salad, spicy wings or calamari.

Drink Specials 0
No drink specials, but know that they have over
130 varieties of tequila!

Atmosphere 3
A handsome and sexy interior worthy of the title
"Matador" greets you upon entering! Stunning,
wrought iron artistry, gilded mirrors and rustic
stucco walls. A stand-out space with compelling,
centrally located, circular fireplace.

Date visited: _____ **My Rating:** _____
Went with: _____
Favorites: _____
Not so much: _____
Other comments: _____
_____

Cerulean Skies

10

Pearl Map
1439 NW Marshall
(503) 705-9840
www.ceruleanwine.com

Happy Hours
2:00–6:00pm Tues-Sun

A Happy Hour favorite!

Food Deals 3
$2.00–$6.00
Great menu line up with items like goat cheese
stuffed lamb and buffalo meatballs, Thai chicken
salad, NW or caprese salads, mac & cheese,
deviled eggs, and desserts like warm cookies!

Drink Specials 3
$3.50 beer; $2.00 tastes; $5.00-$6.00 glasses
$6.00 seasonal wine cocktails

Atmosphere 3
What a cool space! Part gallery, part wine bar.
Art and wine after all, do blend quite nicely.
Big, open industrial-style loft, with beautiful,
built-in decoration from resident artist paintings.
Seasonal outdoor seating, lounge areas, tasting
bar, and just a few tables. Winery in Hood River.

Date visited: _____ **My Rating:** _____
Went with: _____
Favorites: _____
Not so much: _____
Other comments: _____
_____

Cha

10

· · · · · · · · · · · · · · · · · · ·

NW/Nob Hill Map
305 NW 21st Ave.
(503) 295-4077
www.chaportland.com

A Happy Hour favorite!

Happy Hours
3:00–6:00pm Daily; 10:00–11:00pm Fri–Sat
★Sit at the bartop for Happy Hour all the time!

Food Deals 3+
$5.00 / Three for $12.00
The usual suspects in authentic Mexican food:
Tacos, nachos, burrito, quesadilla, taquitos,
torta, tostadas.

Drink Specials 3
$3.50-$5.50 beer; $5.50 wine
$5.50 sangria; $5.50 margarita / mojitos

Atmosphere 3
Same owners as Cha Cha Cha, but Nob Hill's
version is quite refined and elegant overall.
Big, open space with cool, artsy, white divider
and rough, lofty touches. Fun outside patio!

Date visited: _____ **My Rating:** _____
Went with: _____
Favorites: _____
Not so much: _____
Other comments: _____
_____

Coppia

Pearl Map
417 NW 10th Avenue
(503) 295-9536
www.coppiaportland.com

Happy Hours
4:00-5:30pm Tues–Sat

Food Deals 3
$6.00–$8.00
Eight or so fresh and tasty items (pair with wine):
risotto, soups, salads, artisan cheese plates, or
salami and fruit plates. Plus nightly specials.

Drink Specials 3
$3.00 beer; $6.00 red, white, or sparkling wines
$6.00 cocktail of the day

Atmosphere 3
This is the former Vino Paradiso, rebranded to
better emphasize focus on food. The interior
changed a bit, but is more refined and cozy now.
Three seating areas provide different staging
for rotating gallery art. Owned by Pink Martini
vocalist and percussionist, Timothy Nishimoto.

Date visited: _____ **My Rating:** _____
Went with: _____
Favorites: _____
Not so much: _____
Other comments: _____
_____

Davis Street Tavern

Old Town Map
500 NW Davis Street
(503) 505-5050
www.davisstreettavern.com

Happy Hours
4:00–6:00pm Mon–Fri; 3:00-5:00pm Sat-Sun

Food Deals 3
$1.50–$9.00
Stepped-up bar menu includes oysters and mussels, fish tacos, salads, duck wings, cauliflower tempura, olives, beef or pork sandwiches, mac & cheese, steak frites, chocolate truffle.

Drink Specials 2
$4.00 beer; $5.00 wines; $6.00 cocktails

Atmosphere 3
Full of light and Old Town warehouse character, this warm and classy tavern makes for a most perfect spot to congregate and satiate. Brick walls, soaring wood-beamed ceilings, wooden z-shaped bar and giant medieval chandeliers.

Date visited: _____ **My Rating:** _____
Went with: _____
Favorites: _____
Not so much: _____
Other comments: _____
_____

Elephant's Deli

9

NW/Nob Hill Map
115 NW 22nd Ave.
(503) 299-6304
www.elephantsdeli.com

Happy Hours
5:00–7:00pm Mon–Sat

Food Deals 2
$3.95
Nice little array of eats like wood-fired pizza,
fondue, calamari, and mahi mahi bites. Plus a
whole, Whole Foods-like deli with desserts too.

Drink Specials 3
$3.50-$4.50 drafts, $4.00 wines, $6.00 cocktail

Atmosphere 3
It's a super-cute, little, urban bar tucked inside
a quaint, but modern, country store. Eat and
shop, drink and bring home good wine, and
grab gourmet to go! Fun outdoor deck too.
It's really quite a unique place for Happy Hour!

Date visited: _____ **My Rating:** _____
Went with: _____
Favorites: _____
Not so much: _____
Other comments: _____
_____

Fireside

9

NW/Nob Hill Map
801 NW 23rd Ave.
(503) 477-9505
www.pdxfireside.com

Happy Hours
3:00–5:30pm Mon–Fri

Food Deals 2
$3.00-$6.00
Some bites, some meals. Northwest, seasonal
focus with nibbles like a pickle plate, fries, olives,
chickpeas, plus salad and a bread spread. Also
serves up mussels, roast beef or grilled cheese
sandwiches, pizza or kielbasa. S'mores too!

Drink Specials 3
$4.00 drafts; $6.00 wine; $6.00 cocktails (7)

Atmosphere 3
Long, skinny room with windows that open to the
street on warm, sunny days, and two fireplaces for
those all-too-often chilly ones. Very well-designed.
Contemporary tone, with unique showcasings of
wood, art, and fire. Comfy padded chairs and
booths soften the mostly hard edges of the space.

Date visited: _____ **My Rating:** _____

Went with: _____

Favorites: _____

Not so much: _____

Other comments: _____

_____

Fish Sauce

NW/Nob Hill Map
407 NW 17th Ave
(503) 227-8000
www.fishsaucepdx.com

Happy Hours
4:30-6:00pm and 9:00-10:00pm Mon–Sat

Food Deals 3
$2.00-$8.00
Draper Valley wings, tenderloin beef rolls, salad and crispy rolls, sugarcane shrimp, grilled corn, ribs, or salad, all beautifully presented with artful garnishes. Also $3.00 off banh mi sandwiches!

Drink Deals 3
$4.00 drafts, $4.00 sake; $6.00 wines
$7.00-$8.00 signature cocktails

Atmosphere 3
Think Asian and reclaimed wood. The space is intimate and inviting, with beautiful, knotty finished tables, including a super-long, central communal table. Lighting fixtures made from pallets, interesting white chalk murals on black walls, and large, nicely done outside patio.

Date visited: _____ **My Rating:** _____

Went with: _____

Favorites: _____

Not so much: _____

Other comments: _____

_____

website info

www.

happy
hour
guide
book
.com

2014 app and new website
parties
facebook
twitter
contact information
best-of lists
ideas
newsletter

Remember to check our website
every once in a while for changes and closures.

www.happyhourguidebook.com

**And please let us know if you see
information that needs changing!**

Gilt Club

10

Old Town Map
306 NW Broadway
(503) 222-4458
www.giltclub.com

Top cover fave 2013!

Happy Hours
5:00–6:30pm Mon–Fri

Food Deals 3
$2.00–$5.00
An already impressive menu, now made larger.
A good mix of fancy and fun: spicy deviled
eggs, pork rinds, fritto misto, mixed olives, spicy
chicken pops, salad, pork belly, and frito pie!

Drink Specials 3
$2.00-$6.00 beer; $5.00 wine
$5.00 appletini or Moscow mule

Atmosphere 3
Yes, it IS most luscious! Plushness abounds
with deep red walls and velvet drapes with gold
touches & sexy curves galore. WAY swanky!
Very creative touches and overall surroundings.
Famously featured in first episode of "Portlandia!"

Date visited: _____ **My Rating:** _____

Went with; _____

Favorites: _____

Not so much: _____

Other comments: _____

_____

Giorgio's

10

Pearl Map
1131 NW Hoyt
(503) 221-1888
www.giorgiospdx.com

Happy Hours
5:00–6:30pm Tues–Fri

Food Deals 3
$3.00–$10.00
One of the most highly-rated Italian restaurants in town! Happy Hour doesn't quite offer the cheapest prices, but the food is top-notch: soup, Caesar, stuffed meatballs, gnocchi, fusilli, polenta, arancini, pizza, or salt cod fritters.

Drink Specials 3
$3.00 beer of the day; $5.00 wines
$5.00 cocktail of the day

Atmosphere 3
It's a low-key, off-the-radar place that's been around since July 2000. Simple, European café style with black & white tiled floors, dark wood tables, and a long, copper-topped bar.

Date visited: _____ **My Rating:** _____

Went with: _____

Favorites: _____

Not so much: _____

Other comments: _____

_____

Huckleberry Pub

10

Pearl Map
2327 NW Kearney
(503) 228-5553
www.huckleberrypub.com

Happy Hours
3:00–5:30pm Daily

Food Deals 3
$3.00–$6.00
Good food, and kudos to them for posting photos of their Happy Hour grub on their website! What a novel concept that is oddly *so* extremely rare! Anyway... They'll update with the seasons, but offer things like salads, burgers, crostini, sliders, wings, big rings, fries, chili, and chili cheese fries.

Drink Specials 3
$3.50 drafts; $5.00 wine; $3.00 wells
$5.00 house infused cocktails

Atmosphere 3
In a former life, this was the home of the short-lived NW Public House. Homey interior with a couple of big porches. Two stories with the bar upstairs. Streamlined, simple decor, but cozy.

Date visited: _____ **My Rating:** _____

Went with: _____

Favorites: _____

Not so much: _____

Other comments: _____

_____

Irving St. Kitchen

Pearl Map
703 NW 13th Ave.
(503) 343-9440
www.irvingstreetkitchen.com

Happy Hours
4:30–6:00pm Daily

Food Deals 2
$4.00–$7.00
Unique menu items totally matching the theme.
Food changes often: seasonal salad, fried pickles,
steamed mussels, Cajun fries, jambalaya, meatballs and mashed potatoes.

Drink Specials 3
$2.00 tall boy (with $2.00 whisky back)
$6.00 house wines; $5.00 specialty cocktails

Atmosphere 3
Trendy and rustic with TONS of character and
attention to design details. Named Willamette
Week's "Best New Restaurant" in its 2010
Reader's Choice Poll. Lots of nice little nooks
and separate seating areas throughout.

Date visited: _____ **My Rating:** _____
Went with: _____
Favorites: _____
Not so much: _____
Other comments: _____
_____

Isabel

9

Pearl Map
330 NW 10th
(503) 222-4333
www.isabelscantina.com

Happy Hours
4:00-6:00pm Daily

Food Deals 3
$$3.00-$6.00
Isabel's Cantina cookbook features "bold Latin flavors from the New California kitchen," as does her Happy Hour food which may change a bit seasonally: four kinds of tacos, portobello ragòut, salad, soup, chipotle lime chicken or salmon.

Drink Specials 3
$4.00 beer; $6.00 wines; $6.00 specialty cocktails

Atmosphere 2
Located inside a stand-alone building made almost entirely of glass walls; minimalist interior with high ceilings, gray carpet, orange chairs and nice, big seasonal outdoor plaza patio.

Date visited: _____ **My Rating:** _____

Went with: _____

Favorites: _____

Not so much: _____

Other comments: _____

_____

Ivories

Pearl Map
1435 NW Flanders
(503) 241-6514
www.ivoriesjazz.com

Happy Hours
5:00–6:00pm and 9:30pm-close Tues-Sun

Food Deals 2
$2.00 off appetizers, salads, and sandwiches

Drink Specials 3
$3.00-$4.00 drafts; $4.00 wine; $3.00 wells

Atmosphere 3
Jazz Club in the Pearl, that's not too fancy, but
quite nice. It's a big, loft-like space with a stage,
and can feel a little funny being more empty
early on. If you stop in later for a drink, be aware
that cover charges can go into effect as there
is live music there and some are big names
(including the friendly owner, Jim Templeton).

Date visited: _____ **My Rating:** _____
Went with: _____
Favorites: _____
Not so much: _____
Other comments: _____
_____

Jamison's

10

Pearl Map
900 NW 11th St.
(503) 972-3330
www.jamisonpdx.com

Happy Hours
4:00–5:30pm Daily

Food Deals 3
$2.00-$9.00
Seasonal variations with things like three kinds of
unique and tasty flatbreads, kale chips, crepes,
burgers, turkey BLT, meat or cheese and oysters.

Drink Specials 3
$3.00 Sessions; $6.00 wines; $6.00 cocktails

Atmosphere 3
Gorgeous design! Very different than the former
space, Fenouil. Still with an upper-crust look,
but in a very manly and rustic tone. The outside
patio overlooks Jamison square and fountain,
and you can sit there for Happy Hour, or anywhere else in the restaurant. Inside, it's gray
suede and muted, rough woods, brown leather
chairs, a "living wall", and a kick-ass fireplace.

Date visited: _____ **My Rating:** _____

Went with: _____

Favorites: _____

Not so much: _____

Other comments: _____

_____

Jinx

Closed 9

Pearl Map
232 NW 12th Ave.
(503) 922-0178
www.jinxpdx.com

Happy Hours
4:00–7:00pm Mon-Sat

Food Deals 3
$4.00-$7.00
About 10 pan-asian eats like spring rolls, tom ka soup, crab rangoon, wings, satay, pad thai, fried rice, coconut prawns, gyoza, garden salad.

Drink Specials 3
$1.00 off drafts and wine; $4.00 well
$5.00-$6.00 cocktails (10)

Atmosphere 3
New owners have created a warm, inviting lounge. Cool, comfortable environment perfect for small groups of friends to connect or for date night. Gray and plum-colored walls with wood panels, bamboo tabletops, lotus flower lights, pewter wall sconces and globe lights.

Date visited: _____ **My Rating:** _____
Went with: _____
Favorites: _____
Not so much: _____
Other comments: _____
_____

Jo-Bar

10

NW/Nob Hill Map
715 NW 23rd Ave.
(503) 222-0048
www.papahaydn.com/r/6/Jo-Bar

Happy Hours
3:00–6:00pm Daily; also last hour before closing

Food Deals 3
$1.00–$7.00
Expanded menu with 17 items: the famous
Jo Burger, fries, homemade sweet potato chips,
Cobb salad, fondue, French onion soup, steamed
clams, pizza, mac & cheese, wings, olives, nuts.

Drink Specials 3
$4.00 beer; $6.00 house wines
$5.00-$6.00 cocktails (10 selections)

Atmosphere 3
Deep red and olive walls, stunning entry flower
display, original art, huge iron chandelier, open
stone wood oven and rotisserie, full front windows,
outdoor sidewalk seating. Casually chill, yet nice.

Date visited: _____ **My Rating:** _____

Went with: _____

Favorites: _____

Not so much: _____

Other comments: _____

_____

Kells Brewpub

7

Nob Hill/Northwest Map
305 NW 21st Ave.
(503) 208-3227
www.kellsbrewpub.com

Happy Hours
4:00–6:30pm Mon–Fri; 10:00pm–close Mon–Thurs

Food Deals 3
$3.00–$5.00
Irish nachos, wings, BLTC, burger or sandwich
with fries, quesadilla, oyster shooters, sweet
potato fries, hummus.

Drink Specials 0
Sadly, no drink specials

Atmosphere 3
A whole new Kells – inside and out – with an on-
site brewery! Bit by bit, they're playing around
with introducing all kinds of new fun. The inside
of this version of Kells is brand-new and not
all that Irish-y, but still with dark wood booths.
More brews on their way day-by-day...

Date visited: _____ **My Rating:** _____
Went with: _____
Favorites: _____
Not so much: _____
Other comments: _____
_____

Mellow Mushroom

Pearl Map
1411 NW Flanders
(503) 224-9019
www.mellowmushroom.com

Happy Hours
3:00-6:00pm Daily

Food Deals 2
$2.00–$5.00
Mellow menu with garlic knots, pesto bread, Caesar salad, pizza slider, bruschetta with capri salad, wings, or meatball combo.

Drink Specials 3
$2.00 Tecate; $3.75 drafts; $3.00 well drinks; $4.00 Boilermaker; plus other daily deals

Atmosphere 3
Retro-modern-lounge-y with a lot of grooviness going on. Vinyl swivel seats, orange plastic chairs, open kitchen, and wall-to-wall paneling. Half-walls and funky 70s dividers segment out the large, open room. Cool vibe.

Date visited: _____ **My Rating:** _____

Went with: _____

Favorites: _____

Not so much: _____

Other comments: _____

_____

Meriwether's

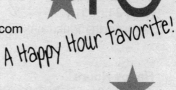

NW/Nob Hill Map
2601 NW Vaughn
(503) 228-1250
www.meriwethersnw.com

A Happy Hour favorite!

Happy Hours
4:00-6:00pm Daily

Food Deals 3+
$3.00–$12.00
OMGWOW! 16 "Pantry Board" items to mix and mingle and another 12 appetizers and such! Seasonal deliciousness like soup, olives, deviled eggs, several salads, fries, burger, stuffed dates, pizza, ribs, steak bites, foccacia, fried pickles, fritters, polenta fries, walnut dip, falafel and more!

Drink Specials 2
$3.50 drafts; $5.00 select wine

Atmosphere 3+
Built on the site of the 1905 World's Fair. Their historic and stately interior exudes a warm and hospitable countryside inn quality. Impressive! Incredibly cozy in the winter. Gorgeous deck out back, but not available for Happy Hour.

Date visited: _____ **My Rating:** _____
Went with: _____
Favorites: _____
Not so much: _____
Other comments: _____
_____

North 45

NW/Nob Hill Map
517 NW 21st Ave.
(503) 248-6317
www.north45pub.com

Happy Hours
4:00–6:00pm Daily; All night on Mondays★

Food Deals 3
$3.00–$6.00
Ten tasty appetizers like calamari, green beans, wings, mac & cheese, sliders, salads, chicken flautas, and pommes frites (yum!)

Drink Specials 2
$3.50 pints of draft pilsner; $5.00 house wines
$4.00 wells; $5.50 "Patio-Rita"

Atmosphere 3
A rich, but homey feel to their travelers-themed bar with framed maps and vacation photos. Very cozy inside/huge patio beer garden in back – which is tented and heated in the winter.

Date visited: _____ **My Rating:** _____
Went with: _____
Favorites: _____
Not so much: _____
Other comments: _____
_____

Oba!

Pearl Map
555 NW 12th Ave.
(503) 228-6161
www.obarestaurant.com

Happy Hours
4:00–6:30pm Daily; 4:00pm–close Sundays ★
9:00pm–close Mon–Thurs; 10pm-close Fri-Sat

Food Deals 3
$3.50–$6.00

A Happy Hour favorite!

A forever classic! Giant menu of deliciousness
(careful – you'll easily leave too full): fish or
chicken baja tacos, nachos, corn cakes with
pork, grilled sweet corn, steak skewers, patatas
bravas, empanadas.

Drink Specials 3
$3.50 drafts; $4.00 house wine
$5.50 flavored Margaritas; $5.00 mojitos

Atmosphere 3
Colorful, Latin-American-style with a festive and
trendy scene. Golden and terra cotta walls, pillars
and white sparkly tree lights. Outdoor sidewalk
dining. "The kind of place you need to hit before
confession."

Date visited: _____ **My Rating:** _____
Went with: _____
Favorites: _____
Not so much: _____
Other comments: _____
_____

On Deck Sports Bar

Pearl Map
910 NW 14th Ave.
(503) 227-7020
www.ondecksportsbar.com

Happy Hours
3:00–6:00pm Mon-Fri; 9:00pm-11:00pm Mon–Thur
Plus Sunday late-night 9:00-10:00pm
Note: No HH during Ducks or Beavers games

Food Deals 3 $2.00–5.00 17 item bar menu:
Nachos, Caesar, chicken strips or burgers w/fries,
taquitos, chips & salsa, pork sliders, fries, tots,
rings, wings, hummus, veggie plate, quesadilla.

Drink Specials 3 $3.00-$4.25 drafts; $4.00 wine
$6.00 cider; $3.75 wells; $4.50 flavored Smirnoff
$5.50 Captain Morgan & Coke

Atmosphere 3 Really as nice as a sports bar
can be: big place with wall-to-wall windows;
hi-tech wavy black ceiling tiles; hi-def TVs.
Wonderful, outdoor deck gets even better
at night! Great place for large group parties.

Date visited: _____ **My Rating:** _____
Went with: _____
Favorites: _____
Not so much: _____
Other comments: _____
_____

Oven & Shaker

Pearl Map
1134 NW Everett
(503) 241-1600
www.ovenandshaker.com

Happy Hours
2:30-5:30pm and 10:00pm–mid Daily

Food Deals 3
$7.00–$10.00
Phenomenally delicious wood-fired pizza, as brought to us by Cathy Whims of Nostrana (Four-time James Beard nominee). About half-off several pizza styles with unique, gourmet spins. A couple of fresh and healthy salads too.

Drink Specials 3
$3.00 daily draft; $5.00 wine; $7.00 cocktails

Atmosphere 3
Rough, exposed woods cover the place with rustic urban charm. An ultra-long bar (45-feet) dominates one full wall, with windows open to the street along the front. It may be more of a late lunch than a Happy Hour given the 4:00pm end-time, but being enormously popular and delicious, it's nice they offer a break. It's great late!

Date visited: _____ **My Rating:** _____

Went with: _____

Favorites: _____

Not so much: _____

Other comments: _____

_____

Paley's Place

Pearl Map
1204 NW 21st Ave.
(503) 243-2403
www.paleysplace.net

A Happy Hour favorite!

Happy Hours
5:30-6:30pm Mon-Thur; 5:00-6:30pm Fri-Sun

Food Deals 3
$2.00-$7.00
Wow! One of the city's best chef's and most
lovely places offers Happy Hour in the bar!
Owned by Vitaley Paley, a James Beard award-
winner, offers a most excellent cheese burger,
oysters on the half-shell, fries, seasonal salad,
bruschetta, cheeses. Ask to see the dinner
menu – it's surprisingly affordable!

Drink Specials 3
$3.00 beer: $5.00 wine: $5.00 cocktails

Atmosphere 3
Opened in 1995 in a large, traditional style home
with large wrap-around porch. He has a cookbook out – try your hand at some classics!

Date visited: _____ **My Rating:** _____
Went with: _____
Favorites: _____
Not so much: _____
Other comments: _____
_____

Papa Haydn

10

NW/Nob Hill Map
701 NW 23rd Ave.; (503) 228-7317

<u>Sellwood</u> 5829 SE Milwaukee; (503) 232-9440
(Similar menu 3–6pm Daily)
www.papahaydn.com

Happy Hours
3:00–6:00pm Mon–Fri

Food Deals 3
$2.00–$7.00
A Portland favorite since 1983 with a most excellent, high-quality Happy Hour! Good size menu with French onion soup, salad, burger, clams, fries, croque monseur or madam (with turkey), mushroom bolognese.

Drink Specials 3
$4.00 drafts; $6.50 wines and wells
$5.00–$6.00 house cocktails

Atmosphere 3
Everything cute in traditional design is represented and ties together beautifully: buttercream walls, upholstered seats, paned glass, thick moldings, stripes and harlequin patterns, and carpeting. Well-known reputation for delicious desserts!

Date visited: _____ **My Rating:** _____

Went with: _____

Favorites: _____

Not so much: _____

Other comments: _____

_____

Paragon

Pearl Map
1309 NW Hoyt
(503) 833-5060
www.paragonrestaurant.com

Happy Hours
4:30–6:30pm and 9:30pm-close Daily

Food Deals 2
$6.00
Bar menu items that change seasonally with things like salad, bruschetta, lamb empenada, ramen, seafood cakes, burger, or crepes.

Drink Specials 3
$3.00–$4.50 drafts; $6.00 house wines
$6.50-$7.50 house infusions, drops or coolers

Atmosphere 3
A forever-favorite in the Pearl finally started Happy Hour! Open-air in the summer = fresh breezes, fun, and excellent views of the Pearl parade outside. Contemporary Northwest style with big open bar, chill music, and bar mirrors overhead to reflect the good-looking crowd.

Date visited: _____ **My Rating:** _____
Went with: _____
Favorites: _____
Not so much: _____
Other comments: _____
_____

Parish

Pearl Map
231 NW 11th Ave.
(503) 227-2421
www.theparishpdx.com

Happy Hours
3:00-6:00pm Daily

Food Deals 3
$3.00–$8.00
Select oysters on the half shell (several kinds,
be sure to stick to the HH ones for the discount);
grilled shrimp, corn, or chicken hearts; plus
wedge salad, burger, slider, soft boiled eggs.

Drink Specials 3
$2.00 Trumer pils; $6.00 house wine or sparkling
$4.00 well drinks

Atmosphere 3
An oyster bar in the Pearl. I like it! Then add in a
New Orleans spin with spicy creole taster plates
and super cute decor? I'm a devoted follower!
Beautiful design with soft blue-greys, dark woods,
and Martha Stewart-worthy signage and slightly
churchy room dividers.

Date visited: _____ **My Rating:** _____
Went with: _____
Favorites: _____
Not so much: _____
Other comments: _____
_____

Park Kitchen

9

Old Town Map
422 NW 8th Ave
(503) 223-7275
www.parkkitchen.com

Happy Hours
5:00–6:00pm Daily

Food Deals 3
$8.00
Seasonal changes with several, seasonal, Americana-nouveau small plates like chickpea fries, grilled peppers, flank steak salad, beets with goat cheese, and salt cod fritters. Bring a friend and get one of everything! One of the best restaurants, but ya gotta pay for it.

Drink Specials 2
$6.00 wine; $6.00 cocktails

Atmosphere 3
Cute, candlelit, and cozy! Coming in from the streets, it's such a sweet, subdued, almost-country respite inside. Café tables outside, with garage doors that open to the park blocks.

Date visited: _____ **My Rating:** _____

Went with: _____

Favorites: _____

Not so much: _____

Other comments: _____

_____

Piattino

Pearl Map
1140 NW Everett
(503) 374-1000
www.piattinopdx.com

Happy Hours
3:00–6:00pm Mon-Sat

A Happy Hour favorite!

Food Deals 3
$3.00–$9.00
Italian small-plates restaurant offers deals on
four of their famously fabulous wood-fired thin
crust pizzas, plus mussels, meatballs, antipasti
board, salads, and bread plates.

Drink Specials 3
$4.00 beer; $5.00-$6.00 wine; $6.00 cocktails

Atmosphere 3
Same owner as the former Shiraz, warming up
the space with gorgeous wood tables, reclaimed
wood fully covering the walls, and a wood-fired
pizza oven front and center at the second bar.
It's very woody!

Date visited: _____ **My Rating:** _____
Went with: _____
Favorites: _____
Not so much: _____
Other comments: _____
_____

Pink Rose

9

Pearl Map
1300 NW Lovejoy
(503) 482-2165
www.pinkrosepdx.com

Happy Hours
4:00-7:00pm and 10:00pm–mid Tues-Sat

Food Deals 3
$3.00-$6.00
Menu may vary somewhat seasonally: pork w/
cheese fries, butter lettuce or brussel sprouts
salad, stuffed mushrooms, bacon- wrapped
dates, chips & dip, and grilled cheese.

Drink Specials 3
$4.00 select draft; $4.00 wines; $4.00 cocktail

Atmosphere 3
A few years ago, this was the all-new, ultra-hip
SoLo Lounge. It's lost some edge and is softer
now, but still retains a dark, underground, clubby
look and feel. The upstairs deck is lovely in the
summer, with its pink umbrella tables, torches,
heat lamps, potted plants and the elevated view
of Lovejoy street passer-bys and traffic.

Date visited: _____ **My Rating:** _____
Went with: _____
Favorites: _____
Not so much: _____
Other comments: _____
_____

Pope House

10

2075 NW Glisan
(503) 222-1056
www.popehouselounge.com

Happy Hours
4:00–7:00pm and 10-close (food only) Daily
★All day Sunday

Food Deals 3
$5.00-$6.00
Yes! Frito Pie! Plus a couple paninis, jambalaya,
hush puppies, sliders, Caesar, mac & cheese.

Drink Specials 3
$3.75 drafts; $5.00 house wines; $3.75 wells
$5.00 Southern-style cocktails; $4.00 whiskeys

Atmosphere 3
This wonderful, old Victorian exudes welcoming
southern hospitality, warmth, and charm, especially at night. Several parlor-like dining/drink-
ing rooms, social central bar, and lots and lots
of whiskey to boot! Still vaguely remembered
fondly as the old Brazen Bean.

Date visited: _____ **My Rating:** _____
Went with: _____
Favorites: _____
Not so much: _____
Other comments: _____
_____

Rae's Lakeview Lounge

8

NW/Nob Hill Map
1900 NW 27th Ave.
(503) 719-6494
www.raesportland.com

Happy Hours
2:00-6:00pm Daily

Food Deals 3
$2.00-$5.00
Huge 16-item menu! Mac & cheese, burgers,
soup, salads, calamari, beef bourguignon, ham
& cheese, black & tan hummus, bread pudding.

Drink Specials 2
$1.00 Millers; $3.00 wine; $3.50 wells

Atmosphere 2
Laid-back, old-school, neighborhood lounge.
Big, open room with divider half-walls adorned
with old photos and topped with games. Parking
lot and outdoor patio, but sadly, no longer any
lake views around (that was back from the
World's Fair days).

Date visited: _____ **My Rating:** _____

Went with: _____

Favorites: _____

Not so much: _____

Other comments: _____

_____

Ringside Steakhouse

7

NW/Nob Hill Map
2165 NW Burnside
(503) 223-1513
www.ringsidesteakhouse.com

Happy Hours
9:30pm–close Daily and 4:00–5:30pm Sun

Food Deals 3+
$2.95–$4.95
A forever favorite menu: steak bites (YUM!),
potato skins, prime rib sandwich, crabcakes,
clams, burger, Caesar, oysters, calamari, jo-jos,
mussels, shrimp, quesadilla, and meatballs.

Drink Specials 0
Sadly, no drink specials

Atmosphere 3
Back to basics and the beloved, old-school,
lounge remains pretty much intact! Renovation
didn't really change things all too much (behind
the scenes re-do excluded). You'll love the place
– dimly-lit, super-cozy interior, and wrap-around
bartender pit. Since 1944. Wow.

Date visited: _____ **My Rating:** _____
Went with: _____
Favorites: _____
Not so much: _____
Other comments: _____
_____

Sal's Famous Italian

● ●

NW/Nob Hill Map
33 NW 23rd Place
(503) 467-4067
www.salskitchen.com

Happy Hours
3:30–5:30pm Daily

Food Deals 3
$5.00
Delicious samplings of all the most popular
dishes: bruschetta, Caesar salad, burger and fries,
spaghetti and meatballs, salumi plate, butternut
squash ravioli, fetticini alfredo (and with chicken).

Drink Specials 3
$3.00 beer; $5.00 house wine
$4.00 well drinks; $7.00 featured cocktails

Atmosphere 3
Hip and quaint old-world Italian trattoria with
gorgeous, faux wall treatments and walls of
classic framed pictures. Sweet space inside,
but in strip mall.

Date visited: _____ **My Rating:** _____
Went with: _____
Favorites: _____
Not so much: _____
Other comments: _____
_____

Seres

10

Pearl Map
1105 NW Lovejoy
(971) 222-7327
www.seresrestaurant.com

Happy Hours
3:00–7:00pm Mon–Sat; All night Tues★
4:00-7:00pm Sun

Top cover fave 2013!

Food Deals 3+
$2.00–$6.50
More than 20 cravable, high-quality, fresh and
organic Pan Asian delights brings everything
under the sun: salt & pepper pork, General Tso's
chicken, Cantonese crispy prawns, spring or
salad rolls, wonton soup, lo mein, pot stickers,
string beans, soups, kung pao chicken, fried rice.

Drink Specials 3
$3.50 drafts; $6.00 wines; $7.00 select cocktails

Atmosphere 3
Pearlesque loft-style with Far East reserve.
High-end but friendly and comfortable. Lofty loft
space with full, floor-to-ceiling windows; natural
tones and tables; gorgeous hanging tile art pieces.

Date visited: _____ **My Rating:** _____
Went with: _____
Favorites: _____
Not so much: _____
Other comments: _____
_____

Serratto

NW/Nob Hill Map
2112 NW Kearney
(503) 221-1195
www.serratto.com

Happy Hours
4:00–6:00pm Daily

A Happy Hour favorite!

Food Deals 3+
$4.00–$8.00
Some of the best food around, at Happy Hour
and beyond! Positively stellar menu items (14):
stone oven pizzas (my personal favorite for Happy
Hour), flame-broiled burgers, salad, calamari,
hummus, deviled eggs, stuffed peppers, French
onion soup, spaghetti bolognese, pommes frites.

Drink Specials 3
$4.00 drafts; $5.00 red or white house wine
$5.00 cocktail specials and wells

Atmosphere 3
Happy Hour is in their more casual "Vineria"
which is only slightly Italian in ambiance,
but extremely pleasant and even romantic.

Date visited: _____ **My Rating:** _____

Went with: _____

Favorites: _____

Not so much: _____

Other comments: _____

_____

Silk

Pearl Map
1012 NW Glisan
(503) 248-2172
www.silkbyphovan.com

Happy Hours
4:00–6:30pm Mon–Sat

Food Deals 3
$4.00–$7.00
Enjoy a large variety of delicious Vietnamese mini-dinners including salad rolls, sliders, hoisin ribs, chicken curry, lemongrass chicken, bahn mi sandwiches (six), wings, pho, crazy noodles.

Drink Specials 2
$4.00 Kirin beer, $5.00 house wines ($20 bottles)

Atmosphere 3
White and natural borderline-retro decor blends contemporary hard lines with silky flow. It's totally mod, gorgeous, and romantic. Enjoy the illuminated and mesmerizing, white "flowing" wall!

Date visited: _____ **My Rating:** _____

Went with: _____

Favorites: _____

Not so much: _____

Other comments: _____

_____

Southland Whiskey Kitchen

9

NW/Nob Hill Map
1422 NW 23rd Ave.
(503) 224-2668
www.southlandwhiskeykitchen.com

Happy Hours
3:30–6:00pm and 10:00pm-close Daily

Food Deals 3
$2.50–$5.00
Southern kitchen vittles like mac & cheese, coleslaw, cornbread, collard greens, grit stix, beans, sliders (four kinds), hush puppies, chili cheese fries, chopped salad, wings, or brisket.

Drink Specials 3
$1.00 off beer, wine, and wells; $6.00 cocktails

Atmosphere 3
Southern style for the Pacific Northwest, right out of a Texas roadhouse, but new and beautiful. Wood parquet walls with a striking zigzag design. Hanging wagonwheel lights and exposed brick add to the charm. Same owners as Casa del Matador.

Date visited: _____ **My Rating:** _____

Went with: _____

Favorites: _____

Not so much: _____

Other comments: _____

Streetcar Bistro

Pearl Map
1101 NW Northrup
(503) 227-2988
www.streetcarbistro.com

Happy Hours
3:00-6:00pm and 10:00pm-mid Daily

Food Deals 2
$3.00-$8.00
About 10 items of all sorts that vary seasonally: salad, soup, wings, pulled pork sandwich, mac & cheese, BLT, seasonal shell fish, charcuterie or cheese boards, burgers, dessert.

Drink Specials 1
$4.00-$5.00 beer (30 of them!); $1.00 off wine
$6.00 cocktails

Atmosphere 3
Sleek modern look in cool new bistro. Muted white pine woods, white leather boxy chairs, and a big bar with about 30 illuminated taps. Nice lounge area with couches and fireplace.

Date visited: _____ **My Rating:** _____

Went with: _____

Favorites: _____

Not so much: _____

Other comments: _____

_____

Thai Smile

9

NW/Nob Hill Map
1639 NW Glisan
(503) 473-8758
www.thai-smiles.com

Happy Hours
4:30-6:00pm Daily

Food Deals 3
$2.50–$6.00
YUM! About 14 delicious specials from the Land
of Smiles (a concept they show well here): crab
rangoon, egg rolls, satay, pot stickers, angel fish
rolls, spring rolls, prawns, tofu dishes.

Drink Specials 3
$3.00 beer; $5.00-$7.25 wines
$5.00-$7.00 cocktails

Atmosphere 3
The HAPPY Hour Guidebook certainly loves the
name! And the place. Formerly Sweet Basil with
new owners and full facelift. Toned down and
comfortable "chic, chill and chilli" restaurant.
Globe lights hanging from the ceiling, green/gray
walls, light wood floors, window and original art.

Date visited: _____ **My Rating:** _____

Went with: _____

Favorites: _____

Not so much: _____

Other comments: _____

_____

TeardropLounge

8

Pearl Map
1015 NW Everett
(503) 970-8331
www.teardroplounge.com

Happy Hours
4:00–7:00pm Mon–Fri

Food Deals 2
$3.00–$6.00
Always-changing the line-up with a couple of gourmet items like pork terrine sandwich or a sugar snap pea salad; plus a couple of little snacks like truffle fries or marinated olives.

Drink Specials 2
$5.00–$6.00 specialty weekly cocktails (3)

Atmosphere 3
Attention to detail in every aspect of design almost brings a tear to my eye... It's gorgeous every step of the way from the bartenders and their magical mixology (the real focus), to the industrial chic and very cool decor. LOVE it!

Date visited: _____ **My Rating:** _____

Went with: _____

Favorites: _____

Not so much: _____

Other comments: _____

_____

Touché

10

Pearl Map
1425 NW Glisan; (503) 221-1150
www.touchepdx.com

Happy Hours
4:00-6:30pm and 10:00pm–close Daily
(11:00pm Fri-Sat)
★All day Sunday (4:00pm–2:30am)

Food Deals 3
$2.50–$6.50
Crazy-huge menu and big servings! Four kinds
of gyros (chicken, lamb, falafel, or veggie),
wood-fired pizza, salads, Mediterranean platter,
spaghetti bolognese, lasagna, burger with fries,
steamed clams, dips/spreads, tiramisu, and more!

Drink Specials 3
$1.00 off drafts; $4.00 wells
$5.00 wines (choice of four)

Atmosphere 3
Happy Hour anywhere in the gorgeous restaurant
downstairs, upstairs in the semi-stately pool
hall, or out on the wonderful new patio(s)! Grand
staircase entrance and six nice, full-size tables.
Great for both stylish pool boys and true sharks.

Date visited: _____ **My Rating:** _____
Went with: _____
Favorites: _____
Not so much: _____
Other comments: _____
_____

Trader Vic's 10

Pearl Map
1203 NW Glisan; (503) 467-2277
www.tradervicspdx.com

Happy Hours
4:00–6:00pm and 10:00pm-close Daily
★All day Sunday (4:00pm–10:00pm)

Food Deals 3+ *Happy Hour of the Year 2014!*
$4.00-$7.00
Twelve exceptionally delicious tiki treats! Glazed
chicken wings, Korean beef tacos, calamari, fries,
char sui pork, sliders, coconut shrimp, stir-fried
chicken in lettuce cups, wontons, salad, beans.

Drink Specials 3+
$4.00 drafts; $5.00 red or white house wines
$6.00 mai tais and signature tropical cocktails

Atmosphere 3+
A Polynesian piece of paradise in the Pearl!
Refined, tropical, tiki elegance mixed with fun,
fascination, and fire. It's fully enchanting and
magical! Thatched ceilings and walls, bamboo
and carved wooden masks everywhere, and
a social, central tiki bar with themed cocktail-
ware. Full walls of windows open to the street.

Date visited: _____ **My Rating:** _____
Went with: _____
Favorites: _____
Not so much: _____
Other comments: _____
_____

Uptown Billiards Club

NW/Nob Hill Map
120 NW 23rd Ave.
(503) 226-6909
www.uptownbilliards.com

Happy Hours
4:00–6:30pm Tues–Sat

A Happy Hour favorite!

Food Deals 3+
Half-price, 20-item bistro menu! Choose from six
sandwiches/burgers, several soups and salads,
five kinds of pizzas, and several bistro items.

Drink Specials 3
$4.00 drafts; $5.00-$6.00 wines
$4.25–$6.00 cocktails ($1.00 off all of them)

Atmosphere 3
Totally different in the pool hall classification with
its upscale class and elegence, spruced up in
2010. There's a nice, big room for playing pool,
a gorgeous wooden bar, a small dining room
and a private, tucked-away billiards room.

Date visited: _____ **My Rating:** _____
Went with: _____
Favorites: _____
Not so much: _____
Other comments: _____
_____

Vault Martini

Pearl Map
226 NW 12th Ave.
(503) 224-4909
www.vault-martini.com

Happy Hours
4:00–7:00pm Daily; ★All day Sunday

A Happy Hour favorite!

Food Deals 3
$3.00-$6.00
A small menu of good drinking accompaniments like a charcuterie or cheese plate, bread and oil, olives, quesadilla, or bacon-wrapped dates. Order several items and share.

Drink Specials 3+
$3.00 Stellas; $5.00 house wines; $3.00 wells $5.00 select cocktails (17 included at Happy Hour, but ask to see the full menu of 80+!)

Atmosphere 3
An absolute stand-out in Portland, and a classic, very classy bar not to be missed – and visited often. Gorgeous space with a fireplace, several lounge areas with very comfortable seating, and fine design and beauty everywhere you look.

Date visited: _____ **My Rating:** _____

Went with: _____

Favorites: _____

Not so much: _____

Other comments: _____

_____

Verde Cucina

Pearl Map
524 NW 14th Ave.
(503) 894-9321
www.verdecocinamarket.com
plus:
Hillsdale: 6446 SW Capitol Hwy; (503) 384-2327

Happy Hours
3:00–5:30pm Daily

Food Deals 2
Small menu limits points: Guac & chips $5.00
Taco of the day $3.00 or roasted veggies $4.00

Drink Specials 2
$1.00 off beer or wine; $4.00 sangritas
$6.00 Margaritas

Atmosphere 2
Formerly Kin and before that Holden's. Simple,
small space with little adornment. Open, central
bar area, roll-up garage doors, orange walls,
wood floors, and black metal chairs.

Date visited: _____ **My Rating:** _____
Went with: _____
Favorites: _____
Not so much: _____
Other comments: _____
_____

Via Delizia

7

Pearl Map
1105 NW Marshall
(503) 225-9300
www.viadelizia.com

Happy Hours
3:00–6:00pm Sun–Fri

A Happy Hour favorite!

Food Deals 3
$4.00–$6.00
Good portions and great food! Bruschetta, salads, ravioli, spaghetti alla bolognese, pork panini, and several flatbreads (steak, chicken or caprese). Be sure to save room for the gelato!

Drink Specials 0
Sadly, no drink deals, but low prices at all times.

Atmosphere 3
A giant tree dominates overhead and creates a pleasant patio piazza scene inside. Hanging tree lights, stone walls, an arched wooden doorway and shutters on windows help transport you to Italy. Cozy little Italian streetside café!

Date visited: _____ **My Rating:** _____

Went with: _____

Favorites: _____

Not so much: _____

Other comments: _____

_____

Voicebox Karaoke

10

NW/Nob Hill Map
2112 NW Hoyt; (503) 303-8220
www.voiceboxpdx.com
New SE Location p.330

Happy Hours
4:00–7:00pm Thurs–Sun ($4.00/hr. Karaoke)
Tuesdays – $10.00 covers your karaoke cost!
★Wednesdays – All night Happy Hour

A Happy Hour favorite!

Food Deals 3
$1.00 off all menu items
Handy and sharable comfort food with a dash
of Asian influence. Lots of snacks and small
plates: Chicken or tofu bánh mì , quesadillas,
sandwiches, pizza, tots.

Drink Specials 3
$1.00 off all beer, wine, saké, and saké cocktails
($3.50 micros, $5.00 house wines)

Atmosphere 3
Rent private "boxes" and never stop singing
(or laughing as the case may be—it's a blast!).
High-style space-age Japanese pop decor with
Pander Bros. art, ultramod hanging lamps and
high-def big-screen TVs. It's a super-happy place!

Date visited: _____ **My Rating:** _____
Went with: _____
Favorites: _____
Not so much: _____
Other comments: _____
_____

Wildwood

NW/Nob Hill Map
1221 NW 21st Ave.
(503) 248-9663
www.wildwoodrestaurant.com

Happy Hours
4:00–6:00pm Mon–Fri (Bar and patio only)

Food Deals 2
$2.00–$10.00
Finally! A real Happy Hour menu with eight
items ranging from snacks to meals! I've been
waiting for an upgrade like this... truffled popcorn,
onion rings, salads, brats, kimchi fried rice,
burgers, potato croquettes, charcuterie board.

Drink Specials 3
$2.00–$4.00 beer; $6.00 select wine
$5.00 choice of 5 signature cocktails

Atmosphere 3
As Northwest good as it gets, but in an understated way. Small bar area with stone, slate,
wood, and gridded windows. Enjoy the patio
outside at Happy Hour! Summer brings Tuesday
and Thursday outdoor BBQs (early dinner hours).

Date visited: _____ **My Rating:** _____
Went with: _____
Favorites: _____
Not so much: _____
Other comments: _____
_____

Wilfs

Pearl (off map)
800 NW 6th Avenue (Union Station)
(503) 223-0070
www.wilfsrestaurant.com

Happy Hours
5:30–7:00pm Tues–Fri

Food Deals 3
$3.50–$6.00
Half-off limited seasonal bar menu with items like soup, salads, three bean veggie chili, risotto fritters, or cheese fries.

Drink Specials 0
Sadly, no drink specials

Atmosphere 3
A beautiful, top-notch Portland classic that falls off the radar, but has a great Happy Hour! Enjoy a fancy evening out in their classy jazz lounge, then stick around to hear some live music later. Truly a special place when you're in the mood for a wonderful night!

Date visited: _____ **My Rating:** _____
Went with: _____
Favorites: _____
Not so much: _____
Other comments: _____
_____

Yama Sushi

Pearl Map
926 NW 10th Ave.
(503) 841-5463
www.yamasushiandsakebar.com

Happy Hours
5:00–6:30pm Mon–Thur

Food Deals 3
$2.00-$6.00
A dozen small hot plates (two ramen dishes, homemade gyoza, calamari, shrimp tempura, edamame, yakitori chicken, and more); and six sushis (four rolls – California, spicy or crunch-spicy tuna, or salmon), plus tempura salmon or tempura snapper.

Drink Specials 2
$3.00 Japanese small beers; $4.00 house wines
$4.00–$7.00 sakés

Atmosphere 3
Nice place with front lounge and dining room divider of old pieces from a Japanese xylophone. Full sushi bar acoss the back, and a long dining area with two rows of tables, cushioned chairs.

Date visited: _____ **My Rating:** _____

Went with: _____

Favorites: _____

Not so much: _____

Other comments: _____

_____

21st Avenue Bar & Grill

NW/Nob Hill Map 721 NW 21st Ave; (503) 222-4121

Happy Hours 3:00–6:00pm Mon–Fri (Drink specials)
Open–6:00pm Daily (Food deals)

Food Deals 2 $4.00 Tons of bar food cheapies like mac & cheese, nachos, totchos, salads, spring rolls, quesadilla, veggie curry – and fried twinkie sundae!

Drink Specials 2 $1.50 PBR; $3.00 micros and wells

Atmosphere 2 Dive bar without too much character, but with a secret, surprisingly cute back patio area!

Basta's Trattoria

NW/Nob Hill Map 410 NW 21st Ave; (503) 274-1572
www.bastastrattoria.com

Happy Hours 5:00-6:30pm; 10:00pm-close Daily

Food Deals 2 No extra discounts at happy hour, just the regular bar menu with about 12 unusual samplings with seasonal updates. Check out owner, Chef Marco Frattaroli's, SE place, Cibo.

Drink Specials 2 $1.00 off all beers; $2.00 off glass of any wine; $6.00 well cocktails

Atmosphere 2 Cool mural paintings; kidney shapes and velvet drapes; outdoor sidewalk seating.

Blitz 21 www.blitzbarpdx.webs.com

Nob Hill/Northwest Map 305 NW 21st; (503) 208-3227

Happy Hours 3:00–6:00pm and 9:00pm-close Daily

Food Deals 2 $1.95–$4.95 All the top bar standards like sliders, burgers, skewers, SW wrap, fish & chips, chips & salsa, cheese fries, hummus and YAY! Totchos!

Drink Specials 3 $2.50 domestics; $3.50 micros $4.50 house wines; $3.00 wells

Atmosphere 2 A nice and casual sports bar on 21st (hence the name). Brick red walls, with a mix of booth, bar, cooshy, and cocktail table seating. Lots of TVs for watching sports, and lots of light.

Blitzbar Pearl

Pearl Map 110 NW 10th Ave; (503) 222-2229
www.blitzbarpdx.net

Happy Hours 3:00–6:00pm and 9:00pm-close Daily

Food Deals 2 $1.95–$4.95 Similar menu as other Blitzes

Drink Specials 3 $2.00 domestics; $3.00 micros
$5.00 house wines; $3.00 wells

Atmosphere 2 Sporty, designed-on-a-dime collegiate
feel with game room. Tables and booths surrounding
one big central bar, spanning two rooms. Patio.

Blue Olive www.blueolivepdx.com

NW/Nob Hill Map 500 NW 21st Ave; (503) 528-2822
and 2712 NE Alberta (503) 206-6168

Happy Hours 3:00pm–close Sun–Thurs
3:00-6:00pm and 9:30pm-close Fri–Sat

Food Deals 2 $4.00–$6.00 About 20 Mediterranean
appetizers including all the greatest hits plus, burger,
salad, soup. Smaller menu at Blue Olive on Alberta.

Drink Specials 3 $4.00 pints and bottles; $5.00 red
or white wine or sangrias; $5.50 wells; $7.50 cocktails

Atmosphere 3 Refined, mellow space with neutral
palette, large screen TV, and ornate empty frames
hanging over the bar. Formerly Virgo & Pisces.

Camellia Lounge www.teazone.com

Pearl Map 510 NW 11th Ave.; (503) 221-2130

Happy Hours 4:00-7:00pm Daily; 2:00pm-close Sun★

Food Deals 2 $5.00–$6.00 A number of discounted
café goodies: black bean burger, Caesar salad, chips,
chipotle bacon shrimp tacos, red potato skins, panini.

Drink Specials 3 $4.00 drafts; $5.00 house wines
$3.00 wells $5.00 unique, signature cocktails

Atmosphere 3 Pass through the super-cute Tea Zone
Café to discover a tucked-away, speakeasy secret:
the Camellia Lounge! Cozy, candlelit charm in the
bar/lounge in back. Store and tea scene in front.

Cha Cha Cha www.chachachapdx.com

Pearl Map 1208 NW Gilsan; (503) 221-2111

Happy Hours 3:00–6:00pm and 8:30-10:00pm Daily

Food Deals 3 $3.95-$5.95 Ole! A full array! Nachos, tostada, tacos, enchillada, burrito, burrito, Caesar.

Drink Specials 2 $3.00 beer; $5.00 wine or wells $5.00 Margaritas (unique and tasty!)

Atmosphere 2 There are now eight ChaChaChas! Convenient location in the heart of the Pearl, but decor and vibe are very casual for this part of the city. Colorful and vibrant with sidewalk seating too.

Daily Café www.dailycafe.net

NW/Nob Hill Map 902 NW 13th Ave; (503) 242-1916

Happy Hours 3:30–6:00pm Mon–Fri

Food Deals 2 $2.00–$5.00 About 10 standards that cover all the bases, plus a daily dessert! Caesar salad, pickle plate, veggie slider, fritto, fries, pasta, ice cream.

Drink Specials 2 $3.50 drafts; $1.00 off wine

Atmosphere 2 It seems more like a breakfast or lunch spot than a place to go for drinks, but it's location, service, food, low prices, and café-style freshness often fit the bill for a refreshing visit.

Dorio www.dorionw.com

NW/Nob Hill Map 1037 NW 23rd Ave; (503) 219-0633

Happy Hours 3:00–6:00pm Mon–Fri

Food Deals 2 Good samplings of tasty Greek food: tyropites (phyllo dough triangles of cheese), hummus plate, meatballs, spinach salad, fries, feta and olives.

Drink Specials 3 $2.00 domestics; $3.00 micros $4.00 wines; $4.00 wells; $6.00 martinis

Atmosphere 2 A kind of urban Greek bistro. It's an L-shaped room, so it's a somewhat awkward use of space, but fine in the front area if you think of it as a bar. Big windows with just a little charm.

Hobo's www.hobospdx.com

Old Town Map 120 NW 3rd Ave.; (503) 224-3285

Happy Hours 4:00–7:00pm Sun–Fri

Food Deals 2 $3.00–$5.00 Classic pub grub done well: calamari, fish tacos, buffalo hot wings, oyster shooters, cheese fries, quesadilla, and mac & cheese.

Drink Specials 2 $1.00 off beer, wine, wells, cocktails

Atmosphere 3 Beautiful, turn-of-the-century, old Portland charm; positioned directly over the haunted Shanghai Tunnels and the starting point for the ghostly Portland Underground Tours.

Jimmy Mak's www.jimmymaks.com

Pearl Map 221 NW 10th Ave; (503) 295-6542

Happy Hours 5:00–6:30pm Mon–Fri

Food Deals 1 10% off regular menu. A different kind of Happy Hour... I could be down with more like 30% off, but can't give many points for trying very hard.

Drink Specials 3 $1.00 off beer ($2.75 domestics; $3.50–$4.25 micros); $5.00 wine; $3.50 well cocktails

Atmosphere 3 Enjoy Jimmy Mak's swanky jazz club finery complete with thick, brilliantly illuminated, red velvet curtains, dark & cushy booth seating, and tiny candlelit cocktail tables. Free pool in bar bar area!

Life of Riley

Pearl Map 300 NW 10th Ave.; (503) 224-1680

Happy Hours 4:00–7:00pm Daily

Food Deals 2 $3.00–$7.00 Tasty basics like buffalo wings, fries, kettle chips, sliders, tofu tacos, oysters.

Drink Specials 2 $2.00 domestics; $3.00 drafts (good tap list!); $1.00 off wine, wells, cocktails

Atmosphere 2 Large and open navy-colored room; semi-retro, semi-Irish decor. Rare, ultra-casual option in contrast to other Pearl restaurants.

Melt www.meltportland.com

NW/Nob Hill Map 716 NW 21st Ave.; (503) 295-4944

Happy Hours 2:00pm–close Mon–Sat

Food Deals $3.00–$6.00 Big deals on their 20+ item appetizer menu with salads, sliders, soups and more.

Drink Specials $4.25 drafts; $5.00 cocktails

Atmosphere New owner gilded/golded up the joint and continues the all-day Happy Hour tradition. Central bar/service station. Popular place! Sidewallk HH.

Muu-Muu's www.muumuus.net

NW/Nob Hill Map 612 NW 21st Ave.; (503) 223-8169

Happy Hours 3:00–7:00pm Daily

Food Deals 2 $3.00-$7.00 BIG small plates menu with a bit of *everything!* Spicy wings, pork tacos, wasabi tuna, salads, calamari, hummus plate, steak bites, potstickers, fish & chips, satay, ribs, tacos.

Drink Specials 3 $2.00 Rainiers; $3.50 microbrews $3.50 wells; $4.00 well martinis

Atmosphere 2 Chill, traveler's-style bar with black tin ceiling tiles, orange hanging lights, velvet drapes, giant urn lamps, and tiny bubble lights.

Paymaster Lounge

Pearl Map 1020 NW 17th Ave.; (503) 943-2780

Happy Hours 2:00–6:00pm Mon–Fri

Drink Specials 2 $3.50 drafts; $3.00 wells

Food Deals 2 $2.00-$3.50 Chili, fries, nachos, queso & chips. Giant and GREAT $7.00 burgers!

Atmosphere 2 Formerly the Moonshine Lounge. Super-casual corner tavern out of step with the rest of the area's general upscale style. Surprising and huge back patio – and it's covered!

Santa Fe www.santafetaqueria.com

NW/Nob Hill Map 831 NW 23rd Ave.; (503) 220-0406

Happy Hours 3:00–6:00pm and 9:00pm–close Daily

Food Deals 2 $3.75–$5.75 Big menu of 15 items covering all the Mexican and texmex basics.

Drink Specials 3 $.50 off drafts; $5.00 wine $3.75 wells; $4.75 Margaritas

Atmosphere 2 A popular, neighborhood watering hole. Good for trivia and outdoor sidewalk seating. Sit anywhere in the restaurant. Good for families too.

Splash Bar www.splashbarpdx.com

Pearl Map 904 NW Couch; (503) 893-5551

Happy Hours 5:00–9:00pm Wed-Sat; Drink deals 'til 10:00pm; All night Wednesday ('til midnight)

Food Deals 2 $1.00 munchie menu: egg rolls, shrimp chips, wings, tacos

Drink Specials 2 $3.00 domestics $4.00 wines; $4.00 wells; plus rotating nightly specials

Atmosphere 2 Decked out Margaritaville nightclub, with a customized VW bus converted into a shot bar. Surf stuff hanging everywhere it possibly can, with a lifesize Captain Morgan statue overseeing the central, high-energy dance floor.

NORTH ▲

1.5 mile

Hop & Vine
Mextiza
Old Gold

Florida
Room

Saraveza

Chapel
Pub

KILLINGSWORTH

Yakuza
Cocotte

Old Town
Pizza

ALBERTA

Alibi

Trebol

Box Social
Las Primas

SKIDMORE

TeSoAriA

Prost!
Bungalo

Equinox

Interurban
Moloko
Sidecar11
Radar
Bar Bar
SamuraiBlue

Crow Bar HUB
5Q

Delta
Mac/Mee-Sen
Uchu

Lincoln
ChaChaCha

Beech
Street

Tasty
n Sons

Por Que No

FREMONT

County Cork
Freehouse
Lucca

Ecliptic Brewing

Liberty Glass

Wine Up

Secret
Society

Widmer

RUSSELL

White
Eagle

820
/Mint

Broder

Tavin's

See Lloyd Center Map page 232

Alberta & Fremont

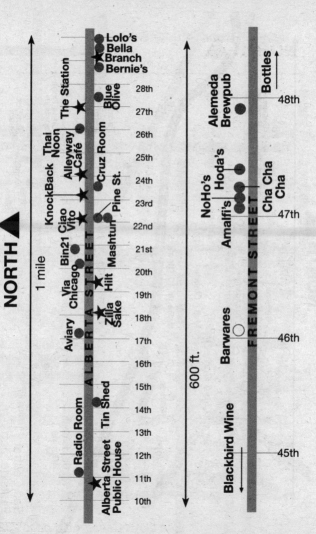

NORTH ▲

1 mile

600 ft.

Alberta Street (left column, south to north):
- Alberta Street Public House
- Radio Room
- Tin Shed
- Aviary
- Zilla Sake
- Via Chicago
- Bin21
- Hilt
- Ciao Vito
- Mashtun
- Pine St.
- Cruz Room
- Alleyway Café
- KnockBack
- Thai Noon
- The Station
- Blue Olive
- Lolo's
- Bella
- Branch
- Bernie's

Street numbers (Alberta): 10th, 11th, 12th, 13th, 14th, 15th, 16th, 17th, 18th, 19th, 20th, 21st, 22nd, 23rd, 24th, 25th, 26th, 27th, 28th

Fremont Street (right column):
- Blackbird Wine
- Barwares
- Amalfi's
- NoHo's
- Hoda's
- Cha Cha Cha
- Alemeda Brewpub
- Bottles

Street numbers (Fremont): 45th, 46th, 47th, 48th

Note: Streets do not align.

Lloyd Center-ish

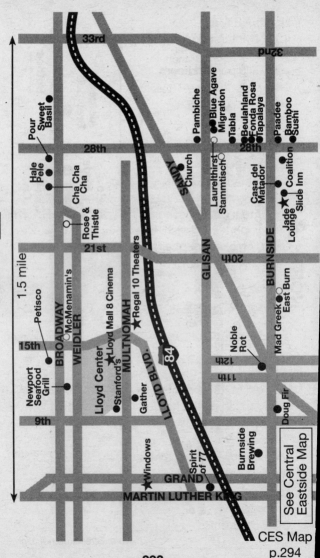

NORTH

1.5 mile

33rd
32nd
28th
28th
21st
15th
9th

Pour Sweet Basil
Hale Pele
Cha Cha Cha
Rose & Thistle
Petisco
Newport Seafood Grill

BROADWAY
WEIDER
MULTNOMAH

McMenamin's
Lloyd Mall 8 Cinema
Regal 10 Theaters
Lloyd Center
Stanford's
Gather

Windows
Spirit of 77
GRAND
MARTIN LUTHER KING

Pambiche
Church
SANDY
Laurelthirst
Stammtisch
GLISAN
20th

Blue Agave
Migration
Tabla
Beulahland
Fonda Rosa
Tapalaya
Paadee
Bamboo Sushi
Casa del Matador
Coalition
Slide Inn
Jade Lounge
BURNSIDE
East Burn
Mad Greek
Noble Rot
12th
11th
4th
Doug Fir
Burnside Brewing

LLOYD BLVD.
84

See Central Eastside Map

CES Map
p.294

232

Alibi Tiki Lounge

North/NE Map
4024 N Interstate
(503) 287-5335
www.alibiportland.com

Happy Hours
3:00–7:00pm Daily

Food Deals 3
$1.95–$4.95
Big Happy Hour menu featuring bar fare with island touches: quesadilla, hot wings, soup, burger, pork sandwich, tater tots, potato skins, shoyu chicken, pepperjack mac & cheese, and more.

Drink Specials 2
$2.00 PBR; $3.00 wells; $5.00 tropicals

Atmosphere 3
Top marks for over-the-top tacky Tiki! Bizarrely dark & divey – a unique Portland treasure! Fun hula girl mural and lots of thatch everywhere. It's so much nicer after the non-smoking law! Karaoke every night starting at 9:00pm.

Date visited: _____ **My Rating:** _____

Went with: _____

Favorites: _____

Not so much: _____

Other comments: _____

_____

Amalfi's

Fremont Map
4703 NE Fremont St.
(503) 284-6747
www.amalfisrestaurant.com

Happy Hours
4:00–6:00pm Tues-Fri; 3:00pm–6:00pm Sat-Sun
9:00pm-close Tues-Sun

Happy Hour of the Year 2011

Food Deals 3
$3.00-$4.00
Enjoy over a dozen zesty Italian eats: mini pizzas, pastas, shrimp scampi, soup, bruschetta, prawns, plus caprese, Caesar and Greek salads.

Drink Specials 2
$4.00-$5.00 beer; $5.00 house red or white wine
Hysterical and creatively-named cocktail list!

Atmosphere 3
For more than 50 years, Amalfi's has served up some of Portland's best Italian food, and is still to this day, a much-beloved icon. Comfy yet contemporary, romantic and still social. Table-top fireplaces both inside and out. Great patio!

Date visited: _____ **My Rating:** _____

Went with: _____

Favorites: _____

Not so much: _____

Other comments: _____

_____

Aviary

10

Alberta Map
1733 NE Alberta
(503) 287-2400
www.aviarypdx.com

Happy Hours
5:00–7:00pm Mon-Fri

Food Deals 3
$2.00-$6.00
You are in for a treat! Happy Hour is taken up a notch with a very unique and eclectic, seasonal menu with items like tempura pumpkin, summer squash fritters, brussel sprout nachos, or oysters. Check out the dinner menu before biting on HH!

Drink Specials 3
$3.00 drafts; $5.00 house wines
$5.00 wells; $6.00 daily cocktail specials

Atmosphere 3
Happy Hour is inside all the way in the back in the very cool, dark and cozy bar area, or outside out front on the plaza style, street-side patio. One of Portland's top "chef-driven" restaurants!

Date visited: _____ **My Rating:** _____
Went with: _____
Favorites: _____
Not so much: _____
Other comments: _____
_____

Bamboo Sushi

Northwest/Nob Hill Map
836 NW 23rd Ave; (971) 229-1925

Lloyd Center Map 310 SE 28th; (503) 232-5255
www.bamboosushi.com

Happy Hours
4:00–6:00pm Mon–Fri (4:30 start SE location)

Food Deals 3 $1.00–$8.00 Bamboo Sushi has
some of the best sushi in town! Nigiri set, inari,
daily hand rolls, vegetable roll, spicy albacore and
NW Philly rolls. Non-sushi items available too,
like tempura, steamed buns, and hanger steak.

Drink Specials 3
$3.00 drafts; $4.00 wine; $4.00–$7.00 sake

Atmosphere 3
Both restaurants are quite similar in layout and
overall style. Serene and cozy with focus on
sustainability and Japanese simplicity. Dark
browns, tans and white; carpeted with patterned
pillows on bench seating and origami fish art.

Date visited: _____ **My Rating:** _____

Went with: _____

Favorites: _____

Not so much: _____

Other comments: _____

_____

Bar Lolo.

Alberta Map
2940 NE Alberta St
(503) 288-3400
www.barlolo.com

Happy Hours
4:00–6:00pm Tues–Fri; ★All night Wed
10:00pm–close Tues–Fri (drinks only)

Food Deals 2
$2.00–$9.00 ($2.00 off)
Unique Spanish nibbles: spiced meatballs,
chicken skewers, calamari, empanadas, sliders,
and patatas bravas.

Drink Specials 3
$3.50 drafts; $5.00 house wines; $4.00 sangria
$5.00 Margaritas

Atmosphere 3
Upscale tapas bar; big, open room with floor-to-
ceiling windows along Alberta Street; simple
style with neutral tones and chalkboard menus.
Originally called Lolo (new owners).

Date visited: _____ **My Rating:** _____
Went with: _____
Favorites: _____
Not so much: _____
Other comments: _____
_____

Bernie's Southern Bistro

9

Alberta Map
2904 NE Alberta
(503) 282-9864
www.berniesbistro.com

Happy Hours
4:00–6:00pm Tues–Sun

Food Deals 3
$4.00
Gourmet southern samplers including Po' Boys,
fried green tomatoes, bread pudding, veggie
salad, sweet potato fries, mac & cheese, fried
pickles, meatloaf sandwich, hush puppies.

Drink Specials 2
$5.00 house wines; $5.00 cocktail specials

Atmosphere 3
Serene and outstanding outdoor garden patio,
and they even let you sit outside for Happy
Hour. Absolutely lovely! Simple, fine-dining,
romantic interior. Casual bar.

Date visited: _____ **My Rating:** _____
Went with: _____
Favorites: _____
Not so much: _____
Other comments: _____
_____

Box Social

10

NE Map
3971 N Williams
(503) 288-1111
www.bxsocial.com

A Happy Hour favorite!

Happy Hours
4:00–6:00pm Daily: 11:00pm–close Sun–Thurs

Food Deals 3
$2.00–$6.00
Small menu, but it's one worth repeating often!
Parmesan popcorn, mixed greens salad, hummus
plate, spinach spread, and a craveable grilled
cheese sandwich served with *yummy* tomato soup.

Drink Specials 3
$4.00 drafts; $4.00 house wine
$4.00 select wells; $6.00 signature craft cocktails

Atmosphere 3
Light, cool and contemporary by day; dark,
sizzling, and seductive by night. The Box Social
bills itself as a friendly and relaxing "drinking
parlour." Fresh, urban style with a welcoming,
neighborhood feel. Exquisite cocktailing!

Date visited: _____ **My Rating:** _____
Went with: _____
Favorites: _____
Not so much: _____
Other comments: _____
_____

Buffalo Wild Wings

• • • • • • • • • • • • • •

8

Lloyd Center
1200 NE Broadway
(503) 432-8179
www.buffalowildwings.com

EIGHT locations throughout Portland:
Cascade Station
9810 Cascades Pkwy; (503) 281-0351
Downtown 327 SW Morrison; (503) 224-1309
Hazel Dell 7704 NE 5th; (360) 597-3486
Beaverton 11995 SW BV Hwy; (503) 352-9503
Wood Village 22849 NE Glisan; (503) 328-9475
Hillsboro 2219 NW Allie; (503) 645-9424
Sherwood 8505 SW Tualatin; (503) 486-5295

Happy Hours
3:00-6:00pm Mon-Fri /9:00pm–mid Daily

Food Deals 2
$3.00 Ten top bar bites + Five for $5.00

Drink Specials 3
$1.00 off beer (decent line-up of microbrews)
$3.00 wine; $3.50 select cocktails (three)

Atmosphere 2
Sporty, collegiate atmosphere that's good clean
fun for everyone; hi-def TVs *everywhere*.

Date visited: _____ **My Rating:** _____

Went with: _____

Favorites: _____

Not so much: _____

Other comments: _____

_____

Church

Lloyd Center-ish Map
2600 NE Sandy Blvd.
www.churchbarpdx.com

Happy Hours
4:00-7:00 Mon-Fri

Food Deals 3 $3.00–$5.00
Creative bites inspired by fixins from the south's bible-belt: fried green tomatoes, ribs, deviled eggs (but of course), hush puppies, fried chicken skin, tofu Hoppin' John, okra chips, pork cracklins, kettle corn. Be a facebook fan for miracle deals like giant, crazily-decked-out $5.00 burgers.

Drink Specials 3
$1.00 off drafts; $3.00 wells; $4.00 house punch

Atmosphere 3
I love Church! And there are so many fun things you can say about it when you go. They really did a great job with the design. Hardly over-the-top church-y, but still had some fun with the theme. It's a bit hipster, with late-night loudness, and turns much more nightclubish in the dark. It's a shame there's so much light...

Date visited: _____ **My Rating:** _____
Went with: _____
Favorites: _____
Not so much: _____
Other comments: _____
_____

Ciao Vito

10

Alberta Map
2203 NE Alberta
(503) 282-5522
www.ciaovito.net

A Happy Hour favorite!

Happy Hours
4:30–7:15pm Daily; 9:00-10:00pm Daily (food)
★All day Sunday

Food Deals 3
$5.00–$8.00
Wow! Giant array of 15 or so seasonal, mostly
Spanish-influenced menu items: beef & potato
or salt cod croquettes, garlic prawns, pork belly
sandwich, octopus, pastas, Spanish omelettes,
patatas bravas, and skirt steak.

Drink Specials 3
Random beer specials; $5.00 wines
$5.00 bartenders choice cocktails

Atmosphere 3
Classic elegance with warmth and style, nice
neighborhood welcoming feel with bright and
funky mural on outside side wall.

Date visited: _____ **My Rating:** _____
Went with: _____
Favorites: _____
Not so much: _____
Other comments: _____
_____

Clyde's Prime Rib

● ●

8

Northeast (off map)
5474 NE Sandy
(503) 281-9200
www.clydesprimerib.com

Happy Hours
4:00–6:00pm Mon-Fri (bar only)

Food Deals 3
$2.50–$7.50
Prime rib is rarely found period, so at Happy
Hour, medium rare at $7.50 is a fantastic find
worth traveling for! Plus sautéed mushrooms,
mac & cheese, burgers, wings, onion rings,
potato skins, and more.

Drink Specials 1
$4.25 daily drink special

Atmosphere 2
Ultra-old-school in a very authentic way. Red-
vinyl, semi-circle booths – and a big parking lot.
Way-retro dining room for dinner only. I'd rate
them higher if they'd let us sit there, but the bar
is getting tired and too dated.

Date visited: _____ **My Rating:** _____
Went with: _____
Favorites: _____
Not so much: _____
Other comments: _____
_____

Cocotte

Northeast (off map)
2930 NE Killingsworth
(503) 227-2669
www.cocottepdx.com

Happy Hours
5:00–6:30pm Tues–Sat (special bar menu)
★5:00pm-close Sun-Mon; 9:00-11:00pm Tues-Sat

Food Deals 3
$3.00-$5.00-$8.00
Nine seasonal items like steamed mussels,
salmon chowder, chicken liver mousse, tartine,
rillettes, cheeses, pickles, olives.

Drink Specials 2
$1.00 off drafts and house cocktails; $5.00 wines
$5.00 apertifs (with a lengthy list to choose from)

Atmosphere 3
Trés cute! Sweet and cozy little corner café with
a wall of paned windows/doors that open to
the street, thick floor length curtains, Country-
French decor and accents, and fresh flowers.
A great word to know, "Cocotte" essentially
means cute little hen/honey/love/stewpan.

Date visited: _____ **My Rating:** _____
Went with: _____
Favorites: _____
Not so much: _____
Other comments: _____
_____

Equinox

10

North/NE Map
830 N Shaver St
(503) 460-3333
www.equinoxrestaurantpdx.com

Happy Hours
4:00–6:00pm Wed–Fri (extended in summer)

Food Deals 3
$3.00–$6.50
Menu with about a dozen exceptionally delicious
items! Varies a bit with the seasons with unique
items like chickpea crepe, beets and bleu, duck
confit sliders, salad, fettuccine, calamari, soup,
truffle fries, mussels, spaetzle, or cheeseburger.

Drink Specials 3
$3.00 drafts; $5.00 wine; $4.00 wells
$5.50 specialty cocktails

Atmosphere 3
Enter through their delightful front patio (where
you can enjoy Happy Hour, weather permitting).
Inside, it's warm and woody throughout with old,
rough wood floors, natural wood tables, and
paneled half-walls. Skylight and garage door.

Date visited: _____ **My Rating:** _____

Went with: _____

Favorites: _____

Not so much: _____

Other comments: _____

_____

Firehouse

North/NE (off map)
711 NE Dekum
(503) 954-1702
www.firehousepdx.com

Happy Hours
5:00–6:00pm Daily

Food Deals 3
$3.00–$11.00
Delicious but limited and somewhat pricey menu.
Items like a roasted beet salad, wood-fired pizza,
meatballs, and fried cauliflower. They grow
herbs and veggies in their own garden!

Drink Specials 3
$3.50–$4.00 select drafts; $5.00 wines
$6.00 daily cocktail

Atmosphere 3
A very cool building from the outside and in, and
on its own triangular block. Firehouse 29 from
the early 1900s has been renovated with lots of
sweat and dreams and now houses one of the
city's cutest Happy Hour places. Open seating
everywhere, including their smokin' patio!

Date visited: _____ **My Rating:** _____
Went with: _____
Favorites: _____
Not so much: _____
Other comments: _____
_____

Fonda Rosa

Lloyd Center-ish Map
108 NE 28th Ave.
(503) 235-3828

Happy Hours
4:30–6:00pm Tues–Sun

Food Deals 3
$5.00–$7.00
Solid neighborhood fave! Mucho mas choices like spinach w/goat cheese, tacoyos, ceviche or veggie tostadas, beet and avocado salad, chicken torta, and tasty tacos with chicken, meat or salmon.

Drink Specials 3
$4.00 drafts; $5.00 wine selections; $4.00 wells
$5.00 Margarita or cosmo; $6.00 sangria

Atmosphere 2
Simple in style with two bars; the narrow room is flanked by windows along 28th for lots of light and has a diner/coffeeshop feel by day, lounge by night.

Date visited: _____ **My Rating:** _____
Went with: _____
Favorites: _____
Not so much: _____
Other comments: _____
_____

Hale Pele

Central Eastside Map
2733 NE Broadway
(503) 662-8454
www.halepele.com

Happy Hours
5:00–6:00pm Tues-Sun

Food Deals 2
$3.00 edamame; $4.00 veggie rice bowl;
$5.00 pork sliders on super-soft Hawaiian bread

Drink Specials 2
$3.00 beer; $6.00-$8.00 Array of tiki cocktails

Atmosphere 3
Owned by master mixologist, Blair Reynolds, of
B.G. Reynolds exotic syrups fame. Formerly
Thatch, it's quite a mecca for tiki aficionados,
decorated with extreme personality and true
respect and aesthetic of 50s/60s-style tiki
lounges. Big tiki Gods, blowfish lights and a fun
back tiki hut for groups (or just two people).
It's about drinks here -- come thirsty!

Date visited: _____ **My Rating:** _____

Went with: _____

Favorites: _____

Not so much: _____

Other comments: _____

_____

Hoda's

8

North/NE Map
4727 NE Fremont
(503) 688-5577
<u>Southeast</u> 3401 SE Belmont; 503-236-8325
www.hodas.com

Happy Hours
2:30–5:30pm Monday–Friday

Food Deals 2
$3.00–$5.00
Short but tasty and traditional menu: hummus, tabouleh bites, fried spicy potatoes, baby kafta burgers, falafel plate, feta salad, and delicious zaatar and spinach pies.

Drink Specials 3
$3.00 beer; $4.00 wines; $5.00 specialty cocktail

Atmosphere 2
Very simple little café spot. Cozy, open room with tile floors and a small corner bar area. Per their website, in Arabic, "Hoda" means enlightenments and many use the word to exchange friendly, warm wishes with one another.

Date visited: _____ **My Rating:** _____
Went with: _____
Favorites: _____
Not so much: _____
Other comments: _____
_____

Interurban 10

Happy Hours
4:00–6:00pm Mon–Fri; 10:00pm–close Sunday

Food Deals 3
$3.00–$5.00
Polenta croquettes, BBQ sandwich, quesadilla,
French onion soup, salad, penne, pups & frites,
grilled broccolini, and hot oatmeal cookies.

Drink Specials 3
$2.00 mini beers; $4.00 jumbo cask draft
$5.00 house wines; $5.00 bubbly cocktails
Plus deals on rotating taster shots of the week

Atmosphere 3
This "publican's table" gives us an urban, industrial hideaway with cozy neighborhood charm.
From the owner of Prost, originally in partnership
with owner of Tasty n' Sons and Toro Bravo.
Long, front bar area with a modern speakeasy
upstairs and big back patio.

Date visited: _____ **My Rating:** _____
Went with: _____
Favorites: _____
Not so much: _____
Other comments: _____
_____

The Knock Back

Alberta Map
2315 NE Alberta
(503) 284-4090
www.theknockback.com

Happy Hours
4:00–6:00pm Tues-Sun

Food Deals 3
$1.00–$5.00
Bar snacks like popcorn, crostini, fries, soup, and burgers or grilled cheese as meals. Plus several salads – good for them (they're good for you)! Wedge with bacon, arugula, kale salads.

Drink Specials 3
$2.00 Tecate, $1.00 off drafts; $4.00 wine
$3.00 wells; $4.00 punch; $6.00 Margarita

Atmosphere 3
Formerly del Inti now turned into a full-on bar. They kept the firepit, and enclosed more of the patio area. Casual enough for guys to happily sit and knock 'em back, but nice (for a bar), so women will like it too. Roll-up garage doors, boxy hanging lamps, booths, mounted boar head.

Date visited: _____ **My Rating:** _____
Went with: _____
Favorites: _____
Not so much: _____
Other comments: _____
_____

Las Primas

North/NE Map
3971 N Williams Ave, #103
(503) 206-5790
www.lasprimaskitchen.com

Happy Hours
3:00–6:00pm Tues–Sun

Food Deals 3
$2.50–$5.00
Delicious, unique food! Flavorful, classic sand-wiches (pepper-rubbed pork, house-made sausage, or veggie), soup, empanadas, salads, – and chorizo saucy fries!

Drink Specials 3
$2.50 Peruvian beer (bottles); $4.00 drafts;
$4.00 house wine; $4.00 sangría
$6.00 pisco sours – choice of six!

Atmosphere 2
Simple restaurant with colorful, hand-painted, welcome mural and Peruvian folk art pieces adorning white walls. Patterned after typical Lima-style sandwich shops with open kitchen, counter service, and cement floors.

Date visited: _____ **My Rating:** _____

Went with: _____

Favorites: _____

Not so much: _____

Other comments: _____

_____

Lincoln

10

North/NE Map
3808 N Williams, #127
(503) 288-6200
www.lincolnpdx.com

Happy Hours 5:30–7:00pm Tues–Fri

Food Deals 3
$2.00–$9.00
Americana home cooking with NW culinary bent and 16-item, seasonal, funky-fresh menu: baked eggs, pigs ears, patty melt, cheese plate, poutine, bruschetta, veggies, rabbit liver mousse, elk heart tartare. Chef/owner Jen Louis was named a Food & Wine Best New Chef in 2012.

Drink Specials 3
$4.00 microbrews; $5.00 house wines
$5.00 wells; $6.00 specialty cocktail

Atmosphere 3
Renovated loft-style warehouse space. Lincoln's interior is on the more basic side of industrial chic, but warmth is added via dark-red walls, natural woods, friendly staff and votive candles. Note: Happy Hour at bartop only (24 seats).

Date visited: _____ **My Rating:** _____

Went with: _____

Favorites: _____

Not so much: _____

Other comments: _____

Lucca

Northeast (off map)
3449 NE 24th Ave.
(503) 287-7372
www.luccapdx.com

Happy Hours
2:30–5:00pm Tues–Fri

Food Deals 3
$2.00–$5.00
Nine small plates with dates, crostini with goat cheese and roasted garlic, pate, olives, bread with roasted garlic oil, salami & cheese plate, and salads. Plus wood-fired pizzas ($9.00).

Drink Specials 3
$3.00 drafts; $4.00 wines; $4.00 wells
$6.00 cosmos and lemondrops

Atmosphere 3
Understated neutrals in wide open room, very relaxing atmosphere with wood-fire oven behind the long bar. Happy Hour here is early, so there will be lots of light coming in the wall-to-wall windows in the front. Cool accent light fixtures. Nice, small group meeting room.

Date visited: _____ **My Rating:** _____

Went with: _____

Favorites: _____

Not so much: _____

Other comments: _____

Mextiza

North/NE (off map)
2103 N Killingsworth
(503) 289-3709
www.mextiza.com

A Happy Hour favorite!

Happy Hours
5:00–6:00pm Wed-Sat and 9:00–10:00pm Fri-Sat

Food Deals 3
$2.00–$5.00
High-quality and delicious small plates brought to us this year by the restaurateur of Autentica and Uno Mas in the Ocean Complex at 24th & Glisan. Pork taco/tortilla, salad, jicama, sope, beans, dumplings, and sautéed calamari.

Drink Specials 3
$1.00 off drafts; $5.00 red or white wine
$5.00 sangria; $5.00 margarita

Atmosphere 3
Cozy, long dining room with cement floors, and tiled back bar area in refurbished old auto body shop. Outside and in, it all looks brand-new, and is a greatly-welcomed addition up north! Large, fenced-in front patio with colorful umbrellas.

Date visited: _____ **My Rating:** _____
Went with: _____
Favorites: _____
Not so much: _____
Other comments: _____
_____

Mint/820

North/NE Map
820 N Russell
(503) 284-5518
www.mintrestaurant.com

Happy Hours
4:00–6:30pm Daily

A Happy Hour favorite!

Food Deals 3
$4.00–$11.00
Expanded, delicious, unique menu: lamb burger,
wild boar sliders, calamari, soup, roasted beet
or spicy Caesar salad, pepitas, sweet potato
fries. Great prices on dinner – check menu! Love!

Drink Specials 3
$2.50 PBR; $5.00 wine; $4.00 well drinks
$7.00 selected cocktails (of "Hip Sips" fame!)

Atmosphere 3
A quintessential Happy Hour and cocktail bar.
Connected to gorgeous and hip Mint Restaurant;
820 is a trendy, upscale ultra-lounge with nice
back deck area to most pleasantly enjoy on a
nice day.

Date visited: _____ **My Rating:** _____

Went with: _____

Favorites: _____

Not so much: _____

Other comments: _____

_____

Miss Delta

8

North/NE Map
3950 N Mississippi Ave.
(503) 287-7629
www.missdeltapdx.net

Happy Hours
4:00–6:00pm Daily; 10:00pm-close Fri-Sat

Food Deals 3
$3.00–$6.50
Exciting and delicious Southern menu! Chicken
& waffles, po' boys, corn fritters, fried okra,
hushpuppies, salads, burger, pork spareribs,
jambalaya, and mac & cheese.

Drink Specials 2
$1.00 off drafts and wells; $5.00 wines

Atmosphere 2
Quaint, old-time N'awlins saloon style. Small
room with long bar with brick walls, rustic wood
floors, antique hanging lamps and for added
effect, mason jar candles.

Date visited: _____ **My Rating:** _____
Went with: _____
Favorites: _____
Not so much: _____
Other comments: _____
_____

257

Moloko

9

North/NE Map
3967 N Mississippi
(503) 288-6272
www.molokopdx.com

Happy Hours
4:00–7:00pm Daily

Food Deals 2
$2.00 off sandwiches
Turkey, salami, tuna, grilled cheese or herbed
chevre sandwiches. Good prices on other
snacks like hummus, chips & salsa, tossed
green salad, nut mix, cheese or salami plates.

Drink Specials 3
$1.50 Rainier; $5.00 wine; $3.50-$4.50 wells
$5.00 select cocktail; $6.00 Bloody Mary, mimosa

Atmosphere 3
A secret Mississippi gem with neon symbols as
signage. Ultra-retro, white and mod interior,
with 60s seating in both vinyl upholstered and
plastic-form lounge chairs. Charming garden
gazebo back deck area is heated in the winter.
They make their own infusions. Cool fish tanks!

Date visited: _____ **My Rating:** _____
Went with: _____
Favorites: _____
Not so much: _____
Other comments: _____
_____

Newport Seafood Grill

10

Lloyd Center-ish Map
1200 NE Broadway; (503) 493-0100
www.newportseafoodgrill.com

0425 SW Montgomery; (503) 227-3474
2865 NW Town Center Loop; Tanasbourne
formerly Newport Bay; (503) 645-2526

Happy Hours
3:00–6:00pm Daily

Food Deals 3 $2.99–$5.99
15 varied menu items including clam chowder, fish & chips, salads, fish tacos, soup, oyster shooters, sliders, burgers, and seasonal items.

Drink Specials 3
Drink specials vary at each location, but good!
Usually $3.99 microbrews and wine; $4.59 wells

Atmosphere 3
Popular, big, and bustling bar areas. Upscale restaurant conveniently located near all the malls. (Beware: drinking and shopping is dangerous!) Also conveniently near movie theaters.

Date visited: _____ **My Rating:** _____

Went with: _____

Favorites: _____

Not so much: _____

Other comments: _____

_____

Noble Rot

10

Lloyd Center-ish Map
1111 E Burnside
(503) 233-1999
www.noblerotpdx.com

Happy Hours
5:00–6:00pm Mon–Fri

Food Deals 3
$2.00–$9.00
Ranges from nibblets to comfort food and
changes with the season: olives, onion rings,
French fries, cheese plate, exceptional paninos,
mac & cheese, hamburger.

Drink Specials 3
$3.50 draft beer; $3.50 red or white wine
$5.50 selection of bartender's specialties

Atmosphere 3
Stunning wall-to-wall, floor-to-ceiling windows
perched high for a wide-open city view; ultra-
cool contemporary-retro interior; illuminated
circular glass art on ceiling. Rooftop outdoor deck
with Happy Hour seating! Sunset Magazine's
Best Wine Bar 2009.

Date visited: _____ **My Rating:** _____

Went with: _____

Favorites: _____

Not so much: _____

Other comments: _____

_____

Noho's

9

Fremont Map
4627 NE Fremont
(503) 445-6646
www.nohos.com

Hidden tropical garden!

Happy Hours
3:00-6:00pm Daily

Food Deals 2
$3.95 Pork or chicken spring rolls or sliders
$4.95 Ribs or grilled chicken
$7.95 Hawaiian style or shoyu poke, sashimi plate

Drink Specials 3
$3.00 drafts; $4.00 wine; $4.00 mai tais

Atmosphere 3
Noho's Hawaiian Cafe is one of Portland's best-kept secrets! Out back, there's a surprise, very lush, tropical garden complete with palm trees, hanging lights, and a group firepit. In the winter, it's all enclosed and has heat lamps. The interior has surfboards hanging on the walls, and is on the more casual side. And heads up -- there are two Portland locations, but this is the one I love! It's a *really* great place to have a party!!!

Date visited: _____ **My Rating:** _____

Went with: _____

Favorites: _____

Not so much: _____

Other comments: _____

_____

Old Town Pizza

8

North/NE Map
5201 NE MLK; (503) 200-5988
<u>Old Town:</u> 226 NW Davis; (503) 222-9999
www.oldtownpizza.com

Happy Hours
MLK: 3:00-6:00pm and 9:00pm-close Daily
Old Town: 9:00pm-close Daily (late-night only)

Food Deals 2
$3.00–$6.00
MLK: Mini-pizzas, Caesar, spinach, or caprese
salads, meatball sliders, spaghetti, sandwiches.
Old Town: $1.50 cheese or pepperoni pizza slices.

Drink Specials 2
$1.00 off house drafts (MLK); they are also a
microbrewery now; $2.50 wells (both locations)

Atmosphere 3
Old Town Pizza is one of Portland's most unique,
historic, and haunted(!) places. The Old Town
location is the former lobby of the Merchant Hotel
(est. 1880). Word is, ghosts reside in the Shanghai
Tunnels below, and maybe at a table or two upstairs! The northside locale extends the vintage
charm with period furniture and accessories.
On-site breweries at both locations!

Date visited: _____ **My Rating:** _____

Went with: _____

Favorites: _____

Not so much: _____

Other comments: _____

_____

Paadee

Lloyd Center-ish Map
6 SE 28th Ave.
(503) 360-1453
www.paadeepdx.com

A Happy Hour favorite!

Happy Hours
5:00–6:30pm Daily

Food Deals 3
$2.00–$7.00
Excellent choices and well-made: Grilled squid or pork skewers, tom yum soup with prawns, sausage selections, fish cakes, noodle dishes. Award-winning food at a top PDX restaurant!

Drink Specials 3
$3.00 drafts; $5.00 house wines
$6.00 specialty cocktails

Atmosphere 3
Cozy industrial-chic, with talented and appropriate interior design choices incorporating subtle Asian stylings. Lots of light, cool bar, curtains, flowers, stained concrete. Long wood tables for groups, smaller 2-4 tops, and sidewalk seating.

Date visited: _____ **My Rating:** _____
Went with: _____
Favorites: _____
Not so much: _____
Other comments: _____
_____

Pambiche

Lloyd Center-ish Map
2811 NE Glisan
(503) 233-0511
www.pambiche.com

Happy Hours
★2:00–6:00pm Mon–Fri; 10:00pm–mid Fri–Sat

A Happy Hour favorite

Food Deals 3
$2.00–$5.00
Mmmmpenadas, fried plantains, salads, bean and
rice dishes, fried chicken and pork, shredded
beef, stew—and don't miss the desserts!

Drink Specials 3
$3.00-$4.00 beer
$5.00 house red and white wines
$6.00 red and white sangrias
$5.50-$7.00 select cocktails
$1.00 off espressos, teas, sodas, juices & shakes

Atmosphere 3
Fun and colorful Cuban café! Outdoor dining
area streetside; bright, cozy and happy inside;
vibrant exterior. Captures the Cuban "feel" well.

Date visited: _____ **My Rating:** _____

Went with: _____

Favorites: _____

Not so much: _____

Other comments: _____

_____

Petisco

North/NE Map
1411 NE Broadway
(503) 360-1048
www.petiscopdx.com

Happy Hours
3:00–6:00pm Tues–Sat

A Happy Hour favorite!

Food Deals 3
$5.00
Ten superb sandwiches served hot or cold, choice of bread, and can be requested as, or with, salads. Two exceptional prosciutto options, roasted portobello, roast beef with roasted red peppers, ham and brie, or deluxe chicken salad. So good! Great HH concept!

Drink Specials 2
$1.00 Millers; $4.00 house wines; $3.00 sangrias
1/2 off wine bottles Sundays after 4:30pm

Atmosphere 2
Cute and casual with European ambiance. Half-sunken basement gives the place added coziness, with a fun patio down below street level. Exposed brick walls, open kitchen and chalkboard menus.

Date visited: _____ **My Rating:** _____

Went with: _____

Favorites: _____

Not so much: _____

Other comments: _____

_____

Pine State Biscuits

7

Alberta Map
2204 NE Alberta
(503) 477-6605
www.pinestatebiscuits.com

Happy Hours
3:00-6:00pm and 10:00pm-close Thur-Sun

Food Deals 2
$2.00-$7.00
The most photographed food on all of Yelp!
Discounts on your favorite menu items like the
Reggie Deluxe. Biscuits and gravy or sandwiches
with fried chicken, flank steak, sausage, ham,
bacon, cheese etc.

Drink Specials 2
$3.50 drafts; $4.00-$6.00 select cocktails

Atmosphere 2
Laid-back, no-frills, counter-service space. Local
art on the walls; lots of wood. Roll-up doors
open to sidewalk seating and a small patio. Or
sit at the bar and watch the cooks make magic!

Date visited: _____ **My Rating:** _____
Went with: _____
Favorites: _____
Not so much: _____
Other comments: _____
_____

Pour Wine Bar

Lloyd Center-ish Map
2755 NE Broadway
(503) 288-7687
www.pourwinebar.com

Happy Hours
4:30–6:30pm Mon–Sat

A Happy Hour favorite!

Food Deals 2
$2.00
Very good and insanely inexpensive, but limited:
cheese panini, marinated olives, and roasted
hazelnuts. Regular menu has some delicious
and affordable options too.

Drink Specials 3
$3.00 pours of select red and white wines
$5.00 off bottles; $2.00 select beer; $15 flights

Atmosphere 3
Striking and sleek 1960s-style Space Odyssey
lounge; mod design with cool, white retro chairs
and walls; string art mural; silver, candlelight,
and real flowers.

Date visited: _____ **My Rating:** _____

Went with: _____

Favorites: _____

Not so much: _____

Other comments: _____

_____

Radar

North/NE Map
3951 N Mississippi
(503) 841-6948
www.radarpdx.com

Happy Hours
5:00–7:00 Tues-Sun

Food Deals 2
$4.00–$5.00
Small menu with some seasonal spins, with current menu as such: deviled eggs (three kinds), roasted radishes, spicy potatoes, pork & grits, and cauliflower fritters. Good regular menu, good food, but limited HH options.

Drink Specials 2
$5.00 wines; $5.00 seasonal cocktails (two)

Atmosphere 2
Narrow room with exposed brick walls and big skylight. Long bar with two-top cocktail tables running along wall, so there's not a lot of room for group seating or many lower dining tables. Small space with flagship painting in back, named after Skip Radar, owner, artist, and pirate. Aarrrr!

Date visited: _____ **My Rating:** _____
Went with: _____
Favorites: _____
Not so much: _____
Other comments: _____
_____

Radio Room

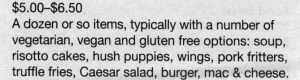

9

Alberta Map
1101 NE Alberta St
(503) 287-2346
www.radioroompdx.com

Happy Hours
3:00–6:00pm Daily

Food Deals 3
$5.00–$6.50
A dozen or so items, typically with a number of vegetarian, vegan and gluten free options: soup, risotto cakes, hush puppies, wings, pork fritters, truffle fries, Caesar salad, burger, mac & cheese.

Drink Specials 3
$3.25 microbrews; $8.00 wine of the week
$3.25 wells

Atmosphere 3
All-out sleek and mod interior fitting of big-city style standards; both upper and lower outdoor decks with bright blue umbrellas and big stone firepit; huge bar with open garage doors; cool movie posters; radio room rumored in rear.

Date visited: _____ **My Rating:** _____

Went with: _____

Favorites: _____

Not so much: _____

Other comments: _____

_____

Samurai Blue

8

Northeast (off map)
3807 N Mississippi
(503) 284-1020
www.samuraibluepdx.com

Happy Hours
★3:00–6:00pm Daily

Food Deals 2
$2.00 hand rolls (three options)
$4.00 gyoza, salmon salad, salmon kama

Drink Specials 2
$1.00 off drafts, warm sake and house wine

Atmosphere 3
Bright orange walls with original and Asian artwork, overhead beams, tsunami wave wall mural and hanging floral room dividers. Black linens and back kitchen open to front rooms.

Date visited: _____ **My Rating:** _____
Went with: _____
Favorites: _____
Not so much: _____
Other comments: _____
_____

Secret Society Lounge

North/NE Map
116 NE Russell
(503) 493-3600
www.secretsociety.net

A Happy Hour favorite!

Happy Hours
5:00–7:00pm / 10:00pm-close Sun–Thurs

Food Deals 2
$3.00–$8.00
Small but unique menu that changes seasonally:
pickled eggs, house flavored popcorn, mac &
cheese, artichoke dip, meatballs, cheese spread.
Simple late-night munchies menu too.

Drink Specials 2
$1.00 off drafts and wine;
$6.00 cocktails

Atmosphere 3
Very cool space! Speakeasy style with candlelit
bookcases, prohibition-era paintings, antique
light fixtures and floral carpet.

Date visited: _____ **My Rating:** _____

Went with: _____

Favorites: _____

Not so much: _____

Other comments: _____

_____

Slide Inn

9

Lloyd Center-ish Map
2348 SE Ankeny
(503) 236-4997
www.slideinnpdx.com

Happy Hours
5:30–7:00pm and 9:00pm–close Wed-Sun
All night Mon-Tues

Food Deals 3
$3.00–$8.00
Big-time gluten-free and veggie options! Also, some heavy aprés ski food. Nibbles like veggie tempura, kale chips, pickled root veggies, yam fries, plus crepes, sliders and sausages, spatzle, gnocchi, mac & cheese, and chili.

Drink Specials 2
$3.50 local brews; $4.00 gluten-free or German pints; $5.00 wine

Atmosphere 3
Formerly il Piatto. Same owners, different concept. Decor-wise, the revamped interior incorporates Alpine Inn elements with a mid-century modern cocktail swank. Simple charm.

Date visited: _____ **My Rating:** _____

Went with: _____

Favorites: _____

Not so much: _____

Other comments: _____

_____

Stanford's

10

Lloyd Center-ish Map
<u>Portland</u>
913 Lloyd Center; (503) 335-0811
1440 N. Jantzen Beach Center; (503) 285-2005
7000 NE Airport Way; (503) 493-4056
<u>Hillsboro</u>
2770 NW 188th Ave.; (503) 645-8000
<u>Lake Oswego</u>
14801 Kruse Oaks Dr.; (503) 620-3541
www.stanfords.com

Happy Hours
3:00–6:00pm and 9:00pm–close Daily (10:00pm
–close Fri & Sat); ★All day Sunday

Food Deals 3 $3.95-$7.95
Now same (giant) menu at all locations: Sliders,
chili fries, cheeseburgers, quesadilla, salads,
mac & cheese, tacos, chicken strips, bruschetta.

Drink Specials 3 (Early HH only)
$4.00 drafts, wine; $5.00 wells; $12.00 pitchers

Atmosphere 3
Classic and popular upscale restaurants with
the Happy Hour action at the central bar.

Date visited: _____ **My Rating:** _____
Went with: _____
Favorites: _____
Not so much: _____
Other comments: _____
_____

The Station

Alberta Map
2703 NE Alberta
(503) 284-4491
www.stationpdx.com

Happy Hours
4:00–7:00pm Daily; All night Monday

Food Deals 3
$4.00–$7.50
Sports bar pub fare with an international spin:
kung pao wings, mac & cheese, pork nachos,
Korean tacos, soup, potato cakes, crayfish tots,
pork belly deviled eggs, hoisin ginger green beans.

Drink Specials 3
$4.00 domestics; $5.00 wine; $2.00 off cocktails

Atmosphere 3
Renamed and sported-up from recent years as
Siam Society. This is the same place with same
owners as Alberta Substation opened in 2012.
Super-high ceilings with rough cement walls
and a towering, illuminated, mirrored wall of
booze. A popular place, so it can be a bit loud,
but a wonderful back beer garden awaits!

Date visited: _____ **My Rating:** _____
Went with: _____
Favorites: _____
Not so much: _____
Other comments: _____
_____

Tabla

10

Lloyd Center-ish Map
200 NE 28th Ave
(503) 238-3777
www.tabla-restaurant.com

Happy Hours
5:00–6:00pm Daily

A Happy Hour favorite!

Food Deals 3
$2.50–$4.50
One of the Northwest's best offers Happy Hour with a fresh, seasonal menu featuring half-off their bar menu! Steve's cheese or charcuterie plates, crostini, tagliatelle with bolognese, Tabla ravioli, salad, veggies, cod fritters.

Drink Specials 3
$3.00 drafts; $6.00 house wines; $12 half carafe
$2.00 off all glass pours; $5.00 wells; $5.00 Negroni

Atmosphere 3
Simple, home-style decor with banquette seating, flowers on tables and at windows, plus original art. Not suitable for groups as Happy Hour is at bar only (plus seasonal sidewalk seating).

Date visited: _____ **My Rating:** _____

Went with: _____

Favorites: _____

Not so much: _____

Other comments: _____

_____

Tapalaya

10

Lloyd Center-ish Map
28 NE 28th Ave
(503) 232-6652
www.tapalaya.com

A Happy Hour favorite!

Happy Hours
4:30–6:00pm Daily
All night Wednesdays if you ride your bike there.

Food Deals 3
$2.00–$5.00
Tapas/bites of New Orleans menu just about
perfect for getting one of everything to share,
like crawfish fritters, mac & cheese, BBQ pork
sandwich, black-eyed pea salad, and fried okra.

Drink Specials 3+
$3.00 drafts; $4.00 red, white, or rosé wine
$2.00 martinis and $3.00 hurricanes (YES!)
$5.00 signature cocktail specials

Atmosphere 3
Laissez les bon temps rouler! Not wild, but fun;
more cozy and cute; neighborhoody and nice.
Live music Thursdays – check calendar.

Date visited: _____ **My Rating:** _____
Went with: _____
Favorites: _____
Not so much: _____
Other comments: _____
_____

Tasty n Sons

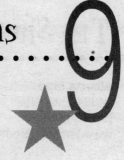

North/NE Map
3808 N Williams
(503) 621-1400
www.tastyntasty.com

Happy Hours 2:30–5:00pm Daily

Food Deals 3
$1.00–$7.00
12 small plates like bacon-wrapped dates, burger, hush puppies, fries, and egg dishes. They're famous for burgers and brunch anytime. Menu changes often, based on the season and the kitchen crew's inspiration! Owners of Toro Bravo.

Drink Specials 2
$1.00 Old Germans; $6.00 wines
$7.00 tasty cocktail specials (4)

Atmosphere 3
Industrial loft-style interior with stained concrete floors, red cinder block walls and roll-up, garage door windows. Sit in the front bar area for nice summer breezes, or side/back area along the open kitchen with butcher's block chef's bar for a view of the cooking! Alert: it's quite loud here.

Date visited: _____ **My Rating:** _____

Went with: _____

Favorites: _____

Not so much: _____

Other comments: _____

_____

Tin Shed

9

Alberta Map
1438 NE Alberta
(503) 288-6966
www.tinshedgardencafe.com

Happy Hours
3:00–6:00pm and 9:00–close Mon–Sat;
3:00–close Sundays★

Food Deals 3
$5.00–$6.00
Fresh and oh-so-tasty! Special mac & cheese of
the day (plus gluten-free option), sliders, potato
cakes, quesadilla, salads, and nachos.

Drink Specials 3
$3.00 microbrews; $4.50 wine; $4.00 wells

Atmosphere 2
Rustic corrugated tin walls; colorful & bright
elsewhere. Loud interior; big and wonderful
outdoor patio with fireplace (family- and dog-
friendly open year-round). Enjoy their lovely
garden in the sunny summertime. Cute!

Date visited: _____ **My Rating:** _____

Went with: _____

Favorites: _____

Not so much: _____

Other comments: _____

Trébol

NE/Mississippi Map
4835 N Albina Ave
(503) 517-9347
www.trebolpdx.com

Happy Hours
5:00-6:30pm and 9:00pm–close Daily

Food Deals 3
$2.00–$6.00
Authentic and interesting Mexican dishes with
soup to nuts, enchiladas, tacos, pork sandwich,
quesadilla, flautas (all fancier than they sound).

Drink Specials 2
$2.00 beers; $5.00 wines and sangrias
$6.00 specialty margaritas; $5.00 mimosas
Note: There are 100+ tequilas here!

Atmosphere 3
Perfect balance of modern and traditional style
with rustic, wood tables, exposed rafters and
vents, gold and orange walls with framed prints,
huge, illuminated bar and cool curtain dividers.

Date visited: _____ **My Rating:** _____

Went with: _____

Favorites: _____

Not so much: _____

Other comments: _____

_____

Uchu Sushi

9

NE/Mississippi Map
3940 N Mississippi
(503) 281-8248
www.uchusushi.com

Happy Hours
2:00-6:00pm Daily; 12:00pm-close Mon–Wed★
9:00pm–close Thur–Sat

Food Deals 3
$4.00–$5.00
Wow! Delightful and very extensive menu offers
14 small plates and 14 sushi rolls! Baked mussels,
egg rolls, wings, poppers, gyoza, calamari, yakitori, several salads, and the full array of classic
sushi rolls. $6.50-$8.00 dinner bowls too.

Drink Specials 3+
$3.00 beers (7 styles); $4.00-$5.00 wines
$3.00 wells; $1.00 off sake; $4.00-$6.00 cocktails

Atmosphere 2
Officially known as Uchu Sushi & Fried Chicken.
Casual, Portland-style, industrial chic. Cement
floors, long front bar, wood tables and roll top
garage doors/window. Iconic, ironic, giant fish
tanks!

Date visited: _____ **My Rating:** _____
Went with: _____
Favorites: _____
Not so much: _____
Other comments: _____
_____

Via Chicago

7

Alberta Map
2013 NE Alberta
(503) 719-6809
www.viachicagopizza.com

Happy Hours
3:00-6:00pm Mon-Fri; 11:00pm-close Fri-Sat

Food Deals 2
$2.00–$5.00
Of course, a slice of pizza, plus salad, hot dog, or bowl of olives. They have a big menu though (so hopefully they will add to this HH soon).

Drink Specials 2
$1.00 off drafts and house wine

Atmosphere 2
Sleek loft-style with cement floors, white and light blue walls, printed chalkboard menu, and roll up garage doors to small patio area. It's not close enough in flavor to any of my Chicago faves, but it *is* a whole lot closer than Chicago!

Date visited: _____ **My Rating:** _____
Went with: _____
Favorites: _____
Not so much: _____
Other comments: _____
_____

Windows Skyroom

8

Lloyd Center Map
1021 NE Grand (Top Floor Red Lion);
(503) 235-2100
www.redlion.com

Happy Hours
4:00–7:00pm Daily (extended until Blazers start
playing, when applicable)

Food Deals 2
$7.00
Fill up on your choice of chicken, pork or beef –
via sliders, tacos and/or nachos. Also quesadillas, chicken strips, wings.

Drink Specials 2 $
1.00 off select beer and wells
$4.00 house wines; Trail Blazer specials

Atmosphere 3 Skyline and river views, sunsets,
and outdoor deck – all very near Convention
Center and Rose Garden Arena in the Red Lion
Hotel. Kinda hotel-y inside, but remodel planned
in mid-to-late 2014. Stargaze out on their stellar
patio in the summer!

Date visited: _____ **My Rating:** _____
Went with: _____
Favorites: _____
Not so much: _____
Other comments: _____
_____

Yakuza

7

North/NE Map
5411 NE 30th Ave
(503) 450-0893
www.yakuzalounge.com

Happy Hours
5:00–6:00pm Wed, Thur, and Sun; plus
10:00-11:00pm Fri-Sat

Food Deals 3
$4.00–$8.00
A touch pricey for HH, but the quality is there!
Cute little menu that changes periodically, with
things like kale salad, veggie or fish hand roll, katsu,
or that incredible burger they are famous for.

Drink Specials 0
No drink specials

Atmosphere 3
This Japanese pub is yet another masterpiece
created by Micah Camden of Beast and DOC
fame, all in the same neighborhood. Interior
has simple wooden bench seating with hanging
draperies to softly separate spaces. Beautiful,
colorful murals adorn walls. Wonderful patio!

Date visited: _____ **My Rating:** _____
Went with: _____
Favorites: _____
Not so much: _____
Other comments: _____
_____

Alberta Street Pub

Alberta Map 1036 NE Alberta; (503) 284-7665
www.myspace.com/albertastreetpub

Happy Hours 3:00–6:00pm Daily

Food Deals 2 $2.00-$7.00 Several English pub-style
choices like fish & chips, Welsh rarebit, salad, burger.

Drink Specials 2 $1.00 off draft, wells, wine

Atmosphere 2 Warm and inviting, dark Irish pub.
High-walled booths enable private conversation.

Alleyway Café

Alberta Map 2415 NE Alberta St.; (503) 287-7760

Happy Hours 3:00–7:00pm Daily

Food Deals 3 $2.00–$5.00 Fresh taste in a long
list of little nibbles with big discounts: sliders, grilled
cheese, sweet potato fries, tacos, chips & salsa,
Caesar, onion rings. Many vegan options also!

Drink Specials 3 $1.50 Rainers; $3.00 micros
$4.00 mimosas, Bloody Marys or mojitos; $3.00 wells

Atmosphere 2 Low-key and ultra-casual neighborhood café with artsy, rotating gallery wares.

Ate-Oh-Ate www.ate-oh-ate.com

Lloyd Center-ish Map 2452 E Burnside; (503) 445-6101

Happy Hours 4:00-6:00pm Daily

Food Deals 2 $2.00-$5.00 Hard-to-find authentic
Hawaiian food! Enjoy nibbles like kalua pig or chicken
sliders, wings, poke, fried rice, or Spam tempura!

Drink Specials 1 $1.00 off drafts; $10.00 bucket o' beer
$5.00 mai-tais. Full bar with unusual beer choices.

Atmosphere 2 Very casual... cafeteria? Quite stark and
Hawaiian theme isn't pushed much in decor. Counter
service only, but brought to us by same owners of
Simpatica and Laurelhurst Market. Hawaii area code 808.

Bar Bar (at Mississippi Studios)

North/NE Map 3943 N Mississippi; (503) 288-3895
www.mississippistudios.com

Happy Hours 4:00-6:00pm Daily

Food Deals 0 Limited menu at Happy Hour prices
at all times: $5.00 burgers or $4.50 salads.

Drink Specials 2 $3.00 drafts; $5.00 Margarita deals
$1.00 off house cocktails

Atmosphere 2 Formerly Mississippi Station. Renovated
and removed all the old station charm, but understated
and nice enough. Great back patio! Concerts next door.

Beech Street Parlor

North/NE Map 412 NE Beech; (503) 946-8184
www.beechstreetparlor.com

Happy Hours 5:00-7:00pm Mon-Sat

Food Deals 1 $1.00 off bar menu that will have your
hunger covered: salads, ham & cheese, tart, hot dog.

Drink Specials 2 $1.00 off drafts/wine; $3.50 wells

Atmosphere 3 Vintage style! It's like an older, vampy,
sister to the Liberty Ale House. Similar in tone to a
speak-easy, but with welcoming front porch, and
several rooms upstairs with parlor couches. Cute!

Bella Faccia Pizzeria

Alberta Map 2934 NE Alberta St.; (503) 282-0600
www.bellafacciapizzeria.com

Happy Hours 4:00–6:00pm Mon–Fri; 3–5pm Sat–Sun

Food Deals 2 50 cents off pizza slices or $4.00 off
whole pizza/pies.

Drink Specials 1 $1.00 off pints

Atmosphere 2 Very casual pizza place with coffeehouse vibe; pleasant back patio and sidewalk seating.

Blue Agave www.blueagavepdx.com

Lloyd Center Map 2828 NE Glisan; (503) 206-85421

Happy Hours 3:00–6:00pm Daily

Food Deals 2 $1.00 off every menu item: About 20 tapas with salads, empanadas, ceviches, flank steak, Spanish omelet, chicken, pork, garlic shrimp, stuffed mushrooms, fried squid, and desserts!

Drink Specials 2 $1.00 off all drinks

Atmosphere 3 Garage-style space partially shared with the courtyard/patio of Migration Brewing. Roll-up doors, floor-to-ceiling windows, light wood tables, terra cotta walls, illuminated bar back, blue floral lamps. Front bar and side restaurant.

Branch Whiskey Bar

Alberta Map 2926 NE Alberta; (503) 206-6266 www.branchwhiskeybar.com

Happy Hours 5:00–6:30pm Sun-Thur; Drink deals only 10:00pm-close Sun-Thur; midnight-close Fri-Sat

Food Deals 2 $2.00-$6.00 Unique menu with items like croquette of the day, duck fat fries, paté, olives, lobster dumplings, mixed greens, curry peanuts.

Drink Specials 2 $4.00 drafts; $5.00 wines $3.00-$5.00 cocktails

Atmosphere 2 Get your whiskey on or branch out to scotch or rye at this small and cozy, brick-walled bar.

Bungalo Bar www.casanaranjapdx.com

NE/Mississippi Map 4205 N Mississippi; (503) 459-4049

Happy Hours 4:00–7:00pm Tues-Sat

Food Deals 0 No Happy hour deals on food.

Drink Specials 3 $3.75 drafts; $6.00 wine; $3.00 wells

Atmosphere 3 Ultra-orange craftsman bungalo with the bar in the living room. It's really all about the front, back, and side deck and patio areas complete with tiki torches, hammock swings, firepits, and umbrellas.

Cha Cha Cha www.chaportland.com

On each of the three map pages in this section
2635 NE Broadway; (503) 288-1045
4727 NE Fremont; (503) 595-9131
3808 N Williams; (503) 281-1655
More locations in NW and SE – see index

Happy Hours 3:00–6:00pm Daily

Food Deals 3 $3.95-$5.95 Big array of homemade Mexican: tostadas, fish tacos, quesadillas, burritos.

Drink Specials 3 $3.00 beer; $5.00 wine; $5 cocktails

Atmosphere 2 Part of the Cha Cha Cha family taken up a notch to the nicer side in the three Northside eateries. Menus vary slightly per location.

County Cork

North/NE Map 1329 NE Fremont; (503) 284-4805
www.countycorkpublichouse.com

Happy Hours 3:00–6:00pm Mon–Fri

Food Deals 3 $3.00–$6.00 Good and big real meals: fish and chips, Murphy's stew, bangers & mash, shepherd's pie with side salads, scotch eggs, wings.

Drink Specials 2 $1.00 off drafts ($3.95 most pints— Imperials); 25 notable beers on a beautiful tap lineup

Atmosphere 2 Big, fun and colorful Irish pub with hand-painted tables, pub decor, bench seating, windows that open to the street, and sidewalk seating.

Cruz Room www.cruzroom.com

NE/North Map 2338 NE Alberta; (503) 208-3483

Happy Hours 4:30–6:30pm Daily (from 4pm Fri-Sat)
Late-night 10:00pm-close Daily

Food Deals 3 $2.00 Tiny tapas taco experiments made with creativity and flavor! Asian style (lemon-grass chicken, coconut milk, spicy peanut-butter slaw); American (potato, bacon and avocado); or Mexican (black bean with roasted corn and jalapeno salsa).

Drink Specials 2 $3.00 drafts; $4.00 house drinks

Atmosphere 2 Long, narrow room is divided into two halves; red bar top and floors. Nice side patio with artist mural.

Free House

NE (off map) 1325 NE Fremont; (503) 946-8161

Happy Hours 4:00–6:00pm Daily

Food Deals 1 $1.00 off entire food menu

Drink Specials 2 $1.00 off all drinks

Atmosphere 2 By definition, a British pub that is owned independently of the breweries that supply it. By neighborhood crowd translation, it rocks! Patio.

Gather www.gatherportland.com

North/NE Map 1000 NE Multnomah; (503) 331-4943

Happy Hours 4:00–6:00pm Mon–Fri

Food Deals 3 $2.50–$7.50 A full half-off their seasonal bar menu, offering several gluten-free choices like quinoa-crusted chicken, wings, mussels and hazelnuts. Also burgers, grilled cheese, pork sliders.

Drink Specials 3 $4.00 drafts, house wines, wells,

Atmosphere 3 Wide open to the lobby, but past that are several nice seating areas. Modern space with a flair for NW taste and style. Recycled boards from an old Jim Beam distillery, giant log beams overhead, and a cool fireplace. Free parking validation (two hours).

Good Neighbor Pizzeria

NE (off map) 800 NE Dekum St.; (503) 285-7400
www.goodneighborpizzeria.com

Happy Hours 4:00-6:00pm and 10:00pm-mid Daily

Food Deals 2 $2.00–$5.00 Italian mini-eats: garlic knots and knots with mozz, salads, pizza, roasted veggie sandwich, roasted potatoes, calzones.

Drink Specials 2 $3.50 drafts; $4.00 bottles of beer $5.00 wines; $3.00 well drinks

Atmosphere 2 Friendly, neighborhood pizza joint with brewery vibe, good beer, 'za and ice cream treats.

Hilt www.thehiltbar.com

Alberta Map 1934 NE Alberta St; (971) 255-1793

Happy Hours 4:00-7:00pm Daily; ★All day Sunday

Food Deals 2 $3.00–$5.00 Menu that's kind of bar-ish and kinda Mediterranean: lamb gyros, beet salad, veggie burger, cheese fries, falafel, and hummus plates.

Drink Specials 2 $1.00 off taps & wells

Atmosphere 2 Not decorated crazily to the hilt, and actually quite non-descript, but a comfortable neighborhood hangout on Alberta with big, outdoor patio.

Jade Lounge www.jadeloungepdx.com

Lloyd Center Map 2342 SE Ankeny; (503) 236-4998

Happy Hours 5:30–6:30pm Daily (drinks)

Food Deals 0 Regular bar menu with some $3-$7 appetizers, some $8-$12 heavier food Food is not Asian anymore, rather similar to next door Slide Inn.

Drink Specials 2 $1.00 off drafts & wine; $4.00 wells; $1.00 PBR and $2.00 microbrews all Sunday★

Atmosphere 2 Asian lounge with jade lanterns hung from high ceilings and low coffee table seating.

Liberty Glass

North/NE Map 938 N Cook; (503) 517-9931

Happy Hours 3:00–6:00pm Daily

Food Deals 2 $3.00-$8.00 Nice menu with a crowd-pleasing array of eats. Cozy, pubby items like trisket nachos, mac & cheese, beets, salad, soups, nibbles.

Drink Specials 1 $1.00 off taps and cocktails

Atmosphere 2 Cute pink house, manned up with antlers and woods. Peaceful, 1776 Colonial pub vibe.

Mac!&Cheesery www.macandcheese.biz

North/NE Map 3936 N Mississippi; 503) 200-5787

Happy Hours 3:00–6:00pm Daily; ★All day Monday
Also during Blazers and Timbers games

Food Deals 2 $3.00–$5.00 Mac & cheese (served with or without hotdogs–remember that?!), pork or burger sliders, chili cheese fries, veggie plate.

Drink Specials 3 $2.50 drafts; $1.00 off wine; $3.00 wells

Atmosphere 2 Long and light room with upper level and natural wood stairs, bar and booths. Very cute touch with kid's metal lunch boxes adorning the walls. Note: All mac and cheeses available gluten free!

Mee-Sen Thai

North/NE Map 3924 N Mississippi; (503) 445-1909
www.meesenpdx.com

Happy Hours 3:00–6:00pm and 9:00pm–close Daily
★All day Tuesday

Food Deals 1 Just 50 cents off small noodle bowls. They have delicious and unique Thai tapas, but eliminated Happy Hour discounts on all but bowls.

Drink Specials 2 $1.00 off beer/wine; $6.00 cocktails

Atmosphere 2 Funky and friendly garage-like space with open doors to a nice stone patio, and built sustainably with materials like old, colorful, barnhouse wood planks – and bicycles!

Old Gold www.theoldgoldpdx.com

North/NE Map 2105 N. Killingsworth; (503) 894-8937

Happy Hours 4:00–7:00pm Mon-Fri

Food Deals 1 $1.00 off sandwiches

Drink Specials 2 $1.00 off drafts, wine and wells

Atmosphere 2 Portland-cool bar next to Mextiza. Growing reputation for great cocktais. Made in Oregon flagship sign with t-shirts for sale and a million whiskeys.

Pause

Northeast (off map) 5101 N Interstate; (971) 230-0705

Happy Hours 4:00–6:00pm Daily

Food Deals 0 Sadly, no discounts at Happy Hour.

Drink Specials 2 $1.00 off drafts and wells

Atmosphere 2 Casual and just a bit retro. Two open room halves with red walls, cement floors. Patio.

Por Que No www. porquenotacos.com

Northeast Map 3524 N Mississippi; (503) 467-4149
Southeast Map 4635 SE Hawthorne; (503) 954-3138

Happy Hours 3:00–6:00pm Daily; Tues 3:00pm–close

Food Deals 1 $.50 cents off tacos; $1.00 off chips and guacamole or salsa. Tasty, simple, authentic Mexican.

Drink Specials 2 $.50 cents off drafts and bottles; $1.00 off sangria and rum drinks; $1.50 off margaritas

Atmosphere 2 A true taqueria vibe, complete with loud music, warm colors, and noisy kitchen clatter. Active sidewalk seating with Happy Hour available. Northeast locaton underwent renovations Fall 2013.

Rontoms www.rontoms.net

Lloyd Center Map 600 E Burnside; (503) 236-4536

Happy Hours 3:00–6:30pm Mon–Sat

Food Deals 2 $4.50 Several seasonal selections like grilled cheese with soup, beet salad, chicken skewers, fondue, pumpkin soup, or wild mushroom risotto.

Drink Specials 1 $1.00 off wells

Atmosphere 2 Big, open room a la 1970s; giant party patio with ping pong; fireplace; lounge chair groupings.

Sidecar 11 www.sidecarpdx.wordpress.com

North/NE Map 3955 N Mississippi; (503) 208-3798

Happy Hours 4:00–7:00pm and 9:00pm-close (food) Daily; ★All day Monday

Food Deals 2 $4.50 Small bar menu of seasonal appetizers yet with a good range of options about half-off. Choose from a couple flatbreads, chicken or steak skewers, tapenade plate, olives, and nuts.

Drink Specials 2 $1.00 off beer, wine and cocktails

Atmosphere 2 Tiny, somewhat hard-to-find place, plus handcrafted, classic cocktails gives Sidecar 11 a certain speak easy appeal at night. By day, too bright.

Spirit of '77 www.spiritof77bar.com

North/NE Map 500 NE MLK Jr Blvd; (503) 232-9977

Happy Hours 4:00–6:00pm Mon–Fri

Food Deals 1 $3.00–$6.00 Chalkboard specials

Drink Specials 2 $4.00 select draft; $5.00 wines or bubbles; $5.00 Margaritas

Atmosphere 3 Big and fun sports bar! Open, warehouse space with exposed wooden beams with scores of hanging lights. A giant lightbulb-filled "Spirit of 77" sign illuminates the bar. Lots of long, thin and high community tables aimed at a *giant* projection screen.

Tavin's www.tavinspub.com

North/NE Map 102 NE Russell; (503) 719-4890

Happy Hours 3:00–6:00pm Daily

Food Deals 2 $3.00-$6.00 Always a rotating menu that may include nachos (chicken or beef), chips & salsa, wings, fries, tacos, hummus, artichoke dip.

Drink Specials 2 $3.75 drafts; $4.00 wine; $3.00 wells

Atmosphere 2 Formerly Afrique, now a very comfortable neighborhood sports pub. Cushioned seats (yay!), high ceilings with lofted seating area, and a traditional, classic bar. Five high-def big-screen TVs.

Thai Noon (My Thai Lounge)

Alberta Map 2635 NE Alberta St.; (503) 282-2021 www.thainoon.com

Happy Hours 4:30–6:00pm Daily

Food Deals 2 $2.75–$7.00 Roughly half-price on Thai basics like egg rolls, wontons, satay, fried rice, pad thai, padkeemow.

Drink Specials 2 $3.00 beers; $2.00 PBRs

Atmosphere 1 Super casual, somewhat spartan lounge next to the Thai Noon restaurant.

Zilla Saké (Sushi)

Alberta Map 1806 NE Alberta; 503-288-8372 www.zillasakehouse.com

Happy Hours 5:00–7:00pm Mon–Fri

Food Deals 2 $1.00–$5.00 California rolls, miso soup, edamame, salad, and spicy squid jerky.

Drink Specials 3 $4.00 Sapporo beer; $4.00 wine $2.50 wells; $4.00 specialty cocktail $6.00–$15.00 Six choices of hot and cold sakes

Atmosphere 2 Cool and artsy zen. Huge sake menu. Dramatic, large-scale art and big screen TV.

SE/Central East Side

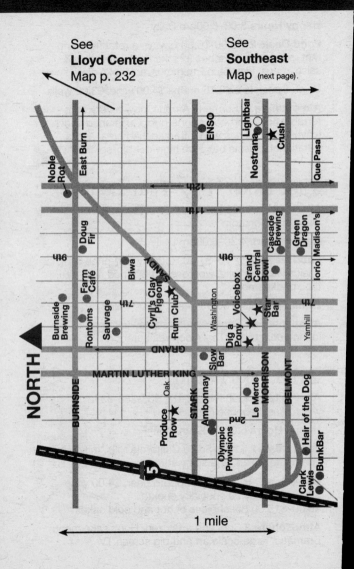

See
Lloyd Center
Map p. 232

See
Southeast
Map (next page).

NORTH

1 mile

294

Southeast

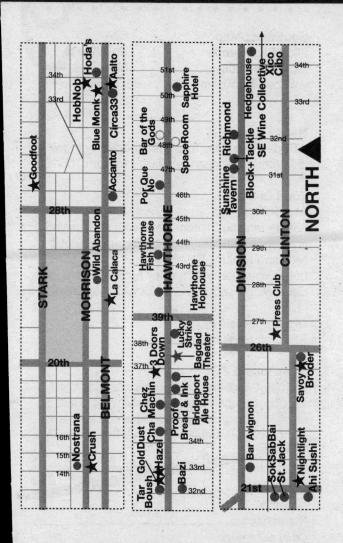

Map 1 (left panel):

34th — Hoda's
33rd — HobNob, Blue Monk, Circa33, Aalto
Goodfoot
Accanto
28th
STARK
MORRISON
Wild Abandon
La Calaca
BELMONT
20th
Nostrana
Crush
16th
GoldDust
15th
14th

Map 2 (center panel):

51st
50th — Sapphire Hotel
49th — Bar of the Gods
48th — SpaceRoom
47th — Por Que No
46th
45th
44th
43rd — Hawthorne Fish House
HAWTHORNE
Hawthorne Hophouse
39th
38th — 3 Doors Down
37th — Lucky Strike
Bagdad Theater
Chez Machin
Cha Cha Cha
Proof
Bread & Ink
Bridgeport Ale House
34th
Tar Boush
Gold Dust
Hazel
Bazi
33rd
32nd

Map 3 (right panel):

34th
33rd
Hedgehouse
SE Wine Collective
Xico
Cibo
Richmond
Block+Tackle
32nd
Sunshine Tavern
31st
30th
DIVISION
CLINTON
NORTH
29th
28th
Press Club
27th
26th
Bar Avignon
Savoy
Broder
SokSabBai
St. Jack
Nightlight
Ahi Sushi
21st

295

Ahi Sushi & Tapas

Southeast Map
2038 SE Clinton
(503) 236-7566
www.sushiahi.com

Happy Hours
4:00-6:00pm Sun, Tues-Wed (hopefully *those* days/hours will change); 9:00-11:00pm Thur-Sat

Food Deals 3
$1.00–$7.00
A wide-ranging 21-item menu with sushi, salads, and tapas. Flavorful, high-quality ingredients. Nice and healthy! Seven kinds of rolls, a giant house salad (only $3!), spicy tuna, skewers, delicious wings, veggie stew, spinach, fried pork.

Drink Specials 2
$1.00 off all drinks

Atmosphere 3
Formerly Vindalho. Cool, illuminated bar! Loft-style space with white, Japanese, ceiling swags, unique lighting choices, upholstered seats, and giant garage doors/windows that open outside.

Date visited: _____ **My Rating:** _____

Went with: _____

Favorites: _____

Not so much: _____

Other comments: _____

_____

Block & Tackle 10

Southeast Map
3113 SE Division
(503) 236-0205
www.blockandtacklepdx.com

A Happy Hour favorite!

Happy Hours
4:00-6:00pm Wed-Sat

Food Deals 3
$1.00–$7.00
Every item makes the city's best-of list, based on both taste and price! Oyster shooters, deviled eggs, fresh greens, clam chowder, shrimp, clams and chorizo in broth, and calamari. Plus $1.00 off oysters on the half shell.

Drink Specials 3
$1.00 Rainers (it goes with the fishing theme)
$5.00 wine; $3.00 wells; $5.00 daily cocktail

Atmosphere 3
Simple and classically modern, with a central, long group table and back bar. Fun, black & white vintage fishing photos, and a big collection of netted glass buoys overhead. Award-winning *Roe* in back – a restaurant within a restaurant!

Date visited: _____ **My Rating:** _____
Went with: _____
Favorites: _____
Not so much: _____
Other comments: _____
_____

Bread & Ink

10

Southeast Map
3610 SE Hawthorne
(503) 239-4756
www.breadandinkcafe.com

Happy Hours
3:30–6:30pm Daily

Food Deals 3
$4.00–$6.00
Focus on locally sourced ingredients and fresh, always changing menu with about 15 items: salads, grilled shrimp, hummus plate, black bean cakes, soup, seasonal veggies, burgers, sandwiches.

Drink Specials 3+
$4.00 microbrews; $5.00–6.50 cocktails
$4.50 red or white wine ($16.00 select bottles)

Atmosphere 3
More than 25 years strong and they finally started a Happy Hour – and it's a good one! A long-time favorite of writer types both because of the name and the mellow and pleasant scene. Open breakfast through late dinner.

Date visited: _____ **My Rating:** _____
Went with: _____
Favorites: _____
Not so much: _____
Other comments: _____
_____

Broder

8

Southeast Map
2508 SE Clinton; (503) 736-3333
www.broderpdx.com

Broder Nord 2240 N Interstate; (503) 282-5555

Happy Hours
5:00–7:00pm Wed–Sat (HH starting in Jan 2014)

Food Deals 3
$4.00–$10.00
Enjoy surf or turf boards, Swedish meatballs, traditional lefse, and aebleskiver. Salad, soup, or potato pancake sides. Legendary for weekend brunches with two-hour waits (but try it at night instead with the all-day breakfast menu)!

Drink Specials 2
$1.50 off draft beer; $1.00 off cocktails

Atmosphere 2
A sweet but sleek Swedish breakfast cafe that turns into a classically cool European-style bar at night. Interesting overhead branch lighting, dark woods, yellow bar stools, blue checker napkins. The new Nord (north) location is the former Gotham Tavern.

Date visited: _____ **My Rating:** _____
Went with: _____
Favorites: _____
Not so much: _____
Other comments: _____
_____

The Brooklyn House

Southeast Map
3131 SE 12th Ave.
(503) 236-6761
www.brooklynhouserestaurant.com

Happy Hours
4:00-6:00pm Tues-Sun

Food Deals 2
$3.00–$9.00
Get $2.00 off five select menu items, currently pork confit with coleslaw, grilled sausage w/ kraut, Caesar or seasonal greens salad, chicken or veggie alfredo. Needs to be a longer list for top points, but I do love the fresh flower garnishes!

Drink Specials 2
$1.00 off beer, wine or wells

Atmosphere 2
The old Berlin Inn, serving European comfort food with committed attention to local sourcing. Homey, three-room house with a small bar, simple artwork, and thick, dark wood moldings. Cute outdoor patio, but near a busy street.

Date visited: _____ **My Rating:** _____

Went with: _____

Favorites: _____

Not so much: _____

Other comments: _____

_____

Café Castagna 10

Hawthorne (off map)
1758 SE Hawthorne
(503) 231-9959
www.castagnarestaurant.com

Happy Hours
5:00-6:00pm and 9:00pm–close Mon–Sat

Food Deals 2
$4.00–$6.00
Menu changes daily per chef's choices, but hosts items like arancini, skewers, meatballs, salads, rillettes, fritters, and be sure to try their famously delicious burger!

Drink Specials 3
$3.00 drafts; $5.00 wines and wells
$5.00 specialty cocktails

Atmosphere 3
Contemporary simplicity with sleek lines, natural colors within a neutral color palette, and big front windows, which give this half of the restaurant more of a café feel.

Date visited: _____ **My Rating:** _____

Went with: _____

Favorites: _____

Not so much: _____

Other comments: _____

_____

Cibo

10

. . . .

Southeast Map
3593 SE Division
(503) 719-5377
www.cibopdx.com

Happy Hours
5:00–6:30pm / 10:00pm–close Daily

Food Deals 3
$3.00-$7.00 Delicious wood-fired pizzas, paninis,
calamari, polenta caprese, sweet potato fries,
bruschetta, prawns.

Drink Specials 3
$3.00 beer, wine and wells; $7.00 cocktails

Atmosphere 3
Pronounced CHEE-bo. Neighborhood bar from
the owner of Basta's, but the casual bar vibe is
a disconnect from the fancy food served. Tables
and booths line the slatted wood walls, all
surrounding the giant central bar/kitchen that
the whole place revolves around.

Date visited: _____ **My Rating:** _____

Went with: _____

Favorites: _____

Not so much: _____

Other comments: _____

_____

Circa 33

• • • • • • • • • • • • • • • • • • •

Southeast Map
3348 SE Belmont Ave
(503) 477-7682
www.circa33bar.com

Happy Hours
4:00–6:00pm Daily; ★All night Monday

Food Deals 2
$3.00–$6.50
Bar menu with slight twists on basics with
seasonal variations: burger, fries, calamari,
mac & cheese, fish & chips.

Drink Specials 3
$3.50 Pilsner; $5.00 house wine
$1.00 off wells; $6.00 planter's punch

Atmosphere 3
Around about the 33rd block, so you'll always
remember where it is, and also relates to 1933,
the year Prohibition was repealed. It's true to
theme and concept, and exudes a genuine
character. Best at night! Alleyway patio too.

Date visited: _____ **My Rating:** _____
Went with: _____
Favorites: _____
Not so much: _____
Other comments: _____
_____

Clarklewis

Central Eastside Map
1001 SE Water Ave.
(503) 235-2294
www.clarklewispdx.com

Happy Hours
4:30–6:30pm Mon–Sat

Food Deals 3
$1.00–$6.00
Menu changes often, with about 12 or so chef's choice nibbles like fresh salads, spaghetti, cauliflower arancini, soup, meatballs, clams or mussels, or a cheese burger.

Drink Specials 3
$4.00 bottled beers; $5.00 house wine
$5.00 martini or gimlet

Atmosphere 3
Sophisticated renovation of old loading dock with northwest and industrial-chic stylings; full, long wall of streetscape gridded windows (open or candlelit), big wooden tables for groups and tucked-away two-tops. A perfect date place!

Date visited: _____ **My Rating:** _____
Went with: _____
Favorites: _____
Not so much: _____
Other comments: _____
_____

Double Dragon 8

Southeast Map
2235 SE Division
(503) 230-8340
www.doubledragonpdx.com

Happy Hours
3:00-6:00pm Mon-Fri; 10:00pm-mid Daily

Food Deals 3
$3.00 1/2 bahn mi sandwiches
$2.00 off all soups, stews, and rice bowls
$3.00 salads and sides
$10.00 burger + beer

Drink Specials 2
$1.00 off drafts; $4.00 wells and rum horchatas

Atmosphere 2
Casual corner cafe with front patio, full wall of
glass at entry, and central bar. Reclaimed wood
lines the walls in artful ways with varying colors
and dimensions, a large Double Dragon stamped
logo, and tiny shelves holding simple treasures.
Comic book tables and anime mural art.

Date visited: _____ **My Rating:** _____
Went with: _____
Favorites: _____
Not so much: _____
Other comments: _____
_____

Farm Café

Central East Side Map
10 SE 7th Ave
(503) 736-3276
www.thefarmcafe.com

Happy Hours
5:00–6:00pm Mon–Fri

A Happy Hour favorite!

Food Deals 3
$2.00–$6.00
Short but sweet menu – fresh goodies change
with the seasons, and even daily: hummus plate,
arancini, fritters, crostini, salads, soup.

Drink Specials 2
$1.00 off draft beer; $5.00 red and white wines
$5.00 choice cocktails

Atmosphere 3+
High-level cuteness alert! Located in a renovated,
old Victorian home dripping with charm. Romantic
and intimate with several meandering, cozy dining
rooms. Big seasonal patio and back bar.

Date visited: _____ **My Rating:** _____
Went with: _____
Favorites: _____
Not so much: _____
Other comments: _____
_____

Grand Central Bowl

• • • • • • • • • • • • • • • •

Central Eastside Map
839 SE Morrison
(503) 236-BOWL (2695)
www.thegrandcentralbowl.com

Happy Hours
3:00–6:00pm and 9:00pm–close (food) Daily

Food Deals 3
$3.95–$5.95
Almost 20 bar basics like sliders, fries, nachos, artichoke dip, onion rings, lettuce wraps, cheese sticks, spicy tuna rolls, and pizzas.

Drink Specials 3
$4.00 select drafts: $4.00 wine; $3.00 wells

Atmosphere 3
A flashy, fancy-smancy bowling mecca! It's a party place in a giant space with several bars, lounges, game rooms and plenty of hi-def, big-screen TVs. Some recent redecorating brings us some nice lounging areas.

Date visited: _____ **My Rating:** _____
Went with: _____
Favorites: _____
Not so much: _____
Other comments: _____
_____

Hokusei Sushi

9

Southeast Map
4246 SE Belmont
(971) 279-2161
www.hokuseisushi.com

Happy Hours
5:00-6:00pm Wed-Sun★All night Monday

Food Deals 3
$2.00–$6.00
Exceptional sushi here, and a big menu, but
prices are all over the board, and (relatively)
not much of it discounted for Happy Hour. Eight
menu items with funny names like wakame salad,
edamame, tatsuta age, harumaki, gyu tan yaki.

Drink Specials 2
$1.00 off drafts and sake (half-off small hot sake)
$5.00 Happy Hour cocktail

Atmosphere 3
Serene, simple, and stark space. Contemporary
design with clean lines, natural woods, open-air
garage door wall, and cement floors. Super-long
group table, pretty artwork, and sushi bar seating.

Date visited: _____ **My Rating:** _____

Went with: _____

Favorites: _____

Not so much: _____

Other comments: _____

_____

Iorio

Southeast Map
912 SE Hawthorne
(503) 445-4716
www.ioriorestaurant.com

Happy Hours
5:00–6:00pm Wed–Fri

Food Deals 3
$5.00-$7.50
Eight plentiful servings of tried and true menu
items plus seasonal and nightly specials: risotto,
porchetta sandwich, creamy polenta, burgers,
pasta, meatballs, salads.

Drink Specials 2
$3.00 drafts; $7.00 wine; $5.00-$7.00 cocktail

Atmosphere 3
Big on red in big, open room with long, central
Italian-family-sized table and window seats.
Low light, dark wood floors, and original paint-
ings depicting country life in bright colors and
ornate gold frames.

Date visited: _____ **My Rating:** _____

Went with: _____

Favorites: _____

Not so much: _____

Other comments: _____

_____

La Calaca Comelona

Southeast Map
2304 SE Belmont
(503) 239-9675
www.lacalacacomelona.com

Happy Hours
4:00-6:00pm and 8:00pm-close Mon–Sat

Food Deals 3
$2.00–$5.00
Authentic, truly delicious Mexican food! Pork
and pineapple tacos (plus other varieties);
grilled cactus, spicy potatoes, mini quesadillas,
taquitos—and grilled grasshoppers!

Drink Specials 3
50 cents off beer; $5.00 wines; $3.50 wells
$4.00 Margaritas and other bartender specials

Atmosphere 3+
Take a Mexican vacation to this Day-of-the-Dead-
inspired taverna named "The Hungry Skeleton."
Bright colorful walls, Mexican-style folk art at
every glimpse and turn, and you can sit anywhere
in the whole loco restaurant early on, but late-
night, Happy Hour is at the bar only. Enchanting
patio out back, but for dinner only.

Date visited: _____ **My Rating:** _____

Went with: _____

Favorites: _____

Not so much: _____

Other comments: _____

_____

Lucky Strike

Southeast Map
3862 SE Hawthorne
(503) 206-8292
www.luckystrikepdx.com

Happy Hours
4:00-6:00pm Daily; 9:00pm-close Sun-Thur;
10:00pm-close Fri-Sat

Food Deals 3
$4.00–$6.00
About a dozen or so eats including pot stickers,
spring rolls, spicy Sichuan (Szechuan) noodles,
kung pao chicken, Guinness pork ribs, dumplings,
stir-fried beans with beef and baby bok choy.

Drink Specials 3
$3.00 beer; $4.00 red and wine wines
$4.00 top-shelf well drinks; $5.00 daily cocktail

Atmosphere 2
A funky space that matches the Hawthorne area
vibe, with a giant wall mural of a tattoo-art dragon
dominating the scene. Lots of small tables and
nice outdoor patio available at Happy Hour.

Date visited: _____ **My Rating:** _____

Went with: _____

Favorites: _____

Not so much: _____

Other comments: _____

_____

Nostrana

Southeast Map
1401 SE Morrison St
(503) 234-2427
www.nostrana.com

Happy Hours
9:00pm–close Daily (Nightly)

Food Deals 3
$3.00–$6.00
It's all about the wood-fired pizza! Get marinara or margherita style (add arugula, prosciutto or anchovies). Also salad, mac & cheese, spiced nuts, roasted olives and cheeses.

Drink Specials 3
$4.00 seasonal ale or pils; $5.00 house wines
$3.00 fresh lemonade; $5.00 select cocktails

Atmosphere 3
Giant, hanger-like space in a mini strip mall with an overhead, complex grid of wood ceiling beams. Interior still manages to feel friendly and intimate with candles, suspended framed art, and a long, communal bar with giant, towering shelves.

Date visited: _____ **My Rating:** _____

Went with: _____

Favorites: _____

Not so much: _____

Other comments: _____

_____

The Observatory

Southeast (Off Map)
8115 SE Stark
(503) 445-6284
www.theobservatorypdx.com

Happy Hours
3:00–6:00pm Daily; 10:00pm–close Sun–Thur

Food Deals 3
$2.00–$6.00
Extra points for being a foodie place, but limited
choices at HH. Seasonal: salad, soup, smoked
whitefish spread, ginger sake mussels, paté.

Drink Specials 3
$1.50 domestics (cans); $3.75 microbrews
$5.00 house wines; $4.00 wells; $5.00 cocktail

Atmosphere 2
Not too lounge-y, and it's probably more of a
restaurant, but their signature cocktails are quite
impressive! Big L-shaped bar dominates this
upscale diner beneath a high-strung globe-light
constellation.

Date visited: _____ **My Rating:** _____

Went with: _____

Favorites: _____

Not so much: _____

Other comments: _____

_____

Olympic Provisions

8

Central Eastside Map
107 SE Washington; (503) 954-3663
1632 NW Thurman; (503) 894-8136
www.olympicprovisions.com

Happy Hours
3:00–6:00pm Tues-Sun

Food Deals 2
$4.00–$7.00
Apertif hour offers sandwiches, a couple of veggie items, and some dessert plates. Things like pork confit, salads, frankfurters, pickled eggs, olives.

Drink Specials 2
$4.00 draft of the day; $5.00 apértifs and soda mixers, house wine options; $6.00 cocktails

Atmosphere 3
Both interiors are similar and follow a trendy NW-gritty-cute look. Cool, industrial spaces with painted white brick walls, lots of cement, old woods, and metal. A funky, illuminated "meat" sign dominates the eastside location. Their new outpost is the old Carlyle. Meet up, or meat-to-go.

Date visited: _____ **My Rating:** _____
Went with: _____
Favorites: _____
Not so much: _____
Other comments: _____
_____

Pacific Pie Company

• • • • • • • • • • • • • •

8

Southeast Map
1520 SE 7th Ave.
(503) 381-6157
www.pacificpieco.com

Happy Hours
3:00–6:00pm Mon-Fri

Food Deals 2
$3.00–$5.00
Five stand-alone items or combo pie with a
pint (or coffee) specials. Deviled eggs, potato
wedges, veggie pasties, sausage rools, bread.

Drink Specials 3
$3.00 drafts; $4.00 wines, $5.00 cocktail

Atmosphere 2
Sigh. Doesn't pie just put a smile on your face?!
And add in a bar? Brilliant! Simple place with
green walls, stained cement floors, natural
wood tables, lots of light, an Aussie flag, and
plenty of pie!

Date visited: _____ **My Rating:** _____
Went with: _____
Favorites: _____
Not so much: _____
Other comments: _____
_____

Press Club

Southeast Map
2621 SE Clinton
(503) 233-5656
www.pressclubpdx.com

Happy Hours
3:00–7:00pm Tues-Sun

Food Deals 3   *A Happy Hour favorite!*
$3.00–$7.00
Fresh salads and soup, crepes or sandwiches
named after famous authors.

Drink Specials 3
$1.00 off beer and wine (i.e. $2.50 imports!)
$6.00 cocktails; plus nightly specials and coffee
Plus $5.00 Bloody Marys all day Sunday

Atmosphere 3
If the ever-so-treasured Powell's Bookstore was
a small neighborhood bar, it would be the
Press Club. There's a sweet, laid-back vibe here
that works well if you are a fan of coffee houses,
bookstores, Paris, or hipster concert venues.

Date visited: _____ **My Rating:** _____
Went with: _____
Favorites: _____
Not so much: _____
Other comments: _____
_____

Proof

Hawthorne Map
3564 SE Hawthorne
(503) 236-6001

Happy Hours
3:00-6:00pm Daily

Food Deals 2
$3.00–$7.00
Same munchies menu as the late night bites
with pulled pork or bison sliders, sweet potato
fries, chips & salsa, mac & cheese, olives &
bread, salad, cheese plate, or fried green beans.

Drink Specials 3
$3.00 drafts; $4.00 wines; $3.50 well drinks
$3.00 pints all day Tuesday

Atmosphere 3
Cool cocktail bar side of connected coffeeshop,
the Cup & Saucer. A special "love-at-first-sight"
kind of place with rotating gallery art adorning
deep red walls. Simple, cozy, and nice.

Date visited: _____ **My Rating:** _____
Went with: _____
Favorites: _____
Not so much: _____
Other comments: _____
_____

The Richmond Bar

Hawthorne Map
3203 SE Division
(503) 208-3075
www.therichmondbar.com

Happy Hours
4:00-6:00pm Daily

Food Deals 2
$4.00–$10.00
Take $1.00 off anything you want on the menu.
All kinds of bar snacks, several salads or pastry
hand pies, plus mac & cheese, brats, garlic
burger, fish sandwich, or a veggie grinder.

Drink Specials 2
Keeping it simple with $1.00 off drinks too
Solid craft cocktails

Atmosphere 3
I love what they've done with the place! It's the
former Matchbox Lounge, now finding renewed
glory as an ultra-cool, vintage-style, old-school
bar. Red wallpaper, retro vinyl banquettes line
the wals, and gorgeous back bar. Order at the
bar as there's no table service right now.

Date visited: _____ **My Rating:** _____
Went with: _____
Favorites: _____
Not so much: _____
Other comments: _____
_____

Rum Club

9

Central Eastside Map
720 SE Sandy Blvd.
(503) 467-2469
www.rumclubpdx.com

Happy Hours
4:00-6:30pm Mon–Sat; ★5:00pm-mid Sunday

Food Deals 2
$2.00–$6.00
Classic cocktail nibbles that change weekly with
unique things like pickled eggs, soup, spiced
nuts, salads, or skewers.

Drink Specials 3
$6.00-$7.00 cocktails (choice of only five, but
they are so good they score top marks!)

Atmosphere 3
Simple but cool, retro-style lounge. Small place
with big horseshoe bar and barely-tropical wallpaper. Cocktail and regular tables, but sit at the
bartop where you can watch the masters at work!
Next door to the former (closed) Beaker & Flask.

Date visited: _____ **My Rating:** _____
Went with: _____
Favorites: _____
Not so much: _____
Other comments: _____
_____

Sapphire Hotel

Southeast Map
5008 SE Hawthorne
(503) 232-6333
www.thesapphirehotel.com

A Happy Hour favorite!

Happy Hours
4:00pm–6:00pm Daily
10:00pm-close Sun–Thurs

Food Deals 3
$3.00–$6.00
Meze platters, soup, several salads, artichoke dip, tandoori spiced chicken, salmon corncakes.

Drink Specials 3
$2.00 PBRs; $5.00 selected wine
$4.00 well drinks; $5.00-$6.00 cocktail specials

Atmosphere 3
Mysteriously sexy and intriguing; trés swanky!
Intimate creative lounge decor. Ex-brothel.
Outdoor sidewalk seating.

Date visited: _____ **My Rating:** _____
Went with: _____
Favorites: _____
Not so much: _____
Other comments: _____
_____

Sauvage

8

Southeast Map
537 SE Ash
(971) 258-5829
www.sauvagepdx.com

Happy Hours
5:00-6:00pm Mon–Fri

Food Deals 2
$2.00–$6.00
Unique eats to complement NW wine palates.
Seasonal changes with items like 1/2 dozen
oysters, wings, market salad, cheeses, pickles.

Drink Specials 2
$5.00 nightly wine special (Full menu has about
50 wines by the glass)

Atmosphere 3
Tucked away in a renovated, old industrial building,
the loft interior is intimate and cozy, with an
urban edge. Brick walls, white tiles, curtains to
soften, and hanging lights made of beer/wine
carboys. Next door to owner's own *Fausse Piste*
Winery.

Date visited: _____ **My Rating:** _____
Went with: _____
Favorites: _____
Not so much: _____
Other comments: _____
_____

Sok Sab Bai

8

Southeast Map
2625 SE 21st Ave. (at Clinton)
(971) 255-0292
www.soksabbai.com

Happy Hours
3:00-6:00pm Mon-Fri; ★All day Monday

Food Deals 3
$3.00–$6.00
Fresh, delicious and healthy choices! Cambodian favorites like banana blossom salad, egg rolls, grilled chicken, Draper Valley spicy wings, beef or tofu skewers, Cambodian sandwiches, and noodle soups.

Drink Specials 2
$1.00 off beer; $5.00 wines; $4.00 sake

Atmosphere 2
Former famous food cart now next to St. Jack's in an old neighborhood home. There's three rooms to sit, plus a private seating area to enjoy seiza-style, seated on floor mats. Simple decor with bright purple walls and bench cushions.

Date visited: _____ **My Rating:** _____

Went with: _____

Favorites: _____

Not so much: _____

Other comments: _____

St. Jack

Southeast Map
2039 SE Clinton
(503) 360-1281
www.stjackpdx.com

Happy Hours
4:00-5:00pm Daily

Food Deals 3
$3.00–$9.00
Classic French bistro hors d'oeuvres: charcuterie plate sampler, mussels, pommes frites, olives, gruyére burger, roasted beet salad; or if you're brave, try the fried tripe!

Drink Specials 3
$4.00 select draft beers; $5.00-$7.00 wines
$6.00-$8.00 choice of four cocktails

Atmosphere 3
Rustic, white, and open bistro space with front pâtisserie/bar area and two romantic restaurant rooms in back. Bright by day with sidewalk café seating, and characteristically candlelit by night. Oregonian's Rising Star 2011 — look for a 2nd location opening early 2014 at 1610 NW 23rd!

Date visited: _____ **My Rating:** _____
Went with: _____
Favorites: _____
Not so much: _____
Other comments: _____
_____

Sunshine Tavern

Southeast Map
3111 SE Division
(503) 688-1750
www.sunshinepdx.com

Happy Hours
5:00-6:00pm and 10:00-11:00pm Daily

Food Deals 3
$2.00–$6.00
Comfort/bar food with a NW-gourmet twist:
pickled eggs, chips, cheese fries with pork and
gravy, romaine salad, crispy oysters, ham &
swiss panini, corn dog, candied hazelnuts.

Drink Specials 3
$4.00 draft beer; $5.00 house wines
$6.00 slushy margarita
$5.00 bartender's choice cocktail

Atmosphere 3
Rain or shine, the sky-high windows let in lots of
light, and the wood walls and booths warm the
place up. After the sun sets, it takes on a totally
different, more intimate glow, perfect for indulging
those late-night munchie cravings.

Date visited: _____ **My Rating:** _____

Went with: _____

Favorites: _____

Not so much: _____

Other comments: _____

_____

TarBoush

Southeast Map
3257 SE Hawthorne
(503) 235-3277
www.tarboushbistro.com

Happy Hours
★ 2:00pm–6:00pm Mon-Fri

Food Deals 3
$4.00–$6.50 (plus $7.50–$12.00 platters)
Unique, mostly vegetarian, Lebanese appetizers
with several full-size meat dishes too: tabbouli,
hummus, baba ghannouj, fava and garbanzo
beans, soups, salad, cheeses, and stuffed pitas.
Desserts too!

Drink Specials 2
$1.00 off beer; $1.50 off wine; $2.00 off cocktails

Atmosphere 3
An absolutely gorgeous and giant Victorian
home on Hawthorne houses this funky and
lively Lebanese restaurant. Nice summer patio
area — and hookahs too!

Date visited: _____ **My Rating:** _____
Went with: _____
Favorites: _____
Not so much: _____
Other comments: _____
_____

Teote

Southeast Map
1615 SE 12th Ave.
(971) 888-5281
www.teotepdx.com

A Happy Hour favorite!

Happy Hours
3:00pm–6:00pm and 9:00-11:00pm Tues-Fri

Food Deals 0 No extra food deals, but it is very affordable, and very, *very* flavorful! Venezuelan-inspired street food. It's love at first sight! And taste. Years later, I've finally found my "new Limo"!

Drink Specials 2
$2.25 Tecates; $2.75 bottles; $.75 off drafts
$1.00 off mixed drinks

Atmosphere 3
This is one of those places I could just tell I'd love. Bright blue exterior, exquisite use of colors and wood textures inside. And a killer back patio that I want to pattern my backyard after! Teote means the end of the journey. They are new and just starting out, and I'm hoping they will add a great Happy Hour (food included), very soon, so I've included them in this book.

Date visited: _____ **My Rating:** _____
Went with: _____
Favorites: _____
Not so much: _____
Other comments: _____
_____

Three Doors Down

Southeast Map
1429 SE 37th Ave
(503) 236-6886
www.3doorsdowncafe.com

Happy Hours
★5:30–9:00pm Tues–Thur; 4:00–9:00pm Sun

Food Deals 3
$2.50–$10.00
Changing 15-item menu of delicious, Italian-focused specials like fettucine, tortiglione, spicy prawns, zuppa de mare, sausage & peppers, eggplant, daily lasagna, arancini, mac & cheese.

Drink Specials 2
$5.00 house wines; $6.00 manhattans / martinis (Beware $6.00 beers *not* included in Happy Hour, but you can get a Rolling Rock for $2.50)

Atmosphere 3
Just off Hawthorne, three doors down on 37th. The Happy Hour bar side is just off the cuter and quieter restaurant side, but has a similar, romantically social, wine bar vibe. Enjoy it all night!

Date visited: _____ **My Rating:** _____
Went with: _____
Favorites: _____
Not so much: _____
Other comments: _____
_____

Township & Range

Southeast Map
2422 SE Hawthorne
(503) 943-2120
www.trpdx.com

A Happy Hour favorite!

Happy Hours
4:00–6:00pm Daily

Food Deals 3
$3.00-$6.00
American diner-style food brought up to new heights: mac & cheese, several salads, brisket or fried chicken sandwiches, burgers, wings, hush puppies, steamed shellfish, paté.

Drink Specials 3
$3.50 drafts; $5.00 wine; $5.00 cocktails (3)

Atmosphere 3
The name is based on a land survey system mapping the Oregon Territory, and accordingly, the restaurant interior design elements include fascinating maps of all kinds. Impressive wood slat walls with a wonderful entrance map done by a local artist. Outside, there's a great patio!

Date visited: _____ **My Rating:** _____

Went with: _____

Favorites: _____

Not so much: _____

Other comments: _____

_____

Vie de Bohème

9

Southeast Map
1530 SE 7th Ave.
(503) 360-1233
www.viedebohemepdx.com

Happy Hours
4:00–7:00pm Tues–Fri

Food Deals 3
$1.95–$5.25
Smallplate menu with about a dozen items made
for sitting and sipping: nuts, olives, or chips;
baguettes with olive oil, brie or chèvre, ham or paté;
pork sliders; hummus; or cheese & salami plate.

Drink Specials 2
$3.00 bottles; $4.00 drafts; $1.00 off wine, wells,
and apéritifs (Recently added taps and full bar)

Atmosphere 3
An urban winery tucked inside a well-appointed
warehouse space. Central dance floor and
Oriental rug stage (big live music venue). Main
level seating with a second, elevated tier, plus a
cozy back wine tasting/library room. The *perfect*
place for parties!

Date visited: _____ **My Rating:** _____

Went with: _____

Favorites: _____

Not so much: _____

Other comments: _____

_____

Voicebox Karaoke
Southeast

A Happy Hour favorite!

Central Eastside Map
734 SE 6th Ave.
(503) 303-8220
www.voiceboxpdx.com

Happy Hours
4:00–7:00pm Thurs–Sun ($4.00/hr. Karaoke)
Tuesdays – $10.00 covers your karaoke cost!
★Wednesdays – All night Happy Hour

Food Deals 3 $1.00 off all menu items
Handy and sharable comfort food with a dash
of Asian influence. Lots of snacks and small
plates: Chicken or tofu bánh mì, quesadillas,
sandwiches, pizza, tots.

Drink Specials 3
$1.00 off all beer, wine, saké, and liquor cocktails
($3.50 micros, $5.00 house wines)

Atmosphere 3
Voicebox's newest location has everything that
makes the Northwest location great, plus a full
bar and *eight* karaoke suites. Each suite has big
TVs and two wireless mics. Features giant
murals by the amazing Souther Salazar!

Date visited: _____ **My Rating:** _____
Went with: _____
Favorites: _____
Not so much: _____
Other comments: _____
_____

White Owl Social Club

Southeast Map
1305 SE 8th Ave.
(503) 236-9672
www.whiteowlsocialclub.com

Happy Hours
3:00-6:00 and 11:00pm-1:00am Daily
(closed Mondays in the winter)

Food Deals 2
$5.00
Special appetizer menu, and they're sensitive
to the needs of those who eat gluten-free and/
or don't eat animals (though they have meat-
eater burgers and sandwiches too). Also a few
sandwiches for $1.00 off regular prices.

Drink Specials 2
$1.00 off drafts; $3.50 wells

Atmosphere 2
Part music venue, part hipster bar, with low-key
Happy Hour. Big open space with red checkerboard floors, long wall of windows, and black
walls. Great outdoor beer garden with firepit!

Date visited: _____ **My Rating:** _____
Went with: _____
Favorites: _____
Not so much: _____
Other comments: _____
_____

Wild Abandon

Southeast Map
2411 SE Belmont
(503) 232-4458
www.wildabandonrestaurant.com

Happy Hours
4:30–6:30pm Mon, Wed–Fri

A Happy Hour favorite!

Food Deals 3
$1.00-$7.00
Choose from about 15 gourmet specialties including shrimp or chicken with peppers over polenta, extra-delicious portobello sandwich(!), soup, burger, several salads, mac & cheese, BBQ pork sandwich, goat cheese torta, or fries.

Drink Specials 3
$2.00–$3.00 beer; $5.00 wine; $5.00 well drinks $5.00–$6.00 array of cocktail specialties

Atmosphere 3
A funky little "Love Shack" as viewed from the street; things change inside with cozy, dimly lit dining. Colorful, glass hanging lamps and a mish-mash of framed prints add to the garage-sale-chic, retro look. Wonderful garden patio in back!

Date visited: _____ **My Rating:** _____

Went with: _____

Favorites: _____

Not so much: _____

Other comments: _____

_____

Xico

8

Southeast (off Map)
3715 SE Division
(503) 548-6343
www.xicopdx.com

Happy Hours
5:00–6:00pm Mon–Fri

Food Deals 2
$2.00-$5.00
Some kind of sope (black bean, pork, or maybe chicken), Sonoran hot dog (about as good as a dog could be and with bacon), loaded chips.

Drink Specials 2
$3.00 Negra Modelo or Pacifico; $6.00 wines
$6.00 Margarita; $7.00 mezcal and a popsicle

Atmosphere 3
Minimalist-mod decor. Cooly hard-edged and contemporary, yet sleek, simple, and serene. Happy Hour no longer restricts us to only the bar area, and you can even enjoy it on their absolutely lovely back patio!

Date visited: _____ **My Rating:** _____

Went with: _____

Favorites: _____

Not so much: _____

Other comments: _____

_____

4-4-2 Soccer Bar www.442soccerbar.com

SE (off map) 1738 SE Hawthorne; (503) 238-3693

Happy Hours 3:00–7:00pm Mon–Fri

Food Deals 1 $3.00–$8.00 Few choices: cevapi/ sandwiches, skewers, artichoke dip.

Drink Specials 2 $2.00 PBR; $1.00 off drafts; $3.00 wells

Atmosphere 2 Well-loved soccer bar! Cozy and fun place with hanging soccer jerseys and memorabilia.

Aalto Lounge www.aaltolounge.com

Southeast Map 3356 SE Belmont (503) 235-6041

Happy Hours 5:00–7:00pm Daily ★

Food Deals 2 $2.00 Simple. Grilled cheese sandwiches with tomato soup or pretzel w/cheese.

Drink Specials 2 $2.00 off house cocktails (3) $10.00 wine bottle options

Atmosphere 2 Compelling and retro-y with artsy vibe, subtle funkiness, loungy ambience. Back patio.

Accanto

Southeast Map 2838 SE Belmont ; (503) 235-4900 www.accantopdx.com

Happy Hours Late-night Happy Hour only 10:00-11:00pm Daily ('til mid Fri-Sat)

Food Deals 3 $3.00–$10.00 Limited menu with items like olives, almonds, charcuterie, deviled eggs, green beans, spaghetti and meatballs, capellini.

Drink Specials 3 $3.50 microbrews; $5.00 red or white wine; $5.00 house-infused cocktail

Atmosphere 2 Next door and same owners as Genoa. Simple Northwest stylings found in many SE PDX foodie restaurants. Open kitchen and back private wine room.

Bar Avignon

Southeast Map 2138 SE Division; (503) 517-0808
www.baravignon.com

Happy Hours 5:00–6:00pm Mon–Fri

Food Deals 3 $2.00–$7.00 Ultra-fresh and gourmet
menu of 10 or so fancy items like mussels, salads,
mussels, marinated olives, daily charcuterie/cheese,
bourbon-caramel popcorn. Oysters on the half-shell.

Drink Specials 3 $4.00–$4.50 drafts (nice choices);
$5.00 wines; $5.50 wells; $5.00 select cocktail

Atmosphere 2 Small, industrial-fresh restaurant with
big bar and small, back table room surrounded by
wine. Coffee-shop-like by day, more romantic at night.

Biwa

Central Eastside 215 SE 9th Ave; (503) 239-8830
www.biwarestaurant.com

Happy Hours 5:00–6:00pm and 9:00-10:00pm Daily

Food Deals 1 $5.00 Ramen or udon deals only

Drink Specials 1 $3.00 Sapporo; $5.00 sake and wells

Atmosphere 2 Spartan NW foodie-style space in half-
basement. Must sit at counter facing open kitchen to
get Happy Hour pricing. Japanese tapas at tables.

Blitz Ladd www.blitzbarpdx.net

Southeast (off map) 2239 SE 11th Ave; (503) 236-3592

Happy Hours 3–6pm Mon-Fri; 9pm-close (food) Daily
(10:00pm-close Fri-Sat)

Food Deals 2 $3.00–$5.00 Similar bar food menu
as other Blitzes

Drink Specials 3 $3.50 drafts, wine, and wells

Atmosphere 2 Huge room with several seating areas.
Plenty of hi-def TVs (including 15 52" screens, plus
a giant 12 ft. projection screen). Plenty of tables and
couches too. Pool, shuffleboard and ping pong.

Blue Monk

Southeast Map 3341 SE Belmont; (503) 595-0575
www.thebluemonk.com

Happy Hours 5:00–7:00pm Daily

Food Deals 2 $5.50 for nice variety: shrimp tacos, bruschetta plate, coconut polenta, and subs.

Drink Specials 3 $3.00 for drafts; $3.00 wells
$5.50 house wine; $4.50 specialty cocktails

Atmosphere 2 Happy Hour downstairs where blue theme continues with pool and cool tunes.

Cha Cha Cha

Southeast Map 3433 SE Hawthorne; (503) 236-1100

Happy Hours 3:00–6:00pm and 8:30-10:00pm Daily

Food Deals 2 $4.00–$6.00 Array of Mexican basics: tostadas, fish tacos, quesadillas, tacos, soup, salads.

Drink Specials 3 $3.00 beer: $5.00 wine;
$5.00 Margaritas

Atmosphere 2 Part of the Cha Cha Cha family as represented with characteristic, southeast style. Very casual with a nice, covered patio just off the street.

Chez Machin Creperie

Southeast Map 3553 SE Hawthorne; (503) 736-9381
www.chezmachincreperie.com

Happy Hours 4:00–6:00pm Mon–Fri

Food Deals 0 No discounts

Drink Specials 2 $1.50 off all beer; $2.00 off wines

Atmosphere 3 Trés cute!!! Dripping with charm like a good creperie should be, with a patio too. Great crepes. Good crowd and low prices, so no need for food deals.

The Conquistador

Southeast Map 2045 SE Belmont; (503) 232-3227

Happy Hours 4:00–7:00pm Daily

Food Deals 1 Cheap food, but no discounts

Drink Specials 2 $3.00 micros; 3.50 wells

Atmosphere 3 I love the vibe here! It was formerly The Globe. It's still not a fancy place, but they opened up the upstairs with a living room lounge right out of the 60s and the whole place has vinyl, curved booths, conquistador paintings, and artifacts everywhere. It's definitely a bar, but they put lots of effort into theme.

Crush www.crushbar.com

Southeast Map 1412 SE Morrison; (503) 235-8150

Happy Hours 4:00–7:00pm Tues–Sun
★All day Tuesdays

Food Deals 3 $2.75–$5.75 Small menu of Happy Hour food: yams w/curry sauce (vegans love it), quesadillas, and flat nachos.

Drink Specials 3 $3.25 microbrews; $4.50 house wines $3.00–$3.50 wells; $4.50 cocktails

Atmosphere 2 Open, artsy lounge with stunning bottle chandelier; a favorite neighborhood hangout.

Delta Café

SE (Not on Map) 4607 SE Woodstock; (503) 771-3101
www.deltacafebar.com

Happy Hours 4:00–6:00pm Mon-Thur
★All night Tuesday includes $5.00 specialty cocktails

Food Deals 3 $3.00–$7.00 Half-priced starters like hush puppies, corn bread, fritters, mac & cheese.

Drink Specials 2 $3.00 drafts or wells (woo hoo!)

Atmosphere 2 They've decked themselves out with very colorful SE PDX-meets-Delta style! Loud, garish and fun with graffiti and folk art everywhere.

Dig a Pony   www.digaponyportland.com

Central Eastside 736 SE Grand Ave.; (971) 279-4409

Happy Hours 4:00–7:00pm Daily

Food Deals 2 $3.00 Small menu of unique bar eats: fried plantains, Cubano sandwich, arugula and pear salad, fries, nuts, churro dessert.

Drink Specials 2 $3.00 choice of drafts; $3.00 wells

Atmosphere 3 Dig the atmosphere. Cool space! Brick walls, big windows, and book nooks, in a giant, rustic-loft style room. Appropriately, there's a very large, horseshoe-shaped bar in the middle. A popular crowd scene, can be loud, and very dark.

Doug Fir   www.dougfirlounge.com

Central Eastside 830 E Burnside; (503) 231-9663

Happy Hours 3:00–6:00pm Daily

Food Deals 2 $2.00–$6.00 Lots of hearty comfort food: burgers, salads, bread pudding, cheese fries.

Drink Specials 3 $3.00 drafts, wine, wells

Atmosphere 3 Twin Peaks meets the Sinatra 50s in classy-kitsch, Northwest lodge theme; couch pits for groups; outdoor patio seating. Order at the bar. Great place to see bands downstairs!

Eastburn   www.theeastburn.com

Central Eastside 1800 E Burnside; (503) 236-2876

Happy Hour 4:00-6:00pm Daily

Food Deals 2 $5.00 Five for five seasonal and fresh menu items: autumn may bring spaetzle, spinach and pear salad, BLTs, elk sliders or red pepper fritters.

Drink Specials 2 $3.50 drafts ($2.50 on Tuesdays) $5.00 wine; $6.00 cocktail

Atmosphere 2 Very casual local place that's more of a bar with one exception – excellent food. There's a true bar in the basement, and great patio with swings!

Gold Dust Meridian

Southeast Map 3267 SE Hawthorne; (503) 239-1143
www.golddustmeridian.com

Happy Hours ★2:00–8:00pm Daily

Food Deals 2 $4.00–$6.00 Huge menu of 16 items
follows period style and includes deviled eggs, grilled
cheese trio (served with soup and salad), green beans,
quesa sundido, fritters, salami plate, mac & cheese.

Drink Specials 2 .50 cents off pints & wells; $1.00 off wine
Daily bartender cocktail special

Atmosphere 3 Marathon Happy Hour joint with a
dark interior that is steeped deep in authentic retro
charm and is at once swanky, chill, and ultra-cool.

Goodfoot

Central Eastside 2845 SE Stark; (503) 239-9292
www.thegoodfoot.com

Happy Hours 5:00–9:00pm Daily

Food Deals 2 $5.00 Select menu items with semi-
healthy pub food. Menu items under $7.00 at all times.

Drink Specials 2 $$2.00 off pitchers; $1.00 off cocktails

Atmosphere 2 Big, open space showcases local artist
rotating galleries and four red felt pool tables (free!).

Hawthorne Fish House

Southeast Map 4343 SE Hawthorne; (503) 548-4434
www.corbettfishhouse.com

Happy Hours 3:00–6:00pm Daily ('til 5:00pm Fri-Sat)

Food Deals 2 $3.95 Wow! Gluten-free fish & chips!
Big menu with fish tacos, catfish sliders, clam or
chicken strips, Caesar salad, and shrimp cocktail,
calamari, shooters, fried oysters, cheese curds, fries.

Drink Specials 2 $4.00 imperial pints, wine and wells

Atmosphere 2 Kinda cute, kinda kitsch-fishy. Café-like
atmosphere with salmon-pink walls adorned with lots
of colorful seafood life.

Hobnob Grille

Southeast Map 3350 SE Morrison; (503) 445-3665
www.hobnobgrille.com

Happy Hours 4:00-7:00pm Daily; mid-2:30am Fri-Sat
★4:00-10:00pm Sunday

Food Deals 2 $2.00–$6.00 Bar food taken up a notch:
sliders (four kinds), chicken wrap, artichoke dip, baby
back ribs, wings, fried pickles or mozzarella sticks.

Drink Specials 2 $4.00 wine; $3.00 cocktail of the day

Atmosphere 2 Very basic interior, almost diner-like in
style. Neutrals, big bar, ping pong. Friendly staff, and
a great place for groups of all sizes.

Iron Horse www.portlandironhorse.com

SE (off map) 6034 SE Milwaukie; (503) 232-1826

Happy Hours 3:00–6:00pm Tues–Sun

Food Deals 2 $3.00–$5.00 Delicious Mexican food:
nachos, salad, bean dip, tacos, poppers, taco salad.

Drink Specials 2 $2.50 domestics; $3.50 microbrews
$3.00 wells; $4.95 margarita

Atmosphere 2 Colorful neighborhood hangout. Choice
of bar, restaurant, or sidewalk seating. Family friendly.

✳ ✳ Remember to check our website
every once in a while for changes and closures.

www.happyhourguidebook.com

And please let us know if you see
information that needs changing.

Landmark Saloon

SE (off map) 4847 SE Division; (503) 894-8132
www.thelandmarksaloon.com

Happy Hours 4:00–7:00pm Mon–Fri; 10:00pm-2:00am
Daily(food)

Food Deals 1 $1.00 off bar menu late-night

Drink Specials 1 $.50 off drafts and wells

Atmosphere 2 Casual, borderline dive-y and locally
loved, neighborhood saloon. Yes – truly a saloon,
country tunes and all. Big outdoor patio with "corn hole."

Le Merde www.montageportland.com

Central East Side 301 SE Morrison; (503) 234-1324

Happy Hours 5:00–6:00pm Daily

Food Deals 2 $4.00–$6.00 Basics from Montage
next door: sevral kinds of mac & cheese, two kinds of
gumbo or hushpuppies, red beans & rice.

Drink Specials 3 $4.00 draft beers, wine and wells
$1.00 off specialty cocktails

Atmosphere 1 Dark and different from adjacent
restaurant, Montage (which is kinda cute), Le Merde
is the lounge side (which is kinda grungy, but cool).

Mad Greek Deli www.madgreekdeli.com

Lloyd Center Map 1740 E. Burnside; (503) 232-0274
<u>Hillsboro:</u> 18450 NW West Union; (503) 645-1650

Happy Hours 4:00–6:00pm Mon–Fri

Food Deals 3 $1.00–$5.00 A dozen cheap and tasty
options: GREEK fries, souvlaki, Greek salad, hummus,
spanakopita, tots, gyros, Greek style pizza, feta fries.

Drink Specials 3 $1.00 off drafts; $4.00 wines
$3.00 wells; $4.00–$6.00 cocktail of the day

Atmosphere 2 Sportsbar-like back area with colorful
team scarves strewn overhead, several big-screen
TVS, and a lively, open bar. Hillsboro location a bit
darker, with counter orders and back bar.

Madison's www.madisonsgrill.com

SE (off map) 1109 SE Madison; (503) 230-2471

Happy Hours
★3:00–6:00pm and 9:00–10:00pm Mon-Sat
$2.50 Tuesdays = 16 taps w/ microbrew deal all night

Food Deals 2 $3.00-$5.00 Cheeseburger, onion
rings, hot wings, tacos, nachos, sliders,chips, tots.

Drink Specials 2 Beers are 75 cents off
$2.75 well drinks; $4.00 select house wines

Atmosphere 2 Friendly, casual hang-out place; brass-
and fern- family style; outdoor wood deck. Free pool!

Muddy Rudder

Southeast (Off Map) 8195 SE 7th Ave; (503) 233-4410
www.muddyrudderpdx.com

Happy Hours 4:00–6:00pm Daily

Food Deals 2 $5.00 Pizza, soup and salad, soup and
half sandwich, or bruschetta.

Drink Specials 3 $3.00 drafts; $4.50 wine; $3.75 wells

Atmosphere 2 Nice, nautical, neighborhood pub.
Cozy, converted home was a true labor of love. Great
place to see live music, and excellent side patio!

Nightlight Lounge

Southeast Map 2100 SE Clinton; (503) 731-6500
www.nightlightlounge.net

Happy Hours ★2:00–7:00pm Daily (3-7pm Sat–Sun)
11:00pm–1:00am Sun–Thurs

Food Deals 2 $3.00–$5.00 Soup, salad, grilled cheese,
Caesar salad, quesadilla, mac & cheese, nachos.

Drink Specials 2 $4.00 microbrews; $1.50 PBRs;
$.50 off well drinks; $1.00 off wine

Atmosphere 2 Artsy, casual, and comfortable,
yet trendy; outdoor dining on nice back deck.

Por Que No

Southeast Map 4635 SE Hawthorne; (503) 954-3138

Happy Hours 3:00–6:00pm Daily; Tues 3:00pm–close

Food Deals 1 $.50 cents off tacos; $1.00 off chips & guac or salsa. Cheap menu at all times!

Drink Specials 2 $.50 cents-$1.50 off beer, horchatas, Margaritas, and rum drinks

Atmosphere 2 A true taqueria vibe, complete with loud music, warm colors, and noisy kitchen ramblings.

Produce Row Café

Central Eastside Map 204 SE Oak St.; (503) 232-8355 www.producerowcafe.com

Happy Hours 4:00-7:00pm and 11:00pm–2:00am (food) Daily ; No late-night HH on Sunday

Food Deals 2 $4.00–$5.00 Small menu with food that goes well with beer: mac & cheese, soup, poutine, burger, sausage, salad.

Drink Specials 2 $1.00 off pints, wine, and wells

Atmosphere 3 Turn-of-the-century beer hall charm mixed with urban Portland vibe. Gorgeous, mahogany front bar with beer selections written on giant mirror. Tin ceilings, wooden beams, tables, and floors.

Que Pasa Cantina

SE (not on Map) 1408 SE 12th Ave.; (503) 230-9212 www.quepasacantinapdx.com

Happy Hours 5:00–6:00pm Mon–Wed; 4:00–6.00pm Thur–Fri; 3:00–6:00pm Sat

Food Deals 2 $5.00 Simple range of the usual but popular, Mexican eats.

Drink Specials 2 $2.00 PBRs / Tecates; $3.00 drafts $3.00 sangria; $4.00 wells; $5.00 Margaritas

Atmosphere 2 Formerly Aqui Mexican. Can't always judge a book by its cover – it's shockingly cute inside! Authentic Mexican taqueria that's quite cozy.

Savoy Tavern www.savoypdx.com

SE Map 2500 SE Clinton; (503) 808-9999

Happy Hours 4:00–6:00pm &10:00pm–close Daily

Food Deals 2 $3.00–$8.00 Nostalgic Americana menu with their famous fried cheese curds, burgers, salad, wings, fries, smoked trout, deviled eggs, mac & cheese.

Drink Specials 3 $4.00 beer; $5.00 wine; $3.50 wells; $5.00 cocktails – plus nightly specials

Atmosphere 2 The bar has character! Kitschy 1950s lodge look by day, but cute & romantic candlelit at night.

Slow Bar www.slowbar.net

Central East Side 533 SE Grand; (503) 230-7767

Happy Hours 3–6pm Mon–Fri; mid–close Sun–Thurs

Food Deals 2 $1.50–$5.50 Pizzetta, green salad, mixed nuts, fries, ceviche, Southern fry, olives. Just get the burger!

Drink Specials 2 $1.00 off all drinks

Atmosphere 2 Dark and smoky, popular, laid-back hipster scene; all black; group seating at window.

Star Bar www.star-bar-rocks.com

Southeast Map 639 SE Morrison; (503) 232-5553

Happy Hours 4:00–7:00pm Daily

Food Deals 3 $2.00-$5.00 There's true dedication to really fresh, seasonal food here! Several stellar sliders, skewers, salads, burgers, tots, fries.

Drink Specials 2 $1.50 PBR; $3.00 micros $5.00 house wines; $3.00 wells

Atmosphere 3 The old Maiden shines on with more of a no-frills, dive bar tone and velvet paintings. Best at night with candlelight and lounge couches.

Out & About

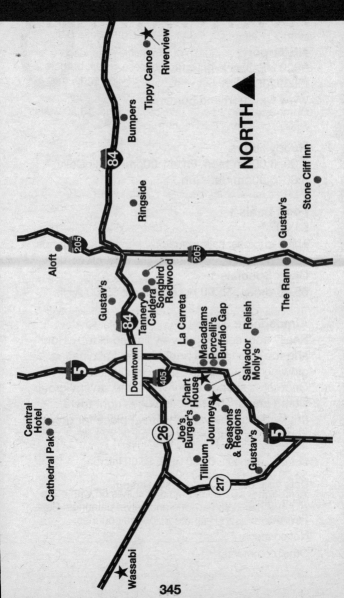

NORTH

Tippy Canoe
Riverview
Bumpers
84
Ringside
205
Aloft
205
Stone Cliff Inn
Gustav's
Gustav's
Tannery
Songbird
Caldera
Redwood
84
La Carreta
The Ram
Macadams
Porcelli's
Buffalo Gap
Relish
Salvador
Molly's
5
Downtown
405
Central
Hotel
Joe's
Burger's
Chart
House
26
Tillicum
Journeys
Seasons
& Regions
Gustav's
Cathedral Park
5
217
Wassabi

Aloft Wxyz Bar

NE/Airport
9920 NE Cascade Parkway
(503) 200-5678
www.wxyzportland.com

Happy Hours
4:00–6:00pm Mon–Fri; 11:00pm–close Daily
5:00–6:00pm Sat–Sun

Food Deals 1
$4.00
Three choices: salsa, guac & chips; tots; hummus.

Drink Specials 1
$5.00 drafts; $5.00 house wines; $5.00 wells

Atmosphere 3+
Really cool space, but very limited Happy Hour
and too open to the bright lobby. Fascinating
glowing bar top puts on its own lightshow.
Geometric shapes everywhere and several group
sitting areas. The MAX line goes right there
(tricky directions via car). Great place for groups
and parties. Check website for live music.

Date visited: _____ **My Rating:** _____

Went with: _____

Favorites: _____

Not so much: _____

Other comments: _____

_____

Buffalo Gap

Southwest/Macadam
6835 SW Macadam
(503) 244-7111
www.thebuffalogap.com

Happy Hours
4:00–6:00pm & 10:00pm–mid Daily
★1:00pm–mid Sunday

Food Deals 3
$2.95–$3.95
Ten of the best basic bar food standards, like
build-your-own tacos, pita pizzas, nachos, BBQ
pork sliders, quesadillas, and chips.

Drink Specials 1
Nightly specials that vary; many revolving
around NFL, Trail Blazers and college games.

Atmosphere 2
Reminiscent of a small-town tourist pub in dining
area; meandering rooms with some down-home
touches; TVs/sports.

Date visited: _____ **My Rating:** _____
Went with: _____
Favorites: _____
Not so much: _____
Other comments: _____
_____

Bumpers

Far Northeast near Edgefield's
21935 NW Halsey; Fairview
(503) 618-1855
www.bumpersgrill.com

Happy Hours
3:00–6:00pm & 9:00pm–close Daily
★All day Sunday

Food Deals 3
$2.95–$4.95
Big menu with several offerings at each price
point: Onion rings, soup, Caesar, fries, calamari,
potato skins, BBQ chicken quesadilla, buffalo
wings, french dip, prawn cigars, BBQ ribs.

Drink Specials 3
$1.00 off draft beers; $4.00 wine; $4.00 wells
$3.00 Margaritas; plus occasional nightly specials

Atmosphere 3
It's in a small strip mall, but it's a nice fine-dining
restaurant. Impressive and giant, 18-foot-long(!),
900-gallon aquarium defining the bar. Two long
rows of bar stools, but only four four-tops, so get
there early. Reservations for groups. Patio seating.

Date visited: _____ **My Rating:** _____

Went with: _____

Favorites: _____

Not so much: _____

Other comments: _____

_____

Caldera Public House

8

Southeast/Mt. Tabor
6031 SE Stark
(503) 233-8242
www.calderapublichouse.com

Happy Hours
5:00–6:00pm & 9:00pm–close Daily

Food Deals 2
$3.00–$9.00
Short list of bar menu items like fries, tots, garlic
bread, hummus plate, calamari, coconut shrimp.

Drink Specials 2
$1.00 off pints, wine, wells and cocktails
$2.00 off pitchers

Atmosphere 3
Kinda hidden over in the far east, but this little
Montavilla neighborhood is continuing to sprout
some new favorites. Inside a turn-of-the-century,
two-story drugstore, Caldera reminds me both
of my old Chicago taverns and some in Ireland.
It has character! And a great back deck too.

Date visited: _____ **My Rating:** _____
Went with: _____
Favorites: _____
Not so much: _____
Other comments: _____
_____

Cathedral Park Kitchen

St. John's
6635 N Baltimore Ave.
(503) 946-8426
www.cathedralparkrestaurant.com

Happy Hours
4:00-6:00pm Mon-Fri

Food Deals 3
$4.00-$8.00 ($2.00 off all small plates -14 items)
International menu of nibbles and meals: ceviche,
scallops, steak bites, spring rolls, samosas,
pan seared broccoli, mushrooms, asparagus,
or brussel sprouts, yucca fries, eggplant w/goat
cheese.

Drink Specials 3
$3.00 beer (bottles): $6.00 wine; $2.00 off cocktails

Atmosphere 3
Unique and gorgeous view of the St. John's
Bridge, the Willamette river, and Forest Park
across the way! Low-key, simple space with
stark white walls with a wall of windows in a
narrow room. New owners, new black tables
and chairs, and changing artwork. Patio.

Date visited: _____ **My Rating:** _____

Went with: _____

Favorites: _____

Not so much: _____

Other comments: _____

_____

The Central Hotel

St. John's
8608 N Lombard
(503) 477-5489
www.centralhotelstjohns.com

Happy Hours
4:00-7:00pm and 10:00pm-close Mon-Fri
★All day Sunday

Food Deals 2
$4.00-$8.00
$1.00 off small plates menu: Most importantly,
cheddar, chives, and bacon smashed potatoes!
Two kinds of ries, mezza plate, goat cheese
gnocchi, fritters, pigs in a blanket, beef tips
skewers, gravlox and latke, and chicken strips.

Drink Specials 3
$3.50 beer: $4.00 wine; $1.00 off cocktails

Atmosphere 3
Relaxed dining and cocktail lounge atmosphere.
Gorgeous vintage-style bar! Nice place that was
soooo needed in St. Johns. Big back room for
bands and kids. Future plans to build a four-
story boutique hotel, hence the name.

Date visited: _____ **My Rating:** _____
Went with: _____
Favorites: _____
Not so much: _____
Other comments: _____
_____

Chart House

10

Near OHSU
5700 SW Terwilliger Blvd
(503) 246-6963
www.chart-house.com

Happy Hours
4:00–7:00pm Daily

A Happy Hour favorite!

Food Deals 3
$4.00–$6.00
Three options at $4.00, $5.00 or $6.00 each:
bruschetta, artichoke hearts, firecracker shrimp,
hummus, prime rib sliders, tacos and calamari.

Drink Specials 3
$4.00 drafts; $5.00 selection of red or white wines
$4.00 wells; $6.00 cocktails; $7.00 martinis

Atmosphere 3
Wow! Definitely one of the best views in the city,
especially on a clear day when you can see Mt.
Hood and Mt. Adams through the floor-to-ceiling,
wall-to-wall windows. Happy Hour is downstairs
in the lounge. Cozy fireplace for winter warmth.
Free valet parking.

Date visited: _____ **My Rating:** _____
Went with: _____
Favorites: _____
Not so much: _____
Other comments: _____
_____

Gustav's

•••••••••••••••••••

Several Locations:
5035 NE Sandy Blvd. (503) 288-5503
12605 SE 97th Ave. (503) 653-1391
10350 SW Greenburg Rd, Tigard (503) 639-4544
1705 SE 164th Ave, Vancouver (360) 883-0222
www.gustavs.net

Happy Hours
3:00–6:00pm and 9:00pm–close Daily

Food Deals 3
$1.99–$5.99
A large array of German specialties and other
hardy, old stand-bys: reuben or shepard's pie,
fish & chips, burgers, schnitzel strips, chicken
skewers, swiss fondue, sliders, potato pancakes.

Drink Specials 0
Only the Vancouver location offers drink specials
(see page 418).

Atmosphere 3
With some imagination and a couple beers from
the strong and authentic European tap line-ups,
you too, can be transported to a genuine Bavarian
bierstube. Gold star for pushing the concept.

Date visited: _____ **My Rating:** _____
Went with: _____
Favorites: _____
Not so much: _____
Other comments: _____
_____

Joe's Burgers

Multnomah Villiage
4439 SW Beaverton-Hillsdale Hwy.
(503) 892-6686
www.joesburgers.com

Downtown: 625 SW 4th Ave.; 503-248-5637
PSU: 540 SW College; (503) 432-8022
Bridgeport: 7409 SW Bridgeport; (503) 598-1111

Happy Hours
3:00–6:00pm and 9:00pm–close Mon–Sat
★All day Sunday

Food Deals 2
$2.00–$4.00
Great burgers, but not on HH menu :-(About
a dozen cheap bar bites like tacos, chili cheese
fries, salads, pizza, mac & cheese bites, chips.

Drink Specials 3
$3.00 drafts; $4.00 wine; $5.00 special cocktails

Atmosphere 3
The old Jopa. Happy Hour is on the patio out
back, or in the bar only (basically a nondescript,
simple room). Overall, outstanding burger joints!

Date visited: _____ **My Rating:** _____
Went with: _____
Favorites: _____
Not so much: _____
Other comments: _____
_____

Journeys

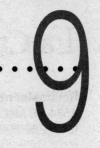

9

Multnomah Villiage
7771 SW Capitol Hwy.
(503) 245-4573
www.journeyspdx.com

Happy Hours
4:00–7:00pm Mon–Sat

Food Deals 3
$5.00–$6.50
Some fresh alternatives too, but they are most famous for their grilled cheese bites (four styles), cheddar and apple plate, hummus, black bean hummus, salad with chicken, soup & salad, artichoke & jalapeno dip, and a charcuterie plate.

Drink Specials 2
$3.50 select beer; $5.00 red or white wines

Atmosphere 3
This is a generous three points, but people *love* it here like it was their own home! It's actually in a cute house – on a tiny hill – with a wonderful outdoor front patio. They have many regulars who are very passionate about this place for its friendliness, games, and wine and beer selections.

Date visited: _____ **My Rating:** _____

Went with: _____

Favorites: _____

Not so much: _____

Other comments: _____

_____

La Carretta

9

Southeast near Sellwood
4534 SE McLoughlin Blvd
(503) 236-8089

Happy Hours
3:00–6:00pm Mon–Fri; 9:00pm–mid Sun–Tues

Food Deals 3
$1.00–$3.00
Less than a dollar each for some decent Mexican food, albeit a bit on the Americanized, greasy side. Less than a dollar each for many items. Small chalkboard menu: taco, enchilada, salad, bean dip, soup or fries. Free chips and salsa!

Drink Specials 3
$1.45 domestics; $1.99 wells and Margaritas! Ask about a cocktail special of the day.

Atmosphere 3
Strikingly bright and colorful exterior! Very festive and traditional Mexican restaurant with tiled table tops, stucco walls, arches, hand-painted murals, a peek at the river, and a drunken parrot.

Date visited: _____ **My Rating:** _____
Went with: _____
Favorites: _____
Not so much: _____
Other comments: _____
_____

Macadams

Southwest/Macadam
5833 SW Macadam
(503) 246-6227
www.macadamsbarandgrill.com

Happy Hours
3:00–6:00pm and 10:00pm–mid Daily
★All night Sunday (3:00–close)

Food Deals 3
$3.00–$6.00
Big bar menu includes pulled pork sliders,
cheeseburger, or chicken strips with fries; brat,
jalapeno-artichoke dip, Buffalo wrap, Caesar,
mac & cheese, tacos, bean dip, calamari.

Drink Specials 3
$4.00 drafts; $4.00 wines; $3.50 wells

Atmosphere 3
Lofted lodge effect with traditional manly-man
tans and browns. Plenty of TVs for watching
your favorite games. Outdoor patio area. Family
friendly in restaurant until 8:00pm.

Date visited: _____ **My Rating:** _____
Went with: _____
Favorites: _____
Not so much: _____
Other comments: _____
_____

Osaka-ya

North/NE Map
7007 SW MacAdam Ave.
(503) 293-1066

Happy Hours
3:00–6:30pm Mon–Fri
★Noon–6:30pm Sat–Sun

Food Deals 3
$2.50–$5.50
Eleven sushi rolls plus ten appetizers! California, Oregon, albacore, tuna and salmon, spicy tuna or salmon, eel and avocado, or all vegetable. Plus, salads, edamame, veggie tempura, gyoza, chicken skewers, salmon roll, and soups. *And* chicken or salmon rice bowls.

Drink Specials 0
Sadly, no drink deals

Atmosphere 2 Driving up, you'll see this white, authentic Japanese house, and inside, the restaurant is pretty nice too. Happy Hour is in the very basic bar though, so lacks the personality going on elsewhere here. Unbeatable food deals though, and at lunchtime on weekends!

Date visited: _____ **My Rating:** _____
Went with: _____
Favorites: _____
Not so much: _____
Other comments: _____
_____

Porcelli's

• • • • • • • • • • • • • • • •

8

North/NE Map
6500 SW Virginia Ave.
(503) 245-2260
www.porcellisristorante.com

Happy Hours
3:00–6:00pm Daily; ★All night Tuesday ('til 9:00pm)

Food Deals 3
$2.00–$5.00
No way! An 8" pizza with four toppings for only
$4.00! Plus, all kinds of other good stuff (and
cheap too): spaghetti, pastrami sub, steamed
clams, antipasto plate, bruschetta, salads, soup.

Drink Specials 2
$1.00 off all drinks

Atmosphere 2
Porcelli's Ristorante & Bar opened in 2009 and
is located in the old Porcelli Grocery on the corner.
There's a big open space when you first walk in,
a long open kitchen, and the bar area is in the
back, so it has a rather awkward layout. Caught
between fancy and casual, it's nice for the area, and
has that Italian romance vibe going after dark.

Date visited: _____ **My Rating:** _____

Went with: _____

Favorites: _____

Not so much: _____

Other comments: _____

_____

Redwood

North/NE Map
7915 SE Stark
(503) 841-5118
www.redwoodpdx.com

Happy Hours
5:00–6:00pm and 10:00pm-close Daily

Food Deals 3
$2.00–$5.00
Chef-owned and loved and it shows (from Broder). Really great line up with spins on some basics like wings, fritters, grilled cheese or pork sandwich; plus some unique items like braised tongue or pork shank sandwiches, fried brussel sprouts., or a veggie burger with yams.

Drink Specials 3
$1.00 off drafts or wine; $3.00 wells

Atmosphere 3
Cool space and beautiful bar! Bright red walls and walls of redwood. High, exposed ceilings, reddish-wood tables and chairs, open kitchen.

Date visited: _____ **My Rating:** _____
Went with: _____
Favorites: _____
Not so much: _____
Other comments: _____
_____

Relish

10

6637 SE Milwaukie Ave
(503) 208-3442
www.relishgastropub.com

Happy Hours
3:00–6:00pm Tues-Sun

Food Deals 3
$3.00–$7.00
Farm-fresh Northwest nibbles like creamed
butter beans, sautéed green beans, grilled
asparagus, chicken penne, sausage meatballs,
bibb lettuce salad, ciabatta bread, olives, and
potato croquettes.

Drink Specials 3
$1.00 off drafts (20 taps!), wines and wells
$6.00 daily cocktail

Atmosphere 3
Cozy and home-like with several traditional-
style dining rooms, and active bar, and a great
summer patio through double french doors.
Sellwood *needed* this wonderful gastropub!

Date visited: _____ **My Rating:** _____

Went with: _____

Favorites: _____

Not so much: _____

Other comments: _____

_____

Ringside Glendoveer

10 ★

Glendoveer
14021 NE Glisan
(503) 255-0750
www.ringsidesteakhouse.com

Happy Hours
3:00–6:00 pm and 8:30pm–close Daily
★11:30am-6:00pm Sat; 11:30am-10:00pm Sun

Food Deals 3
$2.25-5.95
15 menu items: steak bites (YUM!), calamari,
wings, prime rib dip, crab cake, ground steak
burger, chili poppers, garlic bread, Caesar salad,
oysters on the half shell, flatbread, steamed clams.

Drink Specials 3
$5.00 microbrew draft beers, red or white wine,
select well drinks, margaritas or Manhattan

Atmosphere 3
Less dramatic, but bigger and more open than
downtown location with dark, wood paneling
and wall-to-wall windows. Big, open fireplace.
Views of on-site golf course. Great enclosed
patio with wonderful outdoor seating all around!

Date visited: _____ **My Rating:** _____
Went with: _____
Favorites: _____
Not so much: _____
Other comments: _____
_____

Salvador Molly's

Hillsdale (NW of Multnomah Village)
1523 SW Sunset Blvd.
(503) 293-1790
www.salvadormollys.com

Happy Hours
4:00–6:00pm Daily

Food Deals 3
$2.50

A Happy Hour favorite!

YUM!! Unique nibbles from around the globe!
Revolving menu hosts BBQ pork sliders, Caesar
salad, Thai tofu salad, Indian chickpea crepe, or
a veggie quinoa salad. Bold flavors!

Drink Specials 2
$1.00 off drafts; $4.00 cocktail of the day

Atmosphere 3
International fun and flair! Bold vibrant colors in
both food and decor. Entire walls and table tops
are covered in worldly memorabilia. Happy Hour
in bar side only or outside on the deck.

Date visited: _____ **My Rating:** _____
Went with: _____
Favorites: _____
Not so much: _____
Other comments: _____
_____

Seasons & Regions

Just North of Multnomah Village
6660 SW Capitol Hwy
(503) 244-6400
www.seasonsandregions.com

Happy Hours
3:00-5:30pm Daily; 8:30-9:30pm Mon-Sat
8:00-9:00pm Sun

Food Deals 3
$2.95
Seasonal menu (but of course) changes monthly
with sizeable and low-priced portions of items like
smoked salmon, salads, pork sope, Cuban ham
wrap, sloppy joes, fried chicken, or pastas. Many
gluten-free and vegetarian options on regular menu.

Drink Specials 0
Sadly, no drink specials

Atmosphere 3
Sweet café inside, nice tented patio outside.
Has more of a breakfast/lunch bistro vibe with
buttercream walls and well-worn wooden booths.

Date visited: _____ **My Rating:** _____
Went with: _____
Favorites: _____
Not so much: _____
Other comments: _____
_____

Songbird

9

Near Montavilla
6839 SE Belmont
(503) 477-6735
www.songbirdpdx.com

Happy Hours
3:00-5:30pm Tues–Fri

Food Deals 3
$4.00–$7.00
Fresh, seasonal, and tasty treats like roasted
beets or brussel sprouts, salad, fries, ham &
cheese croquettes, quesadilla, burger, portobella
or pulled pork sandwich.

Drink Specials 3
$3.50 drafts (rotating local taps); $6.00 wine
$4.00 wells; $5.00 cocktail-of-the-day

Atmosphere 3
A sweet little neighborhood eatery. Cuteness!
Pretty, new patterned woods throughout, blue
cushioned seats, red barstools, and other white
accents. Sidewalk dining. And put a bird in it –
ask for a signature songbird latte!

Date visited: _____ **My Rating:** _____
Went with: _____
Favorites: _____
Not so much: _____
Other comments: _____
_____

Stone Cliff Inn

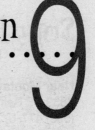

Oregon City east of Clackamas
17900 S Clackamas River Dr.
(503) 631-7900
www.stonecliffinn.com

Happy Hours
3:00-6:00 Mon-Fri

Food Deals 3
$3.00–$6.00
All kinds of happy food: several soups, salads, and sliders, salmon cake, skewers, burger, fries, onion rings, hummus, oysters, calamari.

Drink Specials 2
$4.00-$5.00 beer; $4.00-$5.00 wine; $6.00 wells

Atmosphere 3
Perched up high atop a big, stony cliff with beautiful views of the river and valley below. Parts of the movie "Twilight" filmed here (check facebook pics if you're a fan)! Log cabin lodge with upscale dining. Happy Hour in lounge area.

Date visited: _____ **My Rating:** _____
Went with: _____
Favorites: _____
Not so much: _____
Other comments: _____
_____

The Tannery Bar

8

Only a bit farther out East
5425 E Burnside
(503) 236-3610
www.tannerybarpdx.com

Happy Hours
5:00-7:00pm Daily

Food Deals 2
$4.00-$8.00
Northwest bar trends like olives, house salad,
sheep cheese, fries, Spansih tortilla, truffled
filberts, NW charcuterie plate, ham & brie sando.

Drink Specials 3
$2.00 Rainiers; $4.00 drafts; $5.00 wine
$5.00-$7.00 cocktail of the day

Atmosphere 2
A classic example that represents the NW
bar scene to a T. Overall, a tan color scheme,
reclaimed woods, cement floors, simple and
unpretentious, open kitchen, long community
table, and lit by gas lights.

Date visited: _____ **My Rating:** _____
Went with: _____
Favorites: _____
Not so much: _____
Other comments: _____
_____

Tillicum

8

Raleigh Hills area
8585 SW Beaverton-Hillsdale Hwy.
503-327-8147

Happy Hours
3:00-6:00pm Daily; ★All day Sunday
9:00-11:00pm Mon-Thur

Food Deals 2
$2.99-$5.99
Big menu with more than 15 items. The full bounty
of bar foods with mac & cheese, chips & salsa,
tots, fries, onion rings, wings, sliders, burgers,
veggie plate, sandwich w/soup or salad.

Drink Specials 3
$3.00-3.50 drafts; $4.00 wines; $3.50 wells
$4.50-$5.50 cocktails

Atmosphere 2
Tillicum opened in 1870 as a log cabin tavern, and
has been going strong every since. Recently
purchased by native Oregonians who really know
the bar business. Explore and discover the newly
"rescued" Tilly! Old school meets new vibe.

Date visited: _____ **My Rating:** _____
Went with: _____
Favorites: _____
Not so much: _____
Other comments: _____
_____

Wassabi

10

Hillsboro (Near Tanasbourne)
1861 NW 188th Ave
(503) 747-2354
www.wassabipdx.com

Happy Hours
3:00–6:45pm Daily; 9:00pm–close Mon–Sat

Food Deals 3
$1.00–$5.00
More than 20 delicious Pan-Asian delights! All the
basics plus lots more: springrolls, calamari, rolls
(California, spicy tuna, shrimp, salmon), nachos,
coconut shrimp, veggie tempura, wings, sliders,
chili cheddar fried burrito.

Drink Specials 3
$3.00 domestics; $4.00 micros; $5.00 wines
$4.00 sake; $4.00 wells; $5.00 martinis

Atmosphere 3
Three great spots for Happy Hour! Relax out
on the giant wrap-around patio, in the Ginger
Room Lounge, a contemporary sports bar, or in
the beautiful and serene, fine-dining restaurant.
The number one place to go in Hillsboro by far.

Date visited: _____ **My Rating:** _____

Went with: _____

Favorites: _____

Not so much: _____

Other comments: _____

_____

Cool Dive Bars

These are some fun places that are more casual than those in rest of book, but have style all their own. Ultra-cheap grub and drinks, and some of the best "dive bars" in town!

Ash Street Saloon

Old Town Map
225 SW Ash St; (503) 226-0430
www.ashstreetsaloon.com
4:00–8:00pm Daily $2.00–$3.00 menu items
$1.25 PBRs; $2.75 micros & wells
Good sidewalk seating.

Bar of the Gods

Hawthorne Map
4801 SE Hawthorne; (503) 232-2037
4:00–8:00pm Mon–Fri
$1.50 PBRs; $2.50 wells; 50 cents off menu items
Great back patio.

Beulahland

Lloyd Center-ish Map
118 NE 28th Ave.; (503) 235-2794
4:00–7:00pm Daily $1.00 off menu items
$3.50 pints & $3.00 wells and select cocktails
Funky decked-out walls.

Captain Ankeny's

Old Town Map
50 SW 3rd Ave; (503) 223-1375
4:00–7:00pm Daily Rotating daily specials
$3.00 micros/imports; $3.00 wells
Good tap lineup.

Cool Dive Bars

Florida Room

North/NE Map
435 N. Killingsworth St. ; (503) 287-5658
3:00–7:00pm Daily $3.00-$4.00 snacks
$.50 off cheap wells and taps
Budget beach decor. Known for weekend Bloody Marys.

Gypsy

Old Town Map
625 NW 21st Ave.; (503) 796-1859
4:00–8:00pm Tues–Fri $2.95–$4.95 big bar menu!
$3.50 micros; $2.00 domestics and wells
The Velvet Lounge in bar side is a bit more swanky.

Kelly's Olympian

Old Town Map
426 SW Washington; (503) 228-3669
4:00–7:00pm Mon–Fri $2.00–$4.00 menu
$3.00 well & micros
Motorcycles and garage stuff everywhere. Since 1902.

LaurelThirst Pub

Old Town Map
2958 NE Glisan; (503) 232-1504
Before 5:00pm Mon–Fri $3.75 micros; $2.00 PBR
6:00–8:00pm Free live music
Sidewalk seating.

Lotus Room

Downtown (East) Map
932 SW Third Ave; (503) 227-6185
3:00–7:00pm / 9:00pm–close Daily $2.95–$4.95 apps
$3.00 wells & $3.50 drafts
Huge bar and cool back card room; sidewalk seating.

Cool Dive Bars

Low Brow Lounge

Old Town Map
1036 NW Hoyt; (503) 226-0200
5:00–7:00pm Daily
$1.00 off drafts and wells $5.00 burgers, sandwiches
A famous favorite!

Matador

Old Town Map
1967 W Burnside St; (503) 222-5822
Noon–7:00pm Daily
$2.00 PBRs; $3.00 wells
Bull-fighting-themed dive bar. Really.

Space Room

Southeast Map 4800 SE Hawthorne; (503) 235-8303
www.spaceroomlounge.com
11:00am–7:00pm Daily $2.50 wells $2.25 micros
Blacklight UFO theme.

Tiger Bar

Old Town Map 317 NW Broadway; (503) 467-4111
www.tigerbarpdx.com
5:00–8:00pm Tues–Fri
$3.00–$5.00 Bar eats (good burgers)
$2.25 domestics; $3.00–$3.50 wells
Dark bar with black and brick walls; tiger elements.

Virginia Cafe

Downtown (West) Map
820 SW 10th Ave.; (503) 227-8617
virginiacafepdx.com
4:00–7:00pm Mon–Fri $2.25–$7.00 eats
$1.00 off drafts and wells
It's transplanted, "new" home retains just a bit of
the old, nostalgic charm. More of a café-y dive.

Beaverton

(Cedar Hills Mall Area)

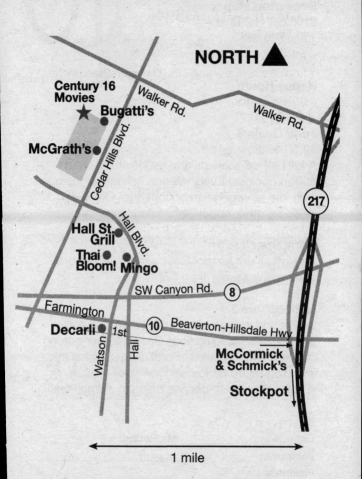

NORTH ▲

Century 16 Movies
Bugatti's
McGrath's
Walker Rd.
Walker Rd.
Cedar Hills Blvd.
217
Hall Blvd.
Hall St. Grill
Thai Bloom!
Mingo
SW Canyon Rd. ⑧
Farmington
Decarli 1st
⑩ Beaverton-Hillsdale Hwy
Watson
Hall
McCormick & Schmick's
Stockpot

|← 1 mile →|

Banya

Beaverton Map
8166 SW Hall Blvd.
(503) 646-6753
www.banyasushi.com

Happy Hours
4:00–6:00 Mon–Thur

Food Deals 3
$2.50-$7.50
A full half-off all sushi and maki with about a
million choices! Every roll and fish under the sun
with lots of vegetarian options too. Other big
deals on other appetizers, salads, and entrees!

Drink Specials 3
Half-off all drinks too! Beer, wine, plus an array
of so many sakes; Try a flight!

Atmosphere 3
Sweet and serene place with pea-green walls
and an ocean colored floor. Cozy little four-person
"rooms" with Japanese floral dividers, plus free-
standing bistro tables with room for groups.
A pleasant respite despite being in a small mall.

Date visited: _____ **My Rating:** _____

Went with: _____

Favorites: _____

Not so much: _____

Other comments: _____
_____

Cafe Murrayhill

On cute little lake in Beaverton (off map)
14500 Murray-Scholls Dr.
(503) 590-6030
www.cafemurrayhill.com

Happy Hours
3:00–6:00pm Daily

Food Deals 3
$5.00
Good-sized portions of Happy Hour faves:
BLT or pork sliders, burgers, fried mushrooms
or onion rings, hummus, calamari, crab cake
or choice of unique pita "sandwiches."

Drink Specials 2
$4.00 beer; $5.00 house wines
Special Monday night deals like 1/2 off bottles

Atmosphere 3
It's totally pleasant in the summer by their little
lake! Outdoor seating with lots of tables and
colorful umbrellas. Nice café-style restaurant in
a small strip mall. Skinny and long dining room
with neutral woods and sherbet-colored walls.

Date visited: _____ **My Rating:** _____
Went with: _____
Favorites: _____
Not so much: _____
Other comments: _____
_____

Big Al's

Beaverton (off map)
14950 SW Barrows Rd.; (503) 748-6118
Vancouver Map 16615 SE 18th; (360) 944-6118
www.ilovebigals.com

Happy Hours
3:00–6:00pm Mon–Fri; 9:00pm–close Daily

Food Deals 2
$4.00–$5.00
Eight great bar menu items: nachos, sliders, mac & cheese, quesadillas, tacos, chicken salad.

Drink Specials 2
$3.00 domestics; $3.00 wells; $5.00 cocktail
Plus some crazy beer deals

Atmosphere 3
Bright lights, loud noises, lots of excitement, and kids everywhere. That being said, they *do* have tons of bowling (glowing and not), pool, and dozens of TVs, so it's fun for adults too. The three, side-by-side, mega-huge movie screens are pretty dang cool to watch sports on!

Date visited: _____ **My Rating:** _____
Went with: _____
Favorites: _____
Not so much: _____
Other comments: _____
_____

B.J. Willy's

Beaverton (off map) (near Cinetopia)
12345 SW Horizon Blvd; (503) 747-7319
West Linn Map
1717 Willamette Falls Dr; (503) 656-4410
22000 Willamette Dr; (503) 650-6020
www.bjwillys.com

Happy Hours
3:00–6:00pm Daily; 9:30pm–close Sun–Thurs

Food Deals 2
$2.99–$5.99
Giant bar menus that vary slightly per location:
chips, fries, tots, rings, wings, sliders, pizzettas,
hummus, mac & cheese, wings, penne, clams.

Drink Specials 3
$1.00 off drafts and well drinks; $4.50 wines
$4.00 margaritas, cosmos and lemon drops

Atmosphere 2
A collection of locally-owned, casual but nice,
hang-out pubs catering to sports nuts, families
and late-nighters. Wood-fired pizza specialists.
Locations all somewhat similar in style and spirit.

Date visited: _____ **My Rating:** _____

Went with: _____

Favorites: _____

Not so much: _____

Other comments: _____

_____

Bugatti's

10

Beaverton Map
2905 SW Cedar Hills Blvd; (503) 626-1400
Hillsboro Map (Tanasbourne)
2364 NW Amber Brook; (503) 352-5252
West Linn Map (opens 4:00pm, no drink deals)
18740 Willamette, West Linn; (503) 636-9555
Oregon City (off map areas)
334 Warner Milne; (503) 722-8222
www.bugattisrestaurants.com

Happy Hours
3:00–6:00pm and 8:00pm–close Daily
All Day Sunday★

Food Deals 3
$3.00–$6.00
Menus vary, but all offer about a dozen items like
prawns, salads, pizzas, pastas, calamari.

Drink Specials 3
$1.00 off drafts; $4.50 wine; $3.50 well cocktails

Atmosphere 3
Basic bar areas compared to the somewhat
fancier attached restaurants. All quite nice though
and more modern than old Italian in style.

Date visited: _____ **My Rating:** _____
Went with: _____
Favorites: _____
Not so much: _____
Other comments: _____
_____

Decarli

• • • • • • • • • • • • • • • 10 • • •

Beaverton Map
4545 SW Watson Avenue
(503) 641-3223
www.decarlirestaurant.com

Happy Hours
4:30–6:00pm and 9:00pm–close Daily ('til
11:00pm Fri-Sat); ★All night Sunday (5–9pm)

Food Deals 3
$2.50–$11.00
Big menu and one of the best in the area: fries,
almonds, olives, bruschetta, meatballs, salads,
several paninis, rib sandwich, pizzettas, burger.

Drink Specials 3
$3.50 draft beer; $2.00 off wine; $4.00 wells
$6.00 specialty cocktail

Atmosphere 3
Warm and welcoming with exposed red brick
walls and an open kitchen. A neighborhood
gem at home in the suburbs, that really seems
more like a friendly, local New York hangout.
Get here early for HH or you might be left out!

Date visited: _____ **My Rating:** _____
Went with: _____
Favorites: _____
Not so much: _____
Other comments: _____
_____

Fireside Grill

6

Beaverton Map
8136 SW Hall Blvd.
(503) 747-4661
www.thefiresidegrillpdx.com

Happy Hours
4:00–6:00pm and 10:00pm–mid Daily

Food Deals 2
$3.00–$5.00
Nice array of bar food: Gorgonzola chips, mini
chef salad, Scotch egg, wings, waffle-fried
chicken, hummus, salad, mac & cheese.

Drink Specials 1
$6.00 house wine

Atmosphere 2
Formerly a McMenamin's place in a small mall,
now an upscale sports bar of sorts. It's all
about the patio here, as the fire is outside in
the middle of a giant stone table. Great deck!
Inside, it's quite simple, with light wood, ski-
lodge paneling, glass doors to the deck, a long
bar, and TVs. No minors.

Date visited: _____ **My Rating:** _____
Went with: _____
Favorites: _____
Not so much: _____
Other comments: _____
_____

Hall Street Grill 10

Beaverton Map
3775 SW Hall
(503) 641-6161
www.hallstreetgrill.com

Happy Hours
3:00–6:30pm and 9:00pm–close Mon–Fri
★All night Sunday (2:00–close)

Food Deals 3
$3.00–$8.00
High-end restaurant = yummy Happy Hour eats!
Coconut prawns, burgers, fries, famous Caesar,
pork belly, reuben bites, gnocchi, tacos, poutine.

Drink Specials 3
$3.00–4.00 beer; $1.00 off wine; $20.00 bottles
$4.00 wells; $5.00 cocktails

Atmosphere 3
Big and bustling Happy Hour scene inside what
is arguably the nicest place in Beaverton. Pacific
Northwest stylings with lots of wood. Fun patio
out back too. Love it!

Date visited: _____ **My Rating:** _____

Went with: _____

Favorites: _____

Not so much: _____

Other comments: _____

_____

Hayden's Lakefront Grill

Tigard Map (Tualatin)
8187 SW Tualatin
(503) 885-9292
www.haydensgrill.com

Happy Hours
3:00am–close Daily

Food Deals 2
$2.95–$9.95
All day bar menu. These are hard to judge when I'm really rating Happy Hour, so a bit off the true regulation playing field. Tricky. Tacos, soup, salad, steak frites, salmon, mussels.

Drink Specials 3
$4.00 select draft; $5.00 house wines
$4.25 martinis

Atmosphere 3
Upscale and upbeat retro spin with color blocking and mod graphics. Good mix of private dining tables and more social cocktail area. Great stop when coming back from wine country! Happy Hour restricted to the lounge only.

Date visited: _____ **My Rating:** _____
Went with: _____
Favorites: _____
Not so much: _____
Other comments: _____
_____

McCormick & Schmick's

• • • • • • • • • • • • • • • • • •

Beaverton Map
9945 SW Beaverton-Hillsdale Hwy.
(503) 643-1322
www.mccormickandschmicks.com

<u>Bridgeport Mall</u>
17015 SW 72nd Ave.; (503) 684-5490

Happy Hours
4:00–6:00pm Daily; 9:00-10:00pm Sun-Thur;
9:00-11:00pm Fri-Sat

Food Deals 3
$2.99-$5.99
Over a dozen menu items at four price tiers:
cheeseburger with fries, fish tacos, quesadilla,
hummus, flatbreads, bruschetta, calamari.

Drink Specials 3
$3.50-$4.50 drafts; $6.00 wine; $4.00 wells
$6.00-$7.00 cocktails

Atmosphere 3
<u>Beaverton</u> – *A very* popular Happy Hour with
fun dining and drinking in upscale warehouse-
style bar. <u>Bridgeport</u> – More in line with the
traditional look of McCormick & Schmick's.

Date visited: _____ **My Rating:** _____
Went with: _____
Favorites: _____
Not so much: _____
Other comments: _____
_____

McGrath's

Beaverton Map
3211 SW Cedar Hills Blvd.; (503) 646-1881
Milwaukee (off map)
11050 SE Oak; (503) 653-8070
Vancouver (off map)
12501 SE Second Circle; (360) 514-9555
www.mcgrathsfishhouse.com

Happy Hours
3:00–6:00pm Mon-Thur; 3:00–5:00pm Friday
9:00pm–close Daily

Food Deals 3
$1.99-$7.99
Unique spins on more than 27 bar menu items!
They have everything! Waay too many to even
begin to list. Bring friends and get a sampler tray.

Drink Specials 3
$3.50–$4.50 drafts; $4.75 wine; $3.75 sangria
$3.95 wells; $5.50 select cocktails

Atmosphere 3
Casually-quaint waterfront fish house decor,
with nautical knick-knacks covering pretty much
every inch of space in their cavernous rooms.

Date visited: _____ **My Rating:** _____
Went with: _____
Favorites: _____
Not so much: _____
Other comments: _____
_____

Mingo

Beaverton Map
12600 SW Crescent (The Round)
(503) 646-6464
www.mingowest.com

Happy Hours
2:30–6:00pm Tues-Fri; 5:00–6:00pm Sun–Mon

Food Deals 3
$5.00–$8.00
Somewhat small-ish but delish menu with soup,
pizzas, burgers, penne pasta, stuffed eggplant,
raviolis, salads.

Drink Specials 3
$4.00 beer; $5.00 red or white wine
$5.00 wells; $6.00 daily cocktail

Atmosphere 3
Pea green walls, over-sized paper sculptures
and lanterns, and window-doors that open to an
inviting piazza with an outdoor Happy Hour bar.
Same owners as Serratto and Mingo in NW PDX.

Date visited: _____ **My Rating:** _____
Went with: _____
Favorites: _____
Not so much: _____
Other comments: _____
_____

Stockpot Broiler 9

Beaverton (Not on Map)
8200 SW Scholls Ferry Rd.
(503) 643-5451
www.stockpot.ypguides.net

Happy Hours
4:00–6:00pm and 9:00pm–close Daily
★All night Monday (3:00–close)

Food Deals 3
$2.95-$4.95
13-item menu of big, cheap servings includes platter of giant onion rings, bruschetta, beef satay, nachos, burgers, Caesar, beef tips, meatballs, fish tacos.

Drink Specials 3
$3.25-3.75 drafts; $5.50 wine; $4.50 wells

Atmosphere 2
A dark lounge even by day with black tables and chairs, bar rails, walls, bricks and fireplace. Golf course views from wonderful seasonal patio. Here and there, it's a bit too early '80s decor with music often reflecting that.

Date visited: _____ **My Rating:** _____

Went with: _____

Favorites: _____

Not so much: _____

Other comments: _____

_____

Thai Bloom!

10

Beaverton Map
3800 SW Cedar Hills Blvd.
(503) 644-8010
www.thaibloomrestaurant.com

Happy Hours
4:00-6:00pm Daily; ★All day Sunday
8:00-close Mon-Thur; 9:00-close Fri-Sat

Food Deals 3+
$1.99-$5.99
Insanely huge menu with over 20 choices and exceptionally delicious food! Nice mix of classics and also some more unusual items. A few stand outs are chicken satay, drunken noodles, dancing shrimp and deliciously crisp spicy tamarind wings.

Drink Specials 3+
$2.99 beer or house wine; $5.00 premium wine
$1.00 off wells; $4.99 specialty cocktails (15+)

Atmosphere 2 Modern lighting, granite horse-shoe-shaped bar surrounded by tables, and floor-to-ceiling windows on three sides. Intriguing photos of Thailand grace the walls. Great patio seating under brick arches perfect for summer imbibing. A very popular and beloved place!

Date visited: _____ **My Rating:** _____
Went with: _____
Favorites: _____
Not so much: _____
Other comments: _____
_____

Vinotopia

8

Beaverton
12345 SW Horizon Blvd
(503) 597-6900
www.cinetopia.com

Happy Hours
3:00–6:00pm and 8:00pm–close Daily

Food Deals 3
$4.00-$5.00
Nine fine bar-style selections: Caesar, wings, artisan pizza, coconut shrimp, fish & chips, hummus, nachos, pulled pork sliders.

Drink Specials 2
$3.50-$4.50 drafts; $4.99 red or white wine

Atmosphere 2
Smallish, elevated bar area with lots of nearby windows. Popular/crowded with restricted seating at Happy Hour (prohibits patio partaking if you want the HH deals). Author's note: Seeing cutting egde, high-action, and 3-D movies at the Cinetopia Theaters is totally worth the drive (there's another one in Vancouver and a BREW-topia too!).

Date visited: _____ **My Rating:** _____
Went with: _____
Favorites: _____
Not so much: _____
Other comments: _____
_____

Bistro 153 www.bistro153.net

Beaverton (Off Map)
3203 SW 153rd Drive; (503) 626-8282; bistro153.net

Happy Hours 2:00–7:00pm and 9pm–close Mon-Fri
★All Day Saturday and Sunday

Food Deals 2 $3.00–$4.00 Big menu of 20+ items:
Sliders (beef, pork, chicken), burger, totchos, salad,
poppers, quesadilla, fries, rings, nachos, wings.

Drink Specials 2 $3.75 micros; $3.50 wine or wells

Atmosphere 2 Bistro-bar located within an office
complex, so there's an active after-work scene. Two
long bartops, carpeted, outdoor seating on patio.

B.J.'s Brewhouse www.bjsrestaurants.com

7390 NE Cornell, Hillsboro; (503) 615-2300

Happy Hour 3:00–7:00pm Mon–Fri and
10:00–closw Sun–Thur

Food Deals 2 $4.00-$6.00 (10 items) Bar basics like
flatbreads, wings, potstickers, sliders, spring rolls.

Drink Specials 3 $4.00 drafts; $6.00 wine; $4.00
wells; $5.00 martinis or mojitos

Atmosphere 3 National chain, so decor matches high-
energy and fun casual standards.

Monteaux's Public House

Beaverton (Off Map) www.monteauxs.com
16165 SW Regatta Lane; (503) 439-9942

Happy Hours 3:00–6:00pm Mon-Sat; Plus late-night
last two hours

Food Deals 2 $3.00–$7.00 Basic bar eats like sliders,
burgers, nachos, hummus, tacos, calamari, wings

Drink Specials 3 $3.00 beer; $11.00 pitchers
$4.00 wine; $4.00 wells

Atmosphere 2 Turn-of-the-century charm mixed
with modern-day neighborhood pub appeal, as
depicted in their hand-painted mural.

Old Chicago

Beaverton (Off Map) www.oldchicago.com
17960 NW Evergreen Pkwy; (503) 533-4650

Happy Hours 3:00–6:00pm and 10:00pm–mid Daily

Food Deals 2 $3.00–$6.00 Big bar menu with
nachos, artichoke dip, pizza, chicken strips, pretzels.

Drink Specials 2 $1.00 off all drafts; $4.00 wine;
$3.00 wells; $5.00 large craft drafts; +Daily drink deals

Atmosphere 2 Sure it's a chain, but with 101 beers
as a theme/tour, Chicago in the name, and 15 TVs.

Outback Steakhouse

Beaverton (Off Map) www.outback.com
11146 SW Barnes; (503) 643-8007

Happy Hours 4–6pm Daily (plus late-night last hour)

Food Deals 2 $4.00-$7.00 Meaty bar menu with
items like cheeseburgers, prime rib sandwich, cheese
fries, shrooms, quesadillas, soup & salad, Caesar.

Drink Specials 3 $3.50-$4.50 drafts; $4.00 wine
$4.00 signature martinis

Atmosphere 2 Follows casually-fun, Outback-style.

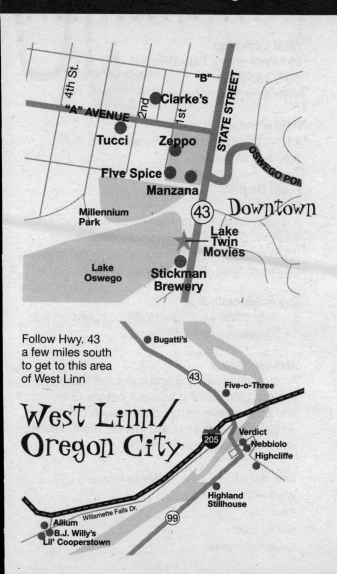

4th St.

"B"

Clarke's

"A" AVENUE

2nd

1st

STATE STREET

Tucci

Zeppo

OSWEGO POI

Five Spice

Manzana

Millennium
Park

(43) Downtown

Lake
Twin
Movies

Lake
Oswego

Stickman
Brewery

Follow Hwy. 43
a few miles south
to get to this area
of West Linn

Bugatti's

(43)

Five-o-Three

West Linn/
Oregon City

205

Verdict

Nebbiolo

Highcliffe

Highland
Stillhouse

(99)

Willamette Falls Dr.

Allium

B.J. Willy's

Lil' Cooperstown

Allium

10

West Linn Map
1914 Willamette Falls Drive
(503) 387-5604
www.alliumoregon.com

Happy Hours
4:00–6:30pm and 8:30pm–close Tues-Sun
★All day Monday

Food Deals 3
$1.50–$8.00
A dozen items brought to you by top area chefs!
Wide range of NW faves: olives, fries, french
onion soup, meat or cheese plates, mixed greens,
pizzas, oysters, burger, clams, fondue.

Drink Specials 3
$3.00 bottles; $4.00 drafts; $4.50 house wines
$4.50 cosmos or lemondrops

Atmosphere 3
An incredibly exciting and welcome addition
to West Linn's dining scene! Contemporary
and open space with harvest-colored walls,
wavy ceilings, chalkboard menus, great lighting,
and a seasonal, outdoor patio.

Date visited: _____ **My Rating:** _____

Went with: _____

Favorites: _____

Not so much: _____

Other comments: _____

_____

Clarke's

8

Lake Oswego Map
455 2nd St.
(503) 636-2667
www.clarkesrestaurant.net

Happy Hours
4:30–6:00pm Mon–Sat

Food Deals 3
$1.00–$6.00
Half-off bar extra-delicious grub menu: burger
with fries, truffled fries, quiche w/soup or salad,
hummus, mac & cheese, shrimp salad.

Drink Specials 2
No corkage fee on Monday (added point for
thinking of this concept!); 25% off wine bottles
Wednesday.

Atmosphere 2
Tiny, but cozy & comfortable modern, bistrostyle
bar area. Neutral tones with wine and bar
as focal points. Outside summer patio seating.

Date visited: _____ **My Rating:** _____

Went with: _____

Favorites: _____

Not so much: _____

Other comments: _____

_____

Five-o-Three

West Linn Map (South)
21900 Willamette Dr.; West Linn
(503) 607-0960
www.restaurant503.com

Happy Hours
4:00–6:00pm Mon–Sat; 9:00–10:00pm Thur–Sat

Food Deals 3
$3.00–$7.00
All kinds of goodies! Soup, salad, 503 burger,
quiche of the day, calamari, salmon cakes, mac
& cheese, pigs in a blanket, clams.

Drink Specials 3
$4.00 drafts; $5.50 house wines; $5.50 wells
$6.00 lemon drops or cosmos

Atmosphere 3
Warm tones with artistic flair looks coolest at
night! Big and welcoming front bar, but you are
welcome to sit anywhere in the restaurant at
Happy Hour. Pleasant and peaceful patio too.

Date visited: _____ **My Rating:** _____
Went with: _____
Favorites: _____
Not so much: _____
Other comments: _____
_____

Highcliffe

West Linn Map (South)
602 7th Street, Oregon City
(503) 212-2008
www.thehighcliffe.com

Happy Hours
2:00–6:30pm Mon–Fri; 4:00pm–6:30pm Sat–Sun

Food Deals 2
$3.00–$6.00
Typical bar food: fries, tots, wings, rings, nachos,
mac & cheese, quesadilla, burgers, pork sliders.

Drink Specials 3
$2.00–$3.50 drafts; $4.00 house wines
$4.50 wells; $4.00 daily cocktail

Atmosphere 3
Housed inside a gorgeous, 1920s former Odd
Fellows Club mansion. Upscale, mellow and
very pleasant with buttercream walls, tin ceiling,
and a 40-foot long bartop. It's tricky traveling
(get good directions), but worth a trip – take a
joyride down south and hang out a while!

Date visited: _____ **My Rating:** _____
Went with: _____
Favorites: _____
Not so much: _____
Other comments: _____

Jefe

Lake Oswego Map
16360 Boones Ferry Rd
(503) 635-1900
www.jefemex.com

Happy Hours
2:00–6:00pm and 8:30pm–close Daily

Food Deals 3
$4.95–$6.95
About half-off 15 items, with some extras exclusive to their Hora Feliz: chicken, beef or fish tacos, quesadilla, calamari, chimichurri shaved steak, ceviche, salad, soup, skewers, or beans & rice.

Drink Specials 3
$4.00 drafts; $5.50 house wines; $6.00 wells
$6.00 sangria, margarita, Moscow mule

Atmosphere 3
Beautifully-designed space with a big central bar, roll-up garage-style doors leading to a pleasant outdoor patio, and *Architectural Digest*-worthy touches featuring slate and stone, iron and wood. Memorable and fascinating wall of suspended wine bottles, flasks built right into stonework, and an open circular fireplace table.

Date visited: _____ **My Rating:** _____
Went with: _____
Favorites: _____
Not so much: _____
Other comments: _____
_____

Tucci

Lake Oswego Map
220 "A" Ave.
(503) 697-3383
www.tucci.biz

Happy Hours
4:00–6:00pm Daily

Food Deals 3
$5.95
Choose from a dozen Italian "bites": Caesar, risotto fritters, crab bruschetta, Tuscan beef skewers, pasta of the day, steamed mussels, calamari, risotto, or pizza.

Drink Specials 3
$5.00 draft beer; $5.00 red or white wine $18.00 carafe; $6.00 house cocktails

Atmosphere 3
A very well-decorated, modernized old Italian-style restaurant. Warm, golden tones, gorgeous tile and iron work, rich dark woods and comfy, upholstered seating.

Date visited: _____ **My Rating:** _____
Went with: _____
Favorites: _____
Not so much: _____
Other comments: _____
_____

Zeppo

Lake Oswego Map
345 First St. Ste 105
503) 675-2726
www.zepporestaurant.com

Happy Hours
2:00–6:00pm and 8:30pm–close Daily

Food Deals 3
$4.95-$6.95
Mixed-quality Italian eats like sausage pizza,
Caesar and caprese salads, bruschetta, risotto
cakes, calamari, chicken or steak skewers.

Drink Specials 3
$3.50 bottles; $4.00 drafts
$5.50 house wines; $6.00 sangria or cocktails

Atmosphere 3
Creative cutlery and kitchenware decor. Warm
and friendly place with central bar, coppertopped
tables and painted concrete floor. Cool Leaning
Tower of Pizza wall art.

Date visited: _____ **My Rating:** _____
Went with: _____
Favorites: _____
Not so much: _____
Other comments: _____
_____

Highland Stillhouse

Oregon City Map
201 S. 2nd Street
(503) 723-6789
www.highlandstillhouse.com

See Brewvana Section, page 69.

Stickmen Brewery & Skewery

Lake Oswego Map
40 N State; Lake Oswego; (503) 344-4449
www.stickmenbeer.com

See Brewvana Section, page 63.

The Verdict

Oregon City Map
110 8th St.; (503) 305-8429
www.verdictbarandgrill.com

Happy Hours 3:00–6:00pm Daily
8:00–9:00pm Sun–Thurs; 9:00–10:00pm Fri–Sat

Food Deals 2 $5.95–$8.95 Pass the bar food: grilled shrimp, seared ahi tuna, cheeseburger, quesadilla, Cajun tots, hummus.

Drink Specials 3 $3.50 drafts; $1.00 off wine & wells Occasional other specials at a whim :-)

Atmosphere 3 Follow the river to the Big V, pursue the patio, and don't bother with any plea-bargaining, because with their "Abatement Period", they cut a deal with everyone. So sit back and relax – they've got you surrounded with guilty pleasures.

Tigard

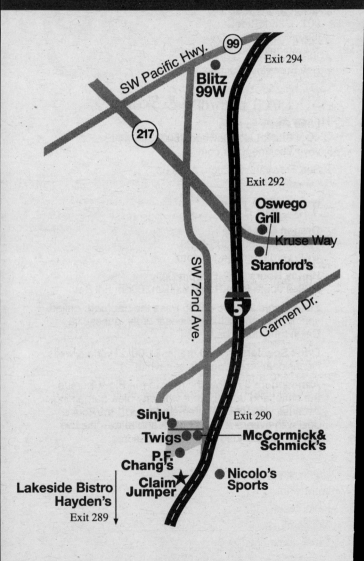

SW Pacific Hwy.

99

Exit 294

Blitz 99W

217

Exit 292

Oswego Grill

Kruse Way

Stanford's

5

SW 72nd Ave.

Carmen Dr.

Sinju

Exit 290

Twigs

McCormick & Schmick's

P.F. Chang's

Nicolo's Sports

Claim Jumper

Lakeside Bistro Hayden's

Exit 289

Blitz 99W

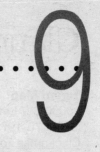

Tigard Map
10935 Sw 68th Pkwy.
(503) 719-5157
www.blitzsportspub.com

Happy Hours
3:00–6:00pm and 9:00pm-close Daily

Food Deals 2
$2.95–$6.95
Top bar standards (15) like nachos, burger or fish & chips, mac & cheese, artichoke-spinach dip, fries, hummus, and YAY! Totchos!

Drink Specials 3
$4.00 drafts, wine or cocktails

Atmosphere 3
A third addition to the growing blitzkrieg taking over the space where Newport Seafood Grill used to be. They remodeled and made it their own, and added a giant, new outdoor deck and a very cool firepit. Unlike many places, you can take your Happy Hour outside! Like the other Blitzes, there are *lots* of big TVs and games too.

Date visited: _____ **My Rating:** _____

Went with: _____

Favorites: _____

Not so much: _____

Other comments: _____

_____

Claim Jumper 10

Tigard Map
18000 SW Lower Boones Ferry, Tualatin
(503) 670-1975
Clackamas Town Center
9085 SE Sunnyside; (503) 654-3700
www.claimjumper.com

Happy Hours
3:00–6:30pm Mon–Fri; 11:00am-3:00pm Sat

Food Deals 3
$2.00–$8.00
Big portions of tasty bar favorites including
three kinds of mini-pizzas, Irish nachos, wings,
bottomless chips & salsa, burger, Caesar, tacos
(chicken, fish or pork), shrimp, and calamari.

Drink Specials 3
$$4.00 drafts; $5.00 wines (6 choices)
$5.00 specialty drinks (8 choices)
$8.00 premium drinks (8 choices)

Atmosphere 3
Inside and out it's rocks and big wooden timbers,
open air and ironworks. Experience the northwest
frontier from the comfort of your barstool.

Date visited: _____ **My Rating:** _____
Went with: _____
Favorites: _____
Not so much: _____
Other comments: _____
_____

Oswego Grill

8

Tigard Map (Lake Oswego)
7 Centerpointe Dr.
(503) 352-4750
www.theoswegogrill.com

Happy Hours
3:00–6:00pm and 9:00pm–close Daily

Food Deals 3
$1.95–4.95
A little bit of everything with 17 items including
fish tacos, artichoke dip, Caesar, soup, flatbreads,
ceviche, pork sliders, or a hot fudge sundae!

Drink Specials 1
$1.00 off drafts

Atmosphere 3
It's the old Chili's off I-5, and almost a kind of new
Stanford's in appearance, but not. Restaurant
side is quite nice and traditional, but bar area
for Happy Hour is a bit cramped and ordinary.
Nice patio in the summer.

Date visited: _____ **My Rating:** _____
Went with: _____
Favorites: _____
Not so much: _____
Other comments: _____
_____

Nicoli's
Grill & Sports Bar

6

Tigard Map (Lake Oswego)
17880 SW McEwan Rd.
(503) 726-GAME (4263)
www.game-time.com

Happy Hours
3:00–6:00pm and 8:30pm–close Daily
And anytime the Seahawks are playing

Food Deals 2
$2.00-$5.00
Deals on game grub like nachos, Caesar, pizzas,
mini corndogs, nachos, sliders, fries, or wings,

Drink Specials 0
Sadly, no drink specials

Atmosphere 3
Formerly Game Time. It's a high-concept family
entertainment complex with arcades and bowling, so if that's up your alley, you'll love it. They
have 45+ hi-def TVs, but may be hard to hear
above loud music and rowdy kids during daytime.
Fun party rooms and two bars.

Date visited: _____ **My Rating:** _____
Went with: _____
Favorites: _____
Not so much: _____
Other comments: _____
_____

PF Chang's

10

Tigard Map
7463 SW Bridgeport Rd.
(503) 430-3020
www.pfchangs.com

Hillsboro (Tanasbourne)
19320 NW Emma Way; (503) 533-4580

Happy Hours 3:00-6:00pm Daily

Food Deals 3
$3.00–$6.00
Big, extensive list of appetizers: Several dim sum
dumplings, wraps and wontons, plus traditional
street fare like ahi tuna crisps, ribs, and rolls.

Drink Specials 3
$2.75-$3.25 beers; $5.00-$6.00 wine
$4.00 wells; $5.00-$6.00 cocktails

Atmosphere 3
An Emperor's Palace appearance, complete
with huge stone lion sculptures and artistic
modern lighting effects. Sit and enjoy the beauty
of the restaurant (kids are welcome) or the bar.
The Pearl location closed 10/13.

Date visited: _____ **My Rating:** _____
Went with: _____
Favorites: _____
Not so much: _____
Other comments: _____
_____

Portland Seafood Co.

10

Tigard Washington Square Mall
9699 SW Washington Square
(503) 620-3474
www.portlandseafoodcompany.com

Mall 205 9722 SE Washington; (503) 255-2722

Happy Hours
3:00-6:00pm and 8:00pm-close Mon-Sat
★Sundays 3:00pm-close

Food Deals 3
$.99-$6.99
About 15 items of all kinds! Oyster shooters, clam chowder, sliders (Cajun blackened cod, salmon, prime rib), salads, fries, chips, dip, taco, prawns, burgers, salmon & noodles, gumbo.

Drink Specials 3
$3.59 drafts and wine; $4.59 wells

Atmosphere 3
They added a touch more modern flair to the former Newport Seafood family look. Streamlined the entrances and contemporized the bar areas. I love what they've doen with the place(s)!

Date visited: _____ **My Rating:** _____

Went with: _____

Favorites: _____

Not so much: _____

Other comments: _____

_____

Sinju

• • • • • • • • • • • • • • • • • 10 • • • •

Tigard Map (Bridgeport)
7339 SW Bridgeport Rd; (503) 352-3815
www.sinjurestaurant.com

<u>Pearl</u> 1022 NW Johnson; (503) 223-6535; 4-6pm
<u>Clackamas</u>11860 SE 82nd; (503) 344-6932
(Same hours but no late-night and all day Sun)

Happy Hours
3:00–6:00pm and 9:00pm–close Daily

Food Deals 3+ *A Happy Hour favorite!*
$1.75–$5.00
12 varieties of sushi rolls and 12 types of nigiri!
Plus, there's another 10 delicious snacks like
miso soup, edamame, gyozas, wings, BBQ platter,
shrimp, and the beautiful, delicious ahi tower.

Drink Specials 3
$3.00 beer; $6.00 wine; $6.00 hot or cold sake
$4.00 wells; $7.00 select specialty drinks

Atmosphere 3
Red! Fiery! I love it! This is the perfect place to
come after a movie at Bridgeport. Great group
room with red cast and open fireplace. Painted
ceilings, wood-slat panels and grids bar it up.

Date visited: _____ **My Rating:** _____
Went with: _____
Favorites: _____
Not so much: _____
Other comments: _____
_____

Thirsty Lion Pub

• •

Washington Square Mall (off map)
10205 SW Washington Square Rd.
(503) 352-4030
www.thirstylionpub.com

Happy Hours
3:00–6:00pm and 10:00pm-close Mon–Fri

Food Deals 3
$3.95–$5.95
Nice pub food menu with items like scotch eggs,
fries, Caesar, edamame, potato cakes, pulled
pork or burger sliders, pizza, calamari, and beer
fondue with soft pretzels.

Drink Specials 0
Sadly, no drink deals

Atmosphere 3
The second version of a big, new national chain
perhaps? Follows established format of the
original in Old Town Portland. Same neighborhood English Pub theme, being even more new,
yuppie and huge. Food, spirits, ales, live music,
and sports on several TVs. 52 taps!

Date visited: _____ **My Rating:** _____
Went with: _____
Favorites: _____
Not so much: _____
Other comments: _____
_____

Twigs Bistro

Tigard Map (Bridgeport)
17003 SW 72nd Ave
(503) 430-0769
www.twigsbistro.com

Happy Hours
3:00–6:00pm and 9:00pm–mid Daily

Food Deals 3
$5.00–$6.00
Sliders (pork, chicken, turkey), hummus, Cajun calamari, fries, and several flatbreads like BBQ chicken or butternut squash. Elsewhere on their menu, they're really good with gluten-free options.

Drink Specials 3
$4.00 draft; $5.00 wines; $5.00 cocktails

Atmosphere 3
Cool, cosmopolitan style appropriate for a martini bar. Great attention to design with pretty color scheme, glowing shelves of glass bottles, and well-selected tiles, upholstery and finishes. Restaurant side (sit anywhere for HH) has a nice, circular, open fireplace. Outdoor seating. Part of small NW chain of 10 locations.

Date visited: _____ **My Rating:** _____

Went with: _____

Favorites: _____

Not so much: _____

Other comments: _____

_____

Cheesecake Factory (off the map/at the mall)

9309 Washington Square Rd; (503) 620-1100
www.thecheesecakefactory.com

Happy Hours: 4:00-6:00pm Mon-Fri
$4.00 beer, $5.00 wine, $5.00 specialty cocktails and
$5.00 wells; Loads of appetizer options $4.95-$6.95
Crazy and vibrant interior design!

Chevy's Fresh Mex (Tigard Map)

14991 Bangy Rd., Lake Oswego (503) 620-7700
12520 SE 93rd Ave., Clackamas (503) 654-1333
1951 NW 185th Avenue, Hillsboro (503) 690-4524
www.chevys.com

Happy Hours: 2:00-7:00pm Daily; 9:00pm–close
$5.00-$8.00 Full array of Mexican appetizers.
$2.99 domestics; $3.99 wine, wells, Margaritas

McCormick & Schmick's (Bridgeport Village)

17015 SW 72nd Ave.; (503) 684-5490
www.mccormickandschmicks.com

Happy Hours: 4:00–6:00pm and 9:00pm–close Daily
Food $2.99–$5.99
Drinks $4.00 drafts; $5.00 wine; $6.00-$7.00 cocktails
See full review on page 88.

✳ Remember to check our website
every once in a while for changes and closures.

www.happyhourguidebook.com

And please let us know if you see ✳
information that needs changing.

Vancouver

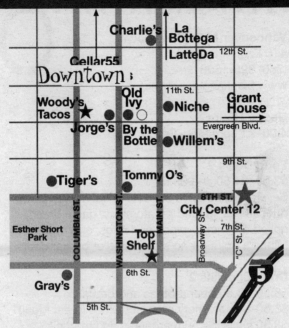

Downtown

Charlie's • | La Bottega
LatteDa — 12th St.

Cellar55

Woody's Tacos ★ • • ○ Old Ivy | 11th St. | Niche • | Grant House

Jorge's | By the Bottle | Willem's • | Evergreen Blvd.

• Tiger's | Tommy O's • | 9th St.

★ 8TH ST.
City Center 12

Esther Short Park

COLUMBIA ST. | WASHINGTON ST. | MAIN ST. | Broadway St. | "C" St.

7th St.

Top Shelf ★

6th St.

5

Gray's

5th St.

See "Waterfront" for Vancouver riverside places.

Far East Vancouver

Cactus Ya-Ya • | MILL PLAIN

Gustav's • | 167th | 15TH STREET

18th • Big Al's

20TH STREET

164TH AVENUE | 176th | 192nd

CASCADE PKWY

14 | Exit 8 | 34TH STREET | • Roots
• 360

411

Black Angus

8

Vancouver Map (Downtown)
415 East 13th Street
(360) 695-1506
www.blackangus.com

Happy Hours
4:00–7:00pm Mon–Fri

Food Deals 2
$3.50, $4.50 and $5.50
Several big bullseye bar eats at each price point:
quesadillas, loaded potato skins, garlic bread,
grilled artichoke, wings and rings, and more.
Minus a point for no steak bites or burger deals.

Drink Specials 2
$3.50-$4.50 beer (bottles and drafts)
$3.50-$5.50 variety of select wines (great idea!)
$3.50 wells; $4.50 margaritas and martinis
Needs some quality NW beer & wine selections.

Atmosphere 3
Heavy western theme follows the founder's
(Seattle's Stuart Anderson) corporate-cowboy
style. Dark and windowless with rough wood
panel walls covered with framed cowboy pics.

Date visited: _____ **My Rating:** _____

Went with: _____

Favorites: _____

Not so much: _____

Other comments: _____

_____

Brewtopia

Vancouver (off map)
8700 NE Vancouver Mall Dr.
(360) 448-4100
www.cinetopia.com

Happy Hours
3:00–6:00pm Daily / 8:00–close Daily

Food Deals 3
$3.99–$5.99
About 10 beer go-withs like calamari, Caesar, fries, bacon mac & cheese, steak frites, nachos, blue cheese dates, spinach salad.

Drink Specials 1
$1.00 off all drafts

Atmosphere 3
You can sample brews from dozens of local and international breweries ($1.90–$2.40 for tasters, with pints $6.50–$7.00). Contemporary and sleek design similar in style to the other Cinetopias, with a couple of small parlor rooms, a 21+ Living Room theater, and two XL grand theaters.

Date visited: _____ **My Rating:** _____
Went with: _____
Favorites: _____
Not so much: _____
Other comments: _____
_____

Charlie's Bistro 9

Vancouver Map (Downtown)
1220 Main Street
(360) 693-9998
www.charliesbistro.com

Happy Hours
3:00–6:00pm Daily / 9:00–11:00pm Fri-Sat

Food Deals 2
$3.00–$6.00
Just a bit of a discount off their bar menu: fritters, wings, shrimp cocktail, Caesar, veggie plate, baked goat cheese crostini, frog legs.

Drink Specials 3
$1.00 off drafts, wine and wells
$5.00 cocktail of the day

Atmosphere 3
Cozy and warm upscale bar area with big stone fireplace and hi-def TV. Long, wooden bar with black & white, historical photos of the founding father/character, Charlie, with family and friends.

Date visited: _____ **My Rating:** _____
Went with: _____
Favorites: _____
Not so much: _____
Other comments: _____
_____

Ginger Pop

Vancouver Map (Downtown)
2520 Columbia House Boulevard
(360) 699-7273
www.gingerpopthai.com

Happy Hours
3:00–6:00pm Daily; 9:00pm–close Fri–Sat

Food Deals 3
$2.00–$8.00
About a dozen fresh and delish Thai treats:
shrimp chips, crispy noodles, salad or egg rolls,
grilled pork, prawns, or chicken, lettuce wraps,
Thai or yum salads, chicken wings and soups.

Drink Specials 3
$3.00-$4.00 drafts; $3.00 wines; $5.00 cocktails

Atmosphere 2
Very diner-like in look and feel, but a little all over
the place with decor ideas. The main walls are
painted a neon green, so the place is cheerful and
bright, and original art mixed with some very
cool lighting jazzes things up too. Patio and roll-
up doors, but it's right next to the parking lot.

Date visited: _____   **My Rating:** _____
Went with: _____
Favorites: _____
Not so much: _____
Other comments: _____
_____

Grant House

Vancouver Map (off map)
1101 Officer's Row
(360) 906-1101
www.thegranthouse.us

Happy Hours
3:00–6:00pm Tues–Fri

A Happy Hour favorite!

Food Deals 3
$1.00-$6.00
Enjoy high-end restaurant quality food and ambiance: fish tacos, calamari, salad, veggie or reuben slider burgers, hummus plate, flat bread. Plus gnocchi or 1/2 pound Grant burger $11.00.

Drink Specials 2
$4.00 drafts; $5.00 wines

Atmosphere 3
Inside the grounds of historic Fort Vancouver. Charming, turn-of-the-century estate (Ulysses S. Grant lived here in the 1850s). Gorgeous patio or wrap-around porch allows Happy Hour patrons to sit outside and savor. Worth a trip!

Date visited: _____ **My Rating:** _____
Went with: _____
Favorites: _____
Not so much: _____
Other comments: _____
_____

Gray's at the Park

Vancouver Map (Downtown)
301 W 6th St
(360) 828-4343
www.graysatthepark.com

Happy Hours
★2:00–6:00pm Daily

Food Deals 2
$3.00–$14.00
Pricey, but top restaurant quality, with a lot of
options in starters, small plates, and salads:
beef brochettes, crabcake, sliders, ahi tuna,
fries, mac & cheese, prawns and pizza.

Drink Specials 3
$4.00 drafts; $5.00 select house wines
$5.00 wells and daily cocktails; $6.00 martinis

Atmosphere 3
Well, the Hilton's are just fancy! A gorgeous, sleek
hotel lobby with contemporary style on through
to the high-class, retro-mod lounge with fireplace.
Across from the south side of Esther Shore Park.

Date visited: _____ **My Rating:** _____
Went with: _____
Favorites: _____
Not so much: _____
Other comments: _____
_____

Gustav's

• • • • • • • • • • • • • • • • **10** • • •

Vancouver Map
1705 SE 164th Ave.
(360) 883-0222
www.gustavs.net
See page 353 for other locations.

Happy Hours
3:00–6:00pm and 9:00pm–close Daily

Food Deals 3
$1.99–$5.99
More than 20 items on the Happy Hour menu,
with mostly German specialties and other
hardy, old stand-bys: reuben or shepard's pie,
fish & chips, burgers, schnitzel strips, chicken
skewers, swiss fondue, sliders, potato pancakes.

Drink Specials 3
$4.00 select drafts; $5.00 house wines
$4.00–$5.00 margaritas, mojitos, other cocktails

Atmosphere 3
With some imagination and a couple beers from
the strong and authentic European tap line-ups,
you too, can be transported to a genuine Bavarian
bierstube. Gold star for pushing the concept.

Date visited: _____ **My Rating:** _____
Went with: _____
Favorites: _____
Not so much: _____
Other comments: _____
_____

Hudson's
(Heathman Lodge)

10

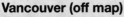

Vancouver (off map)
7801 NE Greenwood Drive
360-816-6100
www.hudsonsbarandgrill.com

Happy Hours
4:00–6:00pm Daily

Food Deals 3
$2.00-$6.00
Wow! More than a dozen items that change up
just a bit depending on the time of year. They
have it all, and for less: cheddar burger, roasted
brussel sprouts, salmon BLTs, fish & chips, salad,
chips, mac & cheese, calamari, Caesar, hummus,
and more!

Drink Specials 3
$3.50 drafts; $5.00 house wines
$5.00 cocktail specials

Atmosphere 3
Very NW-woodsy, earthy, and rustic, both inside
and out, located in the Heathman Lodge. I'd say
Hudson's is probably Vancouver's best Happy
Hour, but it's already often way too crowded.

Date visited: _____ **My Rating:** _____
Went with: _____
Favorites: _____
Not so much: _____
Other comments: _____
_____

Jorge's Tequila Factory

Vancouver (Downtown map)
1004 Washington; (360) 828-5543
No website (needs one!)

Happy Hours
3:30-6:00pm and 9:00–close Daily
★All day Sunday

Food Deals 3 $5.00
Real meals – and delicious, authentic Mexican
ones at that! FajitaDilla, quesadilla, jalapeno
poppers, super or fajita nachos, taquitos, tacos,
Mexican pizza, and more to be added soon.

Drink Specials 3
$2.99 all drafts; $4.00 wine; $4.00 Margarita

Atmosphere 3
Large open room with Happy Hour in the elevated
bar area with lots of bartop seating and just a few
tables. It's really part sportsbar with big-screen
TVs lining the walls. Festive atmosphere with
hanging lights strewn across open rafter ceiling,
brick walls, and giant windows fully lining two
whole sides. Dedicated, nice owner that knows
what to do to pack 'em in. Popular place!

Date visited: _____ **My Rating:** _____
Went with: _____
Favorites: _____
Not so much: _____
Other comments: _____
_____

Lapellah

10

Vancouver (off map)
2520 Columbia House Blvd.
(360) 828-7911
www.lapellah.com

Happy Hours
3:30-6:00pm Daily plus 9:00–11:00pm Fri-Sat

Food Deals 3
$2.00–$6.00
All kinds of delicious and unique options with
seasonal variations: mussels, prawns, burger,
mac & cheese, calamari, flat bread, salads, wings,
olives, fries, and bacon-wrapped jalapenos.

Drink Specials 3
$3.50 drafts; $5.00 select wines
$4.00 wells and $5.00 specialty cocktails

Atmosphere 3
Northwest-style, natural and woody interior is
much like that of their other upscale restaurant,
Roots. Central and long group table dominates
surrounding upolstered booths. Cool lighting.

Date visited: _____ **My Rating:** _____
Went with: _____
Favorites: _____
Not so much: _____
Other comments: _____
_____

Roots

Vancouver Map (Far East)
19215 SE 34th St.; Camas
(360) 260-3001
www.rootsrestaurantandbar.com

Happy Hours
3:00–6:00pm Daily
9:00–11:00pm Fri–Sat

Food Deals 3
$2.50–$8.50
Fresh from the Northwest with about 12 items:
Cheese plate, penne pasta, soup, mussels, fish
& chips, fries, burger, and several salads.

Drink Specials 3
$3.75 draft beer; $6.00 red and white wines
$4.75 well drinks; $5.95 select cocktails

Atmosphere 3
Understated and dimly-lit bar in the Riverstone
Marketplace. Pacific Northwest style inside and
out. Neutral tones and lots of wood and slate.

Date visited: _____ **My Rating:** _____
Went with: _____
Favorites: _____
Not so much: _____
Other comments: _____
_____

Tiger's Garden
Xokdee Lounge

9

• • • • • • • • • • • • • • • •

Downtown Map
312 W. 8th St.
(360) 693-9585
www.tigersgardenrestaurant.com

Happy Hours
4:00–6:00pm Mon–Sat; 4:00–9:00pm Sun★
9:00–11:00pm Mon–Thurs; 9:00pm–mid Fri–Sat

Food Deals 3
$3.50
Appetizers like egg rolls, salad rolls, fried tofu,
wontons, satay, wings, California rolls.

Drink Specials 2
$3.50 drafts; $4.00 wells

Atmosphere 3
Tiger's Garden Restaurant lounge. Once upon
a time it was a wine bar, so lots of comfy, cushy,
couch seating. Swanky! Artistic glass lamps, big
bar, large windows.

Date visited: _____ **My Rating:** _____
Went with: _____
Favorites: _____
Not so much: _____
Other comments: _____
_____

Tommy O's

9

Vancouver Map
801 Washington St.; (360) 694-5107
www.tommyosaloha.com

Happy Hours
3:00–6:00pm Daily; 9:00pm-close Fri–Sat

Food Deals 3
$2.00-$6.00
About 20 tropically-themed eats like skewers,
nachos, beef ribs, fries, coconut shrimp, salad,
burgers, sliders, quesadilla, and sushi rolls.

Drink Specials 3
$3.75 drafts; $4.00 red and white wine
$5.00 specialty cocktails like mai-tais

Atmosphere 2
An only-kinda-Hawaiian bar/lounge next door to
Tommy O's island-style restaurant. Somewhere
along the line, it lost much of its tropical chic
and turned into to being just a plain bar. Sadly,
their other location in east Vancouver closed.

Date visited: _____ **My Rating:** _____

Went with: _____

Favorites: _____

Not so much: _____

Other comments: _____

_____

Vinotopia

8

Vancouver (off map)
11700 Se 7th St.; (360) 213-2800
www.cinetopiatheaters.com

Happy Hours
3:00–6:00pm and 8:00pm–close Daily

Food Deals 2
$4.00–$5.00
Pre-show attractions include Caesar, artichoke dip,
hummus, pizza, nachos, pork sliders, fish & chips.

Drink Specials 3
$3.50 domestics; $4.50 microbrews
$4.99 wine (steward's choice)
FYI – They have an entire room of wall-to-wall
wines to taste! Sample from 88 kinds from all
over the world at $2.00-$8.00 per ounce.

Atmosphere 3
Inside Cinetopia movie theater. Happy Hour
seating currently at the bartop and nearby tables
only, but within sight is the big and open restaurant with stunning fireplace area and occasional
piano player. Serene outdoor garden patio.

Date visited: _____ **My Rating:** _____
Went with: _____
Favorites: _____
Not so much: _____
Other comments: _____
_____

Willem's

Vancouver Map
907 Main St.
(360) 258-0989
www.willemsonmain.com

Happy Hours
3:30–5:30pm Mon and Thur-Sun (closed Tues-Wed)

Food Deals 2
$4.00–$6.00
Frequently changing, five item menu driven by
the Northwest's bounty of seasonal offerings.
Limited menu, and small-ish serving sizes, but
delicious. Things like grilled shrimp, linguini,
chicken liver mousse crostini, grilled romaine
hearts, marinated olives.

Drink Specials 0
Sadly, no drink deals

Atmosphere 3
Romantic, historic, and special place that was
greatly needed in downtown Vancouver! Brought
to us compliments of Chef Willem Paul Klitsie
of Fratelli in the Pearl. Theater chairs, tree trunk
table tops, gold walls, wrought iron, low lighting.

Date visited: _____ **My Rating:** _____

Went with: _____

Favorites: _____

Not so much: _____

Other comments: _____

_____

Woody's Tacos

Downtown Map
210 W Evergreen
(360) 718-8193
www.woodystacos.com

Happy Hours
3:00–6:00pm Mon-Sat

Food Deals 3
$2.00–$3.00

A Happy Hour favorite!

Surprisingly delicious Mexican food for a
shockingly low price! Chips & salsa, garnachas,
mushroom and goat cheese chalupas, shrimp,
chicken or skirt steak skewers, empanadas,
chicken or beef taquitos, and potato croquettes.

Drink Specials 3
$2.50-$3.50 beers; $4.50 wells
$5.50 margaritas; Specials on giant microbrews

Atmosphere 2
Order at Woody's counter, then sit out in the
indoor piazza area where you'll be surrounded
by quaint shops, galleries and artwork. Quite
unique – quiet and sweet, especially at night.

Date visited: _____ **My Rating:** _____
Went with: _____
Favorites: _____
Not so much: _____
Other comments: _____
_____

360° Kitchen & Bar threesixtykitchen.com

Vancouver (East) 3425 SE 192nd; (360) 260-3605

Happy Hours 4:00–6:00pm Daily; 9-10pm Fri-Sat

Food Deals 2 $3.00-$7.00 Pizza of the day, fried oysters, burgers, wings, pork tacos, hummus.

Drink Specials 3 $3.50 draft; $5.00 wine; $5.50 cosmo or lemondrop

Atmosphere 2 Right across the parking lot from sister restaurant, Roots. Colorful and cool with patio.

Cactus Ya-Ya

Vancouver (East)
15704 SE Mill Plain Blvd; (360) 944-9292

Happy Hours 3:00–6:00pm and 9:00pm–close Daily
★All day Sunday

Food Deals 3 $3.95–$5.25 Super-delicious, infamous ya-ya rolls (chicken, salmon or steak), nachos, fish taco, burger, quesadilla, skewers and salads.

Drink Specials 1 Rotating special of the day

Atmosphere 2 A happenin' and very popular area restaurant. Bar side thus gets packed, being some-what small – locals just love it! Popular outdoor patio not for Happy Hour. Artsy Mexicali touches with some cool ironworks, paintings, and sculptures.

La Bottega Cafe www.labottegafoods.com

Downtown Map 1905 Main St; (360) 571-5010

Happy Hours 3:00-5:00pm Daily

Food Deals 2 $4.00–$6.00 Small menu with nice little nibbles: veggie plate, antipasti, olives, crostini and bruschetta, baked polenta.

Drink Specials 2 $1.00 off beer; $5.00 house wine

Atmosphere 2 I vaguely remember a bodega being a grocery store in Spanish. Add in lots of wine bottles for sale and you have bottega! Cute little cafe/store/wine bar.

Shanahan's www.shanahanspubvancouver.com

Downtown Map 209 W McLoughlin; (360) 735-1440

Happy Hours 3:00-8:00pm Daily★

Food Deals 3 $1.99–$4.99 Bar food yes, but crazy-cheap and good! Pork or fish tacos, "Shany fries" (a don't miss), steak bites, chicken quesadilla, pork or chicken sliders, mac & cheese, hummus plate, salad.

Drink Specials 1 $2.50 domestics; $3.00 wells

Atmosphere 2 It's a super-casual, neighborhood, Irish pub with a mysterious, magnetic charm. Something about the place makes you love it, simple as it may be. Resembles most bars in Wisconsin.

The Rock www.therockwfp.com

Vancouver (off Map) 2420 Columbia House Blvd.; (360) 695-7625

Happy Hours 3:00-6:00pm / 9:00pm-mid Mon–Fri ★All day Sun-Mon for football games (3pm-close)

Food Deals 2 $4.49–$8.99 Discounted appetizers plus personal pizzas, mini burgers and wings.

Drink Specials 3+ $3.00 drafts, wine and wells! Plus "bucket" specials ($2.00 off)

Atmosphere 2 Mini chain of Washington wood-fired pizza joints with very fun, casual, collegiate feel.

Top Shelf

Downtown Map 600 Main; (360) 699-7106

Happy Hours 3:00–7:00pm Mon–Fri; ★6pm-mid Sun 10:00pm-mid Mon-Thur

Food Deals 2 $2.50–$4.50 Bar menu with basics like Caesar salad, pork shanks, wings mini gyros, burgers, sliders, hummus, quesadillas, chips & salsa.

Drink Specials 2 $.50 off drafts; $1.00 off wells; $4.00 select martinis

Atmosphere 2 Big U-shaped, central copper-top bar and 18-foot brick walls; comfortable, Irish bar effect; not fancy like the Top Shelf name might imply.

293	Tavin's	399	Verdict
213	Teardrop Lounge	66	Vertigo Brewing
326	Teote	281	Via Chicago
35	TeSoAria	219	Via Delizia
387	Thai Bloom	153	Via Tribunali
293	Thai Noon	45,329	Vie de Boheme
212	Thai Smile	35	Viola Wine
94	Thirst Bistro	425	Vinetopia Vancouver
158	Thirsty Lion	388	Vinotopia Beaverton
408	Thirsty Lion Tigard	372	Virginia Cafe
95	Three Degrees	330	Voicebox East
327	Three Doors Down	220	Voicebox Karaoke
66	Three Mugs Brewing	53	Volcanic Brewing
372	Tiger Bar	369	Wassabi
423	Tiger's Garden	158	West Café
368	Tillicum	75	White Eagle
74	Tin Bucket Brewing	331	White Owl Social Club
278	Tin Shed	64	Widmer Brewing
96	Tippy Canoe	332	Wild Abandon
424	Tommy O's	221	Wildwood
429	Top Shelf	222	Wilf's
214	Touché	426	Willem's
328	Township & Range	282	Windows
215	Trader Vic's	45	Wine:30
279	Trébol	45	WineUp on Williams
397	Tucci	427	Woody's Tacos
63	Tugboat Brewing	333	Xico
409	Twigs	158	XV (15)
280	Uchu Sushi	283	Yakuza
66	Upright Brewing	221	Yama Sushi
216	Uptown Billiards	398	Zeppo
74	Uptown Market	76	Zeus Café
45	Urban Decanter	293	Zilla Sake
152	Urban Farmer		
217	Vault Martini		
218	Verde Cocina		

Notes

Notes

Notes

Notes

"Best-of" Listings

OUTDOOR PATIOS & DECKS

River Decks

Beaches
Cathedral Park Kitchen
Island Café
Jantzen Beach Bar
Joe's Crab Shack
McMenamin's
    on the Columbia
Newport Seafood Grill
Riverview*
Salty's
Stone Cliff Inn*
The Deck
Thirst
Three Degrees

Sky High Decks

Departure
Noble Rot
Windows

Views from Inside

Chart House
Portland City Grill

* No Happy Hour
outside

Pleasant Patios

Amalfi's
Bistro Marquee
Bungalo Bar
Doug Fir
Farm Café
Firehouse
Fish Sauce
Grant House
Jamison
Meriwether's (dinner)
Mextiza
Moloko
Nel Centro
Noho's Freemont
Papa Haydn Sellwood
Radio Room
Stickmen Brewery
Teote
Tin Shed
Yakuza

Delightful Decks

Bernie's
Caldera
Mint/820
Nightlight
The Station
Touché
Wild Abandon

More exceptional patios or decks, but no full Happy
Hours: Channel's Edge, DiPrimi Italian, Hidden Bay,
Prost, Roadside Attraction, Veritable Quandry

"Best-of" Listings

. . . .

AMERICAN FOODS

Best Pizzas

Cafe Castagna
Cibo
Firehouse
Lucca
Nel Centro
Nostrana
Oven & Shaker
Pazzo
Piattino
Serratto
Sunshine Tavern
Touché
Via Tribunali

Steakbites

23 Hoyt
El Gaucho
Morton's
Ringside (3)
Clyde's Prime Rib
Portland City Grill
Ruth's Chris
Urban Farmer

Southern

Bernie's
Bistro Marquee
  (French Creole)
Church
Irving St. Kitchen
Miss Delta
Pope House
Southland Whiskey
Tapalaya

Best Burgers

23 Hoyt
Cafe Castagna
Church
El Gaucho
Grant House
Jake's Famous
Jake's Grill
Joe's Burgers
Little Bird
McCormick & Schmick's
Metrovino
Mint/820 (lambburger)
Morton's
Ringside (all)
Ruth's Chris
Salty's
Saucebox
Serratto
Star Bar

Not my list, but I
hear raves about:
Bar Bar
Gruner
Jo-Bar
Pause
Paymaster Lounge
Slow Bar

"Best-of" Listings

INTERNATIONAL FOODS

Asian/Thai/Vietnamese

Ahi Sushi + Tapas
Bamboo Sushi (2)
Bamboo Thai
Bambuza
Banya
Departure
Dragonwell
E-San
Fish Sauce
Ginger Pop
Hokusei
Luc Lac
Masu
Mee-Sen
Paadee
Saké
Samurai Blue
Saucebox
Seres
Shigezo
Silk
Sinju
Soho
Thai Bloom!
Thai Smile
Yama Sushi

French

Bitro Marquee
Brasserie Montmarte
Chez Machin
Cocotte
Little Bird
St. Jack

German

Gruner
Gustav's (all)
Prost*
Widmer Gasthaus

Indian

Bollywood Theater*
East India Company

Alpine/Northern

Broder
Broder Nord
Slide Inn

"Best-of" Listings
. . . .

INTERNATIONAL FOODS

Italian

Amalfi's
Ciao Vito
Giorgio's
Mama Mia
Piattino
Serratto
Touché
Tucci
Via Delizia

Middle-Eastern

Berbati's
Cypress
Habibi
Hoda's
Karam
Shiraz
TarBoush

South of the Border

Blue Agave
Casa del Matador
Cha
Fonda Rosa
Isabel
La Calaca Comelona
Las Primas
Mextiza
Mi Mero Mole*
Oba
Pambiche
Teote
Trebol

European-Style Pubs

Alberta St. Pub
County Cork
Highland Stillhouse
Horsebrass Pub*
Kell's
Leaky Roof
Moon & Sixpence*
Paddy's
Rose & Thistle Pub
Thirsty Lion

International Flavors

Bluehour
Cruz Room
Living Room Theaters
Muu-muu's
Nel Centro
North 45
Salvador Molly's

"Best-of" Listings

· · · · · · · · · · · · · · · · · ·

LOUNGING AND LINGERING

Cocktails

Bartini
Barwares*
Box Social
Clyde Common
Expatriate*
Gilt Club
Imperial
Interurban
Kask*
La Taq*
Mint/820
Observatory
Olive or Twist*
Richmond Bar
Rum Club
Teardrop Lounge
Vault
Vintage Lounge

Bookish Good Looks

Bread & Ink Café
Dig a Pony
Irving St. Kitchen
Press Club
Tugboat Brewery
Secret Society

New Cool Bars

Church
Lightbar
Multnomah Whiskey
    Library*
Richmond Bar
Raven & Rose

Retro/Mod

Crush
Jinx
Mellow Mushroom
Moloko
The Original
Pour

Retro/Old School

Clyde's Prime Rib
Doug Fir
Driftwood Room
Fish Grotto
Jake's
Gold Dust Meridian
Hubers
Jimmy Mak's
Richmond Bar
Ringside Steakhouse
Ron Tom's
Savoy Tavern & Bistro
Trader Vic's
Wilf's

Speakeasy Style

Beech St. Parlor
Camellia Lounge
Circa 33
Hobo's
Interurban
Sapphire Hotel
Secret Society
Sidecar 11

"Best-of" Listings

• • • • • • • • • • • • • • • • • • • •

OTHER IDEA LISTS

Nautical/Water Theme

Alibi
Beaches
Dan & Louis'
Florida Room*
Hale Pale
Island Cafe
Jantzen Beach Bar
Noho's
The Quay at Red Lion
Sand Bar
Trader Vic's

Fun & Games

Barrel Room*
Big Al's (2)
Cinetopia (3)
Glowing Greens*
Grand Central Bowl
Ground Kontrol Arcade*
Helium Comedy Club*
Living Room Theaters
McMenamin's Edgefield
(+all McMenamin's hotels)
Nicoli's Sports
Punch Bowl Social
Uptown Billiards

*No Happy Hour
or book review*

Nice taps (NOT listed in the Beervana section)

A&L Sports Pub*
County Cork
Gustav's
Higgins
Journeys
Mellow Mushroom
Monteaux's Public House
Muddy Rudder
North 45
Old Chicago
Stammtisch*
Streetcar Bistro
Thirsty Lion
Uptown Billiards

Happy Houses

Brooklyn House
Bungalo Bar
Farm Cafe
Beech St. Parlor
Grant House
Hedgehouse
Huckleberry Pub
Journeys
Latte Da Wine Bar
Liberty Glass
Muddy Rudder
Paley's Place
Pope House
Raven & Rose
Relish
Taste on 23rd
Sok Sab Bai

Are you keeping up?!

● ● ● ● ● ● ● ● ● ● ● ● ● ● ● ● ● ● ● ●

More than 75 additions since the 2013 edition!

- ☐ Ahi Sushi + Tapas
- ☐ B2 Wine Bar
- ☐ Bamboo Thai
- ☐ Bistro Marquee
- ☐ Block & Tackle
- ☐ Brooklyn House
- ☐ Cathedral Park Kitchen
- ☐ Cellar 55
- ☐ Central Hotel
- ☐ Cerulean Skies Winery
- ☐ Church
- ☐ D.E.N.
- ☐ Double Dragon
- ☐ Ecliptic Brewing
- ☐ ENSO Winery
- ☐ Fireside
- ☐ Huckleberry Pub
- ☐ Imperial
- ☐ Joe's Crab Shack
- ☐ Jorge's Tequila
- ☐ Knock Back
- ☐ Korkage
- ☐ Lakeside Bistro
- ☐ Latte Da
- ☐ Luc Lac
- ☐ Nebbiolo
- ☐ Niche Wine Bar
- ☐ Nicoli's
- ☐ Noho's Hawaiian Cafe
- ☐ Old Gold
- ☐ Old Ivy Brewery
- ☐ Old Market Pub
- ☐ Oregon Public House
- ☐ Pacific Pie Co.
- ☐ Paley's Place
- ☐ Piattino
- ☐ Picnic House
- ☐ Pine State Biscuits
- ☐ Portland Seafood Co.
- ☐ Primrose & Tumbleweeds
- ☐ Punch Bowl Social
- ☐ Ración
- ☐ Radar Restaurant
- ☐ Rae's Lakeview
- ☐ Raven & Rose
- ☐ Redwood
- ☐ Relish
- ☐ Richmond Bar
- ☐ Saké
- ☐ Sand Bar
- ☐ SE Wine Collective
- ☐ Shaker & Vine
- ☐ Sok Sab Bai
- ☐ Stone Cliff Inn
- ☐ Tannery
- ☐ Tasty n Alder
- ☐ Teote
- ☐ Thai Bloom
- ☐ Thai Smile
- ☐ The Station
- ☐ Township & Range
- ☐ Twigs
- ☐ Verde Cocina
- ☐ Via Chicago
- ☐ Voicebox East
- ☐ White Owl Social Club
- ☐ Willem's
- ☐ WineUp on Williams

www.happyhourguidebook.com